Remaking the Republic

AMERICA IN THE NINETEENTH CENTURY

Series editors:
Brian DeLay, Steven Hahn, Amy Dru Stanley

America in the Nineteenth Century proposes a rigorous rethinking
of this most formative period in U.S. history. Books in the series
will be wide-ranging and eclectic, with an interest in politics at all
levels, culture and capitalism, race and slavery, law, gender, and the
environment, and regional and transnational history. The series
aims to expand the scope of nineteenth-century historiography
by bringing classic questions into dialogue with innovative
perspectives, approaches, and methodologies.

REMAKING
— THE —
REPUBLIC

Black Politics and the Creation
of American Citizenship

Christopher James Bonner

Happy reading!

C. James B

PENN

UNIVERSITY OF PENNSYLVANIA PRESS

PHILADELPHIA

Published by
University of Pennsylvania Press
Philadelphia, Pennsylvania 19104-4112
www.upenn.edu/pennpress

Printed in the United States of America on acid-free paper
1 3 5 7 9 10 8 6 4 2

Library of Congress Cataloging-in-Publication Data
ISBN 978-0-8122-5206-4

For my parents, Ramona Bonner and James Bonner

CONTENTS

Making Black Citizenship Politics

What is striking is the role legal principles have played
throughout America's history in determining the condition
of Negroes. They were enslaved by law, emancipated by law,
disenfranchised, and segregated by law; and, finally, they have
begun to win equality by law.

—Thurgood Marshall, "Reflections on the Bicentennial
of the United States Constitution," 1987

John Brown Russwurm sat at his desk on a winter day in 1829 to write an
essay explaining why he could no longer live in the United States. Russwurm
had been born in Jamaica in 1799, the child of a white American man and a
woman of African descent. Little is known of his mother. She may have been
free or enslaved, may have been African or of mixed parentage, and may have
died in childbirth or lived to see her son leave Jamaica when he was eight
years old. Russwurm's father gave the child parts of his name and his privilege, sending young John to school in Montreal in the early 1800s, then
inviting his black son to live with his white family in Portland, Maine.[1]

Russwurm was an immigrant, a background that likely shaped his feelings about the possibilities of the United States. When he graduated from
Bowdoin College in 1826, he delivered a commencement address that praised
the accomplishments of the Haitian Revolution and the republic it created.
Haiti, Russwurm said, revealed the "principle of liberty" that dwelt in men
of all colors. Russwurm considered studying medicine and emigrating to
Haiti to help the country become "an empire that will take rank with the
nations of the earth." But by the spring of 1827, he had put down roots in

New York, where he connected with a community of black activists that included Samuel Cornish, a minister and abolitionist who had been born to free black parents in Delaware. Together, Cornish and Russwurm transformed African American politics when they launched *Freedom's Journal*, the nation's first black newspaper, printing its first issue on March 16, 1827.[2]

From the paper's office at No. 5 Varick Street, blocks away from the Hudson River in lower Manhattan, Russwurm and Cornish had considered the "many schemes . . . in action concerning our people."[3] These included a plan to forcibly remove black people to the West African colony of Liberia, the pet project of a group of white politicians who established the American Colonization Society (ACS) in 1816. For most of the life of *Freedom's Journal*, Cornish, Russwurm, and their correspondents denied that the ACS would solve the problems free black people faced. That changed abruptly after Cornish left the *Journal* in Russwurm's hands.[4]

In February 1829, the new editor-in-chief announced his decision to leave the United States in terms that surprised and alarmed other activists. "Our views are materially altered," Russwurm wrote, declaring that he was now "a decided supporter of the American Colonization Society."[5] He believed black people had reached an impasse in working to change their status in the United States. "We consider it a mere waste of words to talk of ever enjoying citizenship in this country: it is utterly impossible in the nature of things."[6] In September 1829, John Brown Russwurm sailed for Liberia and never returned to the United States.[7]

While Russwurm did not believe black citizenship was possible in the United States, other African Americans understood that the meaning of citizenship was unsettled and that this instability might help them change their legal lives. Free black activists in the northern states publicly challenged racial exclusion by calling themselves citizens, invoking the status to claim specific rights. Because the terms of citizenship were uncertain, the status was a flexible and potent tool for African American politics. Black protest spurred conversations about citizenship among state and federal lawmakers, most notably Chief Justice Roger Taney's 1857 effort to deny that any black person could be a citizen in the United States. African American activists used citizenship in ways that shaped the long process of defining the nation's legal structures.[8]

Just weeks after Russwurm embraced colonization, Samuel Cornish returned to New York City and launched the *Rights of All*, the nation's second black newspaper.[9] He offered an alternative vision of the legal possibilities of

African American life in the ways he wrote about citizenship in that paper. Some white Americans believed colonization would compensate Africa for the continent's stolen generations, but Cornish instead demanded that lawmakers "do her sons justice where ever we find them." "Educate this oppressed and afflicted people," Cornish proclaimed, "encourage them in agricultural and mechanical persuits, and there will be no difficulty in making them good and happy citizens."[10] In addition to claiming that black people could be citizens, he declared that the status should entitle them to rights and opportunities. "Our colored citizens have been uniformly denied License as Car[t]men and porters," he wrote, using the status to seek new employment opportunities.[11] He also centered political rights in his vision of citizenship, urging black New Yorkers to seek and to use the right to vote—to "participate in your rights as citizens."[12] Cornish and other free black people saw possibility and power in the concept of citizenship. When Russwurm denied that black people could be citizens, he sparked immediate, forceful opposition because other black activists wanted to use citizenship to seek rights and protections. That form of protest grew out of their opposition to Russwurm and became a critical thread in antebellum black politics.

Free black Americans' overarching political goal was to change the legal circumstances of their lives. The malleable nature of citizenship made the status an important tool in that pursuit. In the era of the American Revolutionary War, lawmakers in several northern states enacted measures to gradually abolish slavery. But legislators and judges also constrained black freedom, denying black men the vote, excluding them from militias, and considering measures that would force African Americans out of their states. Black people relied on the concept of citizenship to challenge those restrictions and seek specific rights and protections. *Remaking the Republic* is the story of that political work as it developed from the 1820s through the 1860s across the free states. This book examines how and why black people called themselves citizens and the meanings of that particular form of their politics. Exploring their political work from this perspective illuminates the legal possibilities of citizen status and the ways African Americans took part in re-creating the legal order of the United States in the nineteenth century. African Americans were active participants in the process of constructing citizenship, determining to whom the status was available and what its content would be.

Black people were able to use citizenship in their politics because there was no agreed-upon definition of citizen status in the law of the early United States.[13] The authors of the U.S. Constitution used the terms "citizen" and "citizens" eleven times in the document. According to the Constitution, citizenship was a criterion for election to Congress or the presidency, a descriptor of those who might sue in federal court, and a status that secured to an individual an unspecified set of "Privileges and Immunities."[14] The framers suggested that citizenship could be an important determinant of an individual's legal life, but they did not clarify the rights or obligations the status entailed or who could call themselves a citizen. Generally, people in the early United States agreed that citizenship described a relationship between individuals and a government, but the conditions and content of the relationship were ill-defined.[15] As late as 1862, U.S. Attorney General Edward Bates acknowledged the persistent vagueness of the status. "Eighty years of practical enjoyment of citizenship, under the Constitution, have not sufficed to teach us either the exact meaning of the word, or the constituent elements of the thing we prize so highly," Bates wrote.[16] That uncertainty provided a space for black politics to operate, enabling African Americans to claim legal protections through citizen status.

Although citizenship could be a path to rights, no decisive legal statement declared that the status must be the foundation for an individual's legal identity. Citizenship remained vague for so long in part because many lawmakers and others did not agree that the status was important for defining identity or securing legal protections. The vagueness stemmed in part from the fact that the framers of the Constitution refused to resolve essential questions about the relationship between states and the federal government. It was unclear how the legal authority of the states related to one another and to that of the national government, and so it was also uncertain to whom an individual should turn to resolve disputes about his or her rights or which level of government would be the operative authority in shaping people's legal lives. State and federal governments legislated and adjudicated questions of rights and obligations, and it was not clear how citizenship might be crafted or administered on either the state or national level or through some combination of the two. Many people in the early United States looked to local courts for justice and had little sense of close ties to the federal government. Generally, authority was decentralized and individuals' legal lives were individual, particular to their contexts, personal connections, wealth, gender, and race.[17] By claiming rights as citizens, black people therefore helped make citizenship more important, pushing the status toward the center of lawmaking discussions, arguing that it should be a cornerstone for individuals' rights and their relationships to American governments. Through their political work, black people built a new republic, one that rested on a legal order in which citizen status connected individuals to the federal government through a web of rights and obligations.

Free black people in the North established community institutions, developed distinctive cultural practices, and organized to practice multiple forms of politics in the nineteenth century. Black northerners did all these things in the face of prejudice, racist violence, legal exclusion, and widespread economic disempowerment.[18] Scholars have explored the myriad ways activists pushed against the limits of freedom and sought to remake their lives. But much of this scholarship has presented activists as striving toward "full citizenship" and has thus obscured the particular ways African Americans used citizen status in pursuit of legal change. Important forms of black protest were possible because there was no accepted legal understanding of citizenship. Further, black protest was potent because it made claims about the foundations of individual Americans' legal identities. Black citizenship politics involved African Americans calling themselves citizens and issuing public demands for formal legal changes, deploying the ill-defined legal status in pursuit of protections they deemed essential.[19]

By understanding the ways black people exploited the uncertainties of citizenship, we can see how their work contributed to the process of defining the status and helped remake the nation's legal order. In the ways black activists used citizenship, they generated and engaged in lawmaking conversations that were part of the long process of determining the legal shape of the republic. Exploring black citizenship politics offers a fuller portrait of African American protest and its transformative potential. This book seeks to specify the work black Americans did when they talked about citizenship and to examine the broadest possibilities of their protest for legal developments in the United States.[20]

This study is built around the work marginalized people did to shape legal development in the early United States. Although African Americans were often excluded from spaces where laws were drafted and court cases decided, black northerners exploited uncertainties of federal law in order to shape its terms.[21] For instance, in 1837, hundreds of black women and men violently rescued an alleged fugitive slave in New York City, challenging the legal process of slavecatching and demanding protections of their personal security. In the 1840s, a black New Yorker named Willis Hodges acquired land in upstate New York as a path to securing the franchise in the state, realizing his vision of a citizenship defined by participation in formal politics.

In the late 1850s, black Bostonians protested the *Dred Scott* decision that denied they could be citizens by celebrating Crispus Attucks, a black hero of the revolutionary era who represented the longstanding, critical presence of black people in the nation. These and other black northerners molded ideas about their legal position and the nature of citizenship through the statements they broadcast in conventions and newspapers as well as through legal and extralegal public displays. By grappling with the concept of citizenship, African Americans pushed their voices into lawmaking discussions at the highest level. They practiced their politics in ways they knew would resonate because of uncertainties about federalism, individual rights, and the future of slavery that stood at the heart of the nation's laws and governments. Free African Americans in the North imagined and helped to build a new legal order through their political uses of citizenship.[22]

*   *   *

Remaking the Republic is rooted in the extensive published record of antebellum black protest. Free African Americans believed that speaking in public was essential to producing change. They used common political forms of the early United States—organizing conventions, printing newspapers, circulating petitions, gathering for public demonstrations—hoping to change ideas about black people and the legal protections to which they were entitled. Black northerners published dozens of newspapers under such weighty titles as the *Rights of All*, the *Colored American*, the *North Star*, the *Ram's Horn*, the *Aliened American*, the *Mirror of Liberty*, and the *Colored Citizen*.

These papers conveyed the thoughts of prominent editors like Samuel Cornish and Frederick Douglass, who had formal education, social connections with white northerners, and access to resources that amplified their voices and concerns. But black newspapers also enabled lesser-known black people to engage the public through letters to the editor as well as by organizing and participating in political events that newspapers covered. State and national conventions brought together dozens of black activists to discuss contemporary challenges and develop political strategies, often including hundreds of people as participants and audience members in formal and informal proceedings. And public protest meetings were designed to be large and open, to present a sizable community interested in pursuing legal change.

Black men's voices emerge clearly and frequently in this archive, while black women often remain at the margins. African American activists, like others in the nineteenth century, tended to view politics as a space for men; newspapers and conventions offered limited opportunities for women to speak directly to the public. Still, women were essential to the functioning of conventions and to the survival of black activists.[23] Further, black women did a great deal of what was seen as traditionally male political work—standing on the front lines during fugitive rescues, attending public meetings where they endorsed and contested men's claims, and organizing in their own spaces to offer their own arguments about black people's proper legal position. I seek to underscore important moments when black women engaged in the public forms of black citizenship politics, to consider what these moments meant to them, and to analyze critically the gendered forms and limitations of particular strategies of black protest.

While a handful of well-connected men produced many of the statements at the heart of this book, the printed record in which their voices are most vivid reflects a wider African American community. Extant sources emerged from a free black population characterized by ideological conflicts, and those tensions helped shape published statements. In collaboration and in conflict, black northerners advocated legal changes that could transform the lives of a broad range of people in the United States. I use printed material to explore the concerns of a large, diverse, politically engaged free black population. Through these sources, I tell the story of the complex communities and ideas that shaped the development of American laws in the nineteenth century.[24]

The printed records of northern black activists make clear that free African Americans were knit together in a political community that crossed state borders. Black people's political concerns were not bound by political geography. Just as lawmakers looked to other states for precedent, black people saw that their advocacy could shape legal developments beyond their local communities. Further, making claims based on a national citizen status was significant for people beyond the specific state in which those claims were made. Most importantly, the infrastructure of black politics relied on interstate networks and labor, reflecting and perpetuating a community of concern that spanned the free states.[25]

This book tells the story of how African American activists reshaped law and society as they worked to enrich their own freedom. In the 1860s, emancipation and Reconstruction created new opportunities for African

Americans to define their relationship with the federal government, and the government took definitive steps to determine the criteria for and rights of citizenship. But the central questions of Reconstruction—the qualities of black freedom and the content of American citizenship—had a long and contentious antebellum history.[26] Black northerners' political work helped to produce the legal changes of the Civil War era. By the time of the war, activists had for decades emphasized that black people should be seen as citizens, that citizen status should link people to the federal government, and that federal authority should protect people's rights. They built the intellectual context for the legal changes of Reconstruction.[27]

This story of free black people's politics reveals the techniques that marginalized groups have used to challenge and remake the structures that excluded them. It is a story of a radical political project working within the rhetorical pathways that the uncertain terms of citizenship provided. African Americans seized the opportunity to remake the republic's legal foundations by working to change understandings of legal belonging in the nation. The nation's laws were, and remain, tenuous and malleable. *Remaking the Republic* is about black people imagining futures as African Americans and using citizenship to build them. Understanding the many ways that people could and did redefine the law illuminates the possibilities of securing justice in exclusionary societies. Bringing together histories of black politics and American laws highlights the ways law has been made and contested by those who were formally excluded from government. It underlines the ways the law, which has so often been a tool to bind black people, also was used to create new possibilities for African Americans' lives.

*   *   *

The first three chapters of this book explore black activists' work to connect with an expanding set of communities in pursuit of rights. First, I consider the ways black New Yorkers used citizenship to protest disfranchisement. People in New York joined those in other states who faced similar restrictions. Together, they argued that because they had built their communities, they were citizens, and that citizenship must entail formal political rights. Chapter 2 connects black politics to debates about the nation's expansion in the early 1840s. As lawmakers considered the annexation of Texas and the changing geography of slavery, black activists challenged state-level legal restrictions with appeals to federal authority, arguing that they should possess rights through a national citizen status. To foster black political unity and a relationship with the federal government, they presented themselves as a body of African American citizens, a national community bound together by a shared legal status. In the spring of 1848, revolutions across Europe captured Americans' attention. Chapter 3 builds around Frederick Douglass's thoughts on Europe and the ways activists attacked the hypocrisy of a nation of slaveholders who praised a new birth of freedom abroad. Traveling and reading about Europe influenced the ways black people imagined citizenship and worked for legal change in the late 1840s.

The second half of the book focuses on a set of protest strategies black activists used amid a series of legal and political watersheds during the mid-nineteenth century. Slavecatchers posed the most urgent threat to black northerners' freedom. Activists used citizenship to argue for legal protections, including a jury trial for any person alleged to be a fugitive from slavery. Chapter 4 examines that work in the 1830s and 1840s alongside extralegal rescues, which also implicitly demanded legal protections of black freedom. The potency of those multiple forms of black politics led southerners in Congress to push through the Fugitive Slave Act of 1850, a law that created a substantial new apparatus to arrest black people in the North and ship them into bondage in the South. Similarly, black citizenship politics produced other moments of crisis and opportunity in the next two decades. In May 1857, Chief Justice Roger Taney erected a new legal barrier designed to silence African Americans' arguments about citizenship when he ruled in *Dred Scott v. Sandford* that black people could never be American citizens. Chapter 5 traces black responses to Taney's ruling. Activists denied Taney's authority, working to ensure that the terms of citizenship remained a ground for debate and a useful political tool. While *Dred Scott* encouraged some to consider following John Russwurm to West Africa, the Civil War offered profound opportunities to remake black people's legal lives. Activists sought enlistment and equal pay by presenting themselves as citizens, expecting that that status and their sacrifice would secure their rights in peacetime. Chapter 6 shows how antebellum forms of politics persisted into the Civil War era and how they molded urgent discussions about the content of citizenship and the significance of suffrage.

In June 1866, Congress agreed to the Fourteenth Amendment, which conferred citizenship on black people who were born in the United States and ensured "the equal protection of the laws" to American citizens. This story closes in the aftermath of that measure, as black people experienced the

possibilities and limits of citizen status. The vagueness of the Fourteenth
Amendment, the brutality of white resistance to black rights, and the failures
of legal enforcement increasingly demanded that African Americans continue
the work they had done in the antebellum period, struggling to mold the
terms of citizenship and make the status meaningful in their lives.

CHAPTER 1

An Integral Portion of This Republic

When John Russwurm announced his support for colonization, Samuel Cornish went immediately to work to refute the claim that black people could not be American citizens. Cornish had left the newspaper business, but in the spring of 1829, he returned to New York City and launched the *Rights of All*. That paper facilitated black people's efforts to establish a clear legal position for themselves in the United States. From the late 1820s through the 1830s, in the *Rights of All* and his subsequent work, Cornish deployed many of the principal strategies of early antebellum black politics. He stood at the forefront of black protest that linked people across the free states. He spoke to black and white Americans and used citizenship to fight disfranchisement and colonization, the central components of black exclusion.

Cornish and other black Americans rejected John Russwurm's pessimism because they saw possibility in the vagueness of citizenship.[1] Black people were citizens because they contributed to American communities, activists argued. Further, they claimed citizen status should provide them with specific rights, in particular equal access to the vote. For Cornish and his colleagues, there was a simple logic to their claims. No definitive legal statement existed to exclude African Americans from citizen status. Activists used that ambiguity to pursue specific legal protections, responding directly to the terms of the laws that excluded them and urging those in positions of power to see black people as part of a community of citizens entitled to rights. Black citizenship politics in the early antebellum period wove together a range of projects—anticolonization, agrarianism, moral uplift, and the pursuit of the vote. Cornish knit together a cohort of black activists whose work helped shape the terms of citizenship as they sought opportunities to live as African Americans.

*   *   *

Samuel Cornish did essential work to create the political tools black activists used to make public claims about the terms of citizenship. Cornish was born free in the slaveholding society of Delaware in 1795. When he was around twenty years old, he began training for the ministry at Philadelphia's First African Presbyterian Church. Cornish honed his voice in the church, then spread it in a range of activist work. He was an early advocate of black state and national conventions, a cofounder of the American Anti-Slavery Society, and a leader of the New York Committee of Vigilance, which worked to protect free people from slavecatchers.[2] In the 1820s and 1830s, Cornish helped to produce a black print culture that was central to activists' efforts to claim rights through citizenship.

In May 1829, just two months after John Russwurm closed *Freedom's Journal*, Cornish introduced the nation's second black newspaper. His new project presented both subtle and overt opposition to Russwurm's ideas. Cornish greeted readers of the *Rights of All* with a masthead quoting Proverbs 14:34: "Righteousness exalteth a nation: but sin is a reproach to any people." The first half of that verse had run atop the *Journal*, and it might have seemed a simple choice for an antislavery minister. But invoking Proverbs 14 conveyed complex meanings beyond an expression of devotion. The chapter begins, "Every wise woman buildeth her house: but the foolish plucketh it down with her hands." Throughout, Proverbs 14 offers guidelines for individuals and communities. Cornish's chosen masthead linked the new paper to its predecessor and, for readers familiar with the Bible, might have brought to mind his unwise former colleague.[3] He launched the *Rights of All* in direct opposition to Russwurm, who had abandoned the nation that had once been his home and had torn down the activist "house" he had established in the office of *Freedom's Journal*.

In a message introducing readers to the paper, Cornish described it as a tool for "the general improvement of Society" and announced his intent to focus on black people, the most "oppressed and afflicted" members of the population. He acknowledged that he could be criticized for having left his post at the *Journal*, and he encouraged readers and patrons to judge his new venture on its own merit, independent of any earlier work. But he chose to raise the issue of "the late Editor" of *Freedom's Journal*, declining to mention Russwurm by name. "To me the subject is equally strange as to others," he wrote, calling Russwurm's support for the ACS one of the "novelties of the day." Cornish concluded that he and "the intelligent of my brethren gener-ally," were convinced that for most black people, colonization was "in no wise calculated, to meet their wants or ameliorate their condition."[4]

From its beginnings, then, Cornish used the *Rights of All* to marginalize Russwurm and the claim that black people could not be citizens, presenting audiences with African Americans who were determined to change the cir-cumstances of their lives in the United States. He was invested in "this great Republick" and in determining what work he might contribute "towards the improvement of all its parts."[5] When editors from the *New York Observer and Chronicle* said the new paper resulted from "the change of the 'Freedom's Journal' in respect to African colonization," Cornish denied their claim, which he called a "gratuitous censure."[6] But it is instructive to read his paper, and with it much of early antebellum black protest, as an extended response to the assertion that black Americans could not be citizens. Colonizationists looked to compensate Africa for her stolen generations with exiled black Americans, but Cornish urged Americans to "do her sons justice where ever we find them." "Educate this oppressed and afflicted people," he demanded, "encourage them in agricultural and mechanical persuits, and there will be no difficulty in making them good and happy citizens."[7] Many black Ameri-cans were outraged at those who seemed to prioritize Africa over their native country. "Mr. Russwurm tells us, he knows no other home for us than Africa," one black Philadelphian noted. "As his usefulness is entirely lost to the people, I sincerely pray that he may have the honor to live and also die there."[8]

Cornish often contested Russwurm's arguments without printing his former colleague's name. The editors of the *Observer* had overlooked Russ-wurm's claims about citizenship and had thus misrepresented black Ameri-cans' concerns. For Cornish, the *Observer*'s announcement of his paper was a "gratuitous censure" because it reduced black politics to a reactionary move-ment against the ACS and ignored the work of claiming and shaping citizen-ship in the United States. He demanded that those in power "do justice" for African Americans by offering opportunities for education and labor, and he called on black people to seize those opportunities in order to solidify their claims to citizen status. Together, individuals and governments would reshape the terms of African Americans' lives. He surely hoped that the *Observer* would reprint his alternative portrait of African Americans' concerns.

Cornish initiated a public correspondence with the editors of the *Observer* in the hope of broadening the readership of the *Rights of All*. The

Observer was a weekly paper connected to the Presbyterian Church that did not typically cover black politics, but its editors were sympathetic to colonization and had earlier shown interest in Russwurm and *Freedom's Journal.*[9] By writing about that paper, Cornish spoke to white New Yorkers who were apparently uninterested in the work of changing black people's lives in the country. Newspapers in places including Baltimore, Boston, and Norwich, Connecticut, announced the launch of the *Rights of All* and encouraged Cornish to see the potential reach of his paper.[10] Cornish printed letters from an array of black and white correspondents interested in legal change. Generally, he crafted the paper with a diverse readership in mind and with the goal of widening his subscriber base. He published columns advising African Americans on proper conduct, expecting that black people would read them. But he frequently addressed free black northerners in his calls for more subscribers. Cornish understood that people often read a single copy of a newspaper aloud to an audience of friends and acquaintances. He likely hoped that some of those friends and acquaintances might choose to become subscribers themselves.[11] He also printed reasoned arguments against unjust laws, perhaps hoping his words would reach white voters and lawmakers who did not favor racial equality. And in the summer of 1829, Cornish may also have been writing to John Russwurm, who remained in New York making final arrangements for his move to Liberia. Perhaps Cornish held out hope that he might convince his former colleague of the error of emigration.

His work set the tone for later black editors who would similarly address an array of topics and target a range of black and white audiences.[12] In general, black newspapers needed an interracial readership for financial stability. Editors and contributors also understood that, through print, they might change the minds of those in the power structure who remained prejudiced as well as shape conversations and policy regarding African Americans. And people like Cornish reached a far broader audience than a list of subscribers indicates because of the ways ideas circulated in antebellum print culture.[13]

Cornish subtly attacked Russwurm throughout the *Rights of All*, including in a message encouraging black Americans to follow the example of Jewish people in London who petitioned Parliament for legal equality. "Americans we truly are, by birth and feeling," Cornish wrote. He urged black people to assert more forcefully their desire for legal protections in the United States. He commanded his readers, "Let no man talk of impossibility; with God, all things are possible."[14] Many black activists expressed similar optimism rooted in their Christian faith. To Cornish, the pessimistic Russ-wurm did not belong in a community of black Christian men and women. Cornish's criticism was indirect, but his target was clear. In August 1829, with Russwurm making final preparations to leave the country, Cornish wrote, "Any coloured man, of common intelligence, who gives his countenance and influence, to [Liberia] . . . should be considered as a traitor to his brethren, and discarded by every respectable man of colour."[15] Protesting the ACS and, by implication, Russwurm, he offered an alternative vision of black Americans' future and laid the foundation for black citizenship politics.

Colonization was part of a broader project of restricting black people's unfettered movement and access to space in the United States.[16] Pennsylvania lawmakers proposed two measures in 1832, one that would limit protections available to alleged fugitive slaves and the other to outlaw new black migra-tion into the commonwealth.[17] Activists turned again to print culture for their response, collecting signatures on a petition against those measures.[18] James Forten delivered their message to the state legislature. Born free in 1766, Forten ran a profitable sail-making shop in Philadelphia, had served on a privateer during the American Revolution, and had previously organized in opposition to an effort by state lawmakers to outlaw new black migrants in the 1810s. In 1832, Forten and his fellow activists delivered their petition to state lawmakers and had it published, convinced that their concerns were meaningful beyond the population of free black Pennsylvanians.

Forten reminded lawmakers that their state constitution declared that all men were "born equally free and independent" and that, under its terms, "every man shall have a remedy by due course of law."[19] The petitioners denied that free black people endangered the state and vehemently rejected the prevailing argument that they had "promoted[ed] servile insurrections."[20] The petitioners might have chosen Forten as their representative because he had made a specific, memorable contribution to the nation by fighting in the Revolutionary War. His personal history reflected African Americans' emotional ties to the nation, the less tangible but no less powerful feelings that bound people to their home. "They feel themselves to be citizens of Pennsylvania [and] children of the state," Forten explained.[21] The phrase conjured an image of activists throwing themselves on the mercy of the legis-lature, asking that the state reciprocate their feelings. But it also charged the state for dereliction of its duties. They made an emotional appeal designed to change the law, arguing for a citizen status that imposed responsibilities on individuals as well as on the government. From the petitioners' perspective, it was no more just for Pennsylvania to reject James Forten than it was for a mother to abandon her infant. Citizenship should bind American people and governments in a web of obligations. Perhaps the strength of that appeal pushed lawmakers to reconsider. Perhaps logic moved legislators, convinced that it would not benefit their state to exclude people like Forten who had fought to create the nation. Pennsylvania officials rejected the proposed law to bar black migration into the state.[22] But white northerners would continue to promote similar exclusionary measures that threatened black people's claims to rights as citizens.

*   *   *

Forten's military service was part of a history that refuted the idea that African Americans had little to offer society as prospective citizens. Colonizationists and those who wanted to bar black people from particular states argued that African Americans were disproportionately poor, violent, and immoral. The personal histories of people like Forten helped refute those ideas. Activists argued that people who offered useful contributions to their communities were entitled to citizen status. In 1832, the Pennsylvania petitioners presented data that denied charges of black poverty, including evidence that African Americans were only 4 percent of the 549 people who had received poor relief from the state in 1830, far less than their 8 percent of the state's population. Forten estimated that African Americans paid more than enough in taxes to support poor black Pennsylvanians, and he noted that many black people turned to African American benevolent societies for relief rather than seeking state aid. The petitioners said black Pennsylvanians owned more than $100,000 in real property and that many worked in skilled mechanical trades despite prejudice that limited their opportunities for apprenticeships.[23] Black self-sufficiency was a foundation for claims to legal protections.

Because African Americans were valuable members in their communities, black removal would harm people across the nation. Samuel Cornish built the *Rights of All* around the argument that African Americans were important, enthusiastic contributors to the United States. In July 1829, when government officials gathered to amend New York City's charter, Cornish encouraged them to provide equal employment opportunity in the city. "The pursuit of an honest living," he hoped, "will be secured to all our citizens." He printed an editorial the morning the officials planned to meet in which he emphasized black people's desire to work in specific jobs for their own benefit and to help their city develop. "Our colored citizens have uniformly been denied License as Car[t]men and porters," Cornish wrote. As he sat at his desk drafting that editorial, Cornish must have imagined lawmakers traveling through lower Manhattan on their way to the meeting: perhaps some would pick up an unfamiliar newspaper or overhear a discussion about the opinionated black editor and be convinced that black people were essential workers for the city. Cornish wanted people to reexamine their ideas about black Americans and about citizenship as a legal status. It was likely no coincidence that he published this message just as the New York Workingmen's Party emerged in the city, a group of white laborers who organized to secure political and economic power. He wanted to capitalize on extant discussions about the relationship between work and formal political rights.[24] He outlined a capacious citizenship that would have appealed to many readers, one defined by individuals' contributions to their communities. He sought job opportunities for black Americans in ways that aligned with his political goals.[25]

New York in the 1820s was a city on the move, where cartmen and porters performed critical tasks. They transported lumber, sand, and other building supplies, and they carried groceries and household goods between shops and residences in the expanding city. Licensed cartmen decided who could join their guild, and by tradition, they were entitled to the freemanship, a remnant of colonial law that provided political privileges, including voting rights, in recognition of a person's work.[26] Cornish's demand that black New Yorkers have access to jobs as cartmen asked lawmakers to connect black people to a new legal status. African Americans wanted to do the hard, necessary work that made the city grow. In return, Cornish sought black access to a specific job that had historical ties to formal political power. In this message, he crafted a citizenship that gave political weight to black labor, connecting it to rights through the city's legal traditions. He asked the city to enact a law that would limit the influence of prejudice and make employment opportunities and formal political voice available to working black New Yorkers.

Here and elsewhere, Cornish used traditionally male work to claim rights through citizenship. He spoke from the context of male-dominated public politics of the nineteenth century. Indeed, although these activists thought in transformative ways about people's legal statuses, in many cases, they elided or obscured questions about women's rights. To some extent, Cornish and other black male activists worked for change within the limits of accepted

American ideas about political power. In his direct response to legal restrictions imposed on black men, he seemed uninterested in the possibility that women should engage in formal politics.

As they demanded work opportunities, black activists also spoke extensively about issues of morality. They used personal uplift programs to pursue legal change. As northern state lawmakers enacted laws that gradually ended slavery, they also imposed limits on black freedom, including, for example, measures that disfranchised black people and excluded black men from state militias. White northerners worried that the horrors of slavery had rendered black people unfit for freedom. Black activists looked to alleviate those concerns through a series of programs aimed at their "moral improvement." They worked to spread Christianity, literacy, and standards of personal conduct among freed people. They promoted specific virtues such as temperance, religious devotion, frugality, and industriousness.[27] Activists made arguments about citizenship in conjunction with that moral reform work. Uplift programs reflected concerns about morality and the desire to eliminate the legal restrictions on black northerners' freedom. Black activists' moralizing was part of their efforts to use citizenship in pursuit of specific legal changes.[28]

As he designed the layout for the first issue of the *Rights of All*, Cornish gave prominent place to a statement that linked morality, labor, and citizenship. Directly beneath his introductory statement, he copied an article from the *Boston Courier* that celebrated agrarian life, and he offered comments in support of that message. Rural landowners lived enviably independent lives, he said, vastly different from the geographic and economic restrictions urban residents felt. A farmer could "have the happiness to see his offspring [become] useful and virtuous citizens," but Cornish anticipated that a city dweller would more likely raise "fashionable vagabonds." He echoed a common concern that black people cared more about ostentatious displays of wealth than about the work necessary to earn it. Cornish argued that families who had the means should display their "respectability" by embracing an agrarian lifestyle: leaving cities, purchasing land, and preparing their children "for an investment in the right of soil." A number of black New Yorkers had already made new homes in the countryside, and he hoped others would follow suit, "until our portion of city dissipation is transformed into country respectability and usefulness." Cornish's concerns about respectability and personal conduct reflected Christian beliefs that many black northerners shared. And even readers who disliked Cornish's tone might have been glad to read the editor's concrete plan for black people to escape the challenges they faced in cities. He closed one call for black agrarianism with an advertisement for 12,000 acres of land being sold in hundred-acre plots "in a fertile county in the state of New-York," available at a price of 20 shillings an acre. People in towns and cities could form associations to purchase plots, he suggested.[29] Writing from his Manhattan office, Cornish took hold of the notion of agrarian virtue to advance his political ends. Farming could offer black people a path to citizen status and then onward to legal protections. Cornish rhetorically opened a place for black Americans in a citizenry defined by morality and useful work.[30]

Cornish's was one voice in a chorus of free black people who promoted moral improvement and connected legal protections to a person's contributions to a community. For instance, a group of women who established the African Female Benevolent Society in Troy, New York, in 1833, declared that through divine principles of human equality, they were "entitled to the same rights and privileges" as "our fellow beings who differ from us in complexion alone." They would embrace "such virtues as will render us happy and useful to society" to contest the legal manifestations of prejudice.[31] Society members chose Elizabeth Wicks to speak at the organization's first anniversary. As she reflected on their work in the previous year, Wicks declared, "My friends, I think I see an opening in behalf of our oppressed race."[32] She urged action, asking young people not to let their "youth be wasted away without improvement and utterly lost to every valuable and noble purpose." Wicks reminded her fellow society members of the broad significance of their work, saying, "Let our minds travel south and sympathise with the present state of the two millions of our brethren who are yet in bondage." She encouraged New York's black women to think of their moral reform work as an antislavery crusade.[33] The Society published Wicks's address and their constitution together in a pamphlet, hoping that other black women in Troy would read about and join their efforts. Wicks and her fellow black women demanded legal change, working against racial prejudice and against the arguments of other activists that suggested men should lead the charge of black protest. They were undiscouraged by Cornish's gendered politics and convinced that they could use moral improvement as a path to legal protections, regardless of prevailing ideas about who should possess rights.

Black people connected their uplift politics across a broader geography when they launched the American Moral Reform Society (AMRS) in 1835.[34] At their annual meeting the following year, AMRS members proclaimed that education was "the most valuable blessing that we, as a people, can bestow upon the rising generation." Speaking at that gathering, William Watkins added to education "moral training," arguing that together, those programs could remedy "the universal depravity of the human heart" and its influence on the nation's laws.[35] Born in Maryland in 1801, the son of a free black minister, the precocious Watkins established a school for black children when he was only nineteen. He did the dangerous work of black politics in a slave state and remained attuned to the concerns of African Americans beyond Maryland's borders.[36] Watkins believed that individuals' character shaped their communities. "It is unquestionable," he declared in 1836, "that those children who are early taught to remember their Creator . . . to fear God and keep his commandments . . . will be far more likely than others, in adult life to be good citizens and exemplary christians."[37] A citizen must be morally upright, he said. Watkins and other delegates to the AMRS meeting laid a foundation in personal conduct for the nebulous legal status of citizenship. By creating a society dedicated to moral reform, black people implicitly argued that they were capable of being good citizens because they were so concerned with morality. Further, making personal conduct a foundation for citizenship denied claims that there was an insurmountable racial barrier to the status.

Watkins described for his audience a man named Henry Blair, who Watkins presented as a model black citizen. Blair was also a free black Marylander who had recently patented a mechanized corn planter and had his device exhibited in the nation's capital. According to Watkins, Blair held himself to a high moral standard, and his invention revealed black people's intellectual capacity. Watkins conjured for his audience an image of Blair standing beside his device, "triumphantly refuting" ideas of black inferiority. So long as black people worked to become "more intelligent, more useful, more respectable," none could say they were unfit for life in the United States.[38] Blair's intellect and morality were mutually reinforcing traits. "The attractions of the gaming table and the ale house are not, in [Blair's] view, to be compared with those to be found in his own domicil—in the rich volumes of a well selected library." Black people thus educated and morally restrained would "cease to grovel . . . [and] command respect and consideration from all who respect themselves and whose good opinions are worth having." Blair offered a lesson for black Americans. "Give the rising generation a good education," Watkins declared, "and you instruct them in, and qualify them for, all the duties of life—you make them useful citizens and productive christians."[39] Morality and intellect were inseparable, and improvement in both realms suited black people for citizen status in the United States.

Watkins hoped that his address, published separately from the AMRS proceedings, could influence those who doubted "'that *all* men are created *equal.*'"[40] His was part of a tradition of proclaiming equality in print, a history in which words produced real change. He spoke to fellow reformers and to white opponents of racial equality. Watkins, along with Samuel Cornish and Elizabeth Wicks, suggested that black people could enjoy citizen status if they pursued moral improvement and education. Their arguments laid foundations for people to claim legal protections through citizen status. Their vision of citizenship placed the power for change in black people's hands, working to ensure that prejudice could not prevent African Americans from securing legal change. Activists thus made arguments about the social foundations of citizenship as a step toward using the status to claim rights.

*   *   *

Moral uplift challenged the advocates of colonization and specified the responsibilities of an American citizen. From that foundation, activists outlined the rights citizenship should entail, focusing particularly on formal political participation. Black New Yorkers pursued uplift politics in direct response to state restrictions on black suffrage embedded in the 1821 constitution. When a delegate to that year's constitutional convention proposed to limit the franchise to white men over age twenty-one, he sparked a heated debate over the terms and significance of civic participation. John Ross favored disfranchising black men because "they are a *peculiar* people," who were "seldom, if ever, required to share in the burdens or defense of the State." Others echoed Ross's doubts that black people would reliably promote the common good as voters.[41] Delegates voted against that proposal, but it made black suffrage a question for debate. They appointed a committee to define new qualifications for voting, and its membership included many who had supported the sweeping racial exclusion. Committee members proposed a "freehold qualification" requiring black New Yorkers to own $250 in real property in order to vote.[42] One delegate worried that under the proposal, "37,000 of our free black citizens, and their posterity, for ever, shall be degraded by our constitution." Prejudice would prevent many black New Yorkers from earning the wealth required to vote, others observed. But the measure passed, in part because men like Martin Van Buren believed that the property requirement "held out inducements to industry" among black New Yorkers.[43]

Black activists thus understood the promotion of moral uplift and industrious labor as ways to refute the arguments that had been used to disfranchise them. And they understood that they might use citizenship to claim formal political rights. When Cornish and Russwurm announced *Freedom's Journal* in 1827, they intended to "urge our brethren to use their right to the elective franchise as free citizens."[44] They framed suffrage as a fundamental aspect of citizen status, and they did not mention the freehold qualification, which they saw as an illegitimate denial of an essential right. In August 1828, Russwurm published the voting regulations in states from Maine to Mississippi. "In every case," he concluded, "voters are required to be citizens of the United States, by birth or naturalization."[45] Linking suffrage and citizenship would open the polls to black Americans if they could claim citizen status through their personal conduct. Uplift ideology emerged from conservative ideas about personal conduct, but activists deployed it in radical challenges to the exclusionary legal order and in pursuit of formal political rights. If they showed people like Martin Van Buren the myriad ways they contributed to their communities as well as the extent to which they were diligent and frugal, they would solidify their claims to suffrage. Just six months before Russwurm decided to emigrate, he seems to have agreed with Cornish that through uplift ideology, citizenship could offer a path to black rights.

But Russwurm ultimately grew tired of talking about citizenship and demanding black suffrage, leaving the project to Cornish and the *Rights of All*. Cornish made the radical claim that delegates to the 1821 Constitutional Convention had acted "very wrong and illegally." "A State has the right of appointing qualifications of its voters," he said, but it was illegal to make color one of those distinctions, just as it was illegal "to require of A. six feet stature, and not require of B. the same."[46] This was a transformative vision of the law for the young republic, a claim that discrimination on the basis of natural traits was fundamentally unjust. In his pursuit of suffrage, Cornish made a sweeping argument in favor of racial equality before the law.

Cornish published specific critiques of state laws that presented barriers on a path to justice. His editorial seeking opportunities for black men as "cartmen and porters" not only reflected ideas about the freemanship but also responded directly to the text of New York's 1821 constitution. Article II, Section 1 of the constitution established basic qualifications for voters—male citizens, twenty-one years old, residents in the state for at least six months, who had paid a property tax. The constitution also allowed any man to vote who had been exempted from taxation, performed militia duty, been exempted from the militia because he was a fireman or had worked in building public roads. At the end of that list, the constitution declared that "no man of colour" could vote without meeting the $250 property requirement.[47] White men's work offered them a variety of routes to the polls; labor was critical to lawmakers' ideas about voting and citizenship in the early antebellum period. And so when Samuel Cornish promoted black agrarian self-sufficiency or called for people to do useful work in their communities, he demanded rights in the terms state lawmakers had established. Talking about specific kinds of men's work delivered a targeted attack on black exclusion. Disfranchisement was unjust because black men were walking the very paths to suffrage that lawmakers had built for white men. Cornish was redefining the community, pushing lawmakers to think of "men of colour" within the category of "male citizens" that comprised the electorate.

Searching for an example that connected personal conduct, citizen status, and suffrage, Cornish turned to the government of British Honduras, the Central American colony that would become Belize. He quoted the white editor of the New York *Albion*, who was surprised that "the coloured population there seems to have equal privileges with the white, and are actually struggling with them for political ascendancy." Any person, black or white, who had been born in the colony and possessed $3,000 worth of property could be elected to the colonial legislature. While Cornish might have disagreed with the property qualification, the fact that it was universal reflected the truth of human equality. "Why should there be any distinction among the worms of the *dust*," he wrote, "the occupants of Jehovah's footstool, save that which results from merit?" Christianity decreed all men to be equal and offered a foundation for their personal conduct. "Cultivated minds and sanctified hearts, would so qualify our brethren in Honduras for the exercise of their rights, as to leave the *Albion*, no cause for surprise." He concluded, "The same causes . . . will produce the same effects in this country."[48] Protestantism was central to Cornish's political ideology, as it was for many northern black activists. He put his faith to work, advocating "sanctified hearts" because they showed people's fitness for political rights.

Lawmakers in northern states deprived black people of specific rights and, as in Pennsylvania, tried to enact laws to bar African Americans from living in their states. Activists recognized that they could use uplift politics to oppose residency restrictions in the same ways they pushed for equal voting rights. Black New Yorkers' struggles for suffrage paralleled fights against laws that restricted black movement and residency. In 1807, Ohio enacted a law requiring black emigrants to pay a $500 bond within twenty days of entering the state. Lawmakers justified the law with claims about personal conduct, arguing that the bond was insurance against the criminality, poverty, and general misconduct they anticipated of African Americans. The law lay dormant for two decades, but in 1829, officials began planning to enforce it, perhaps fearing a black population boom.[49] On hearing that news, a black man in Pittsburgh wrote to Samuel Cornish to denounce the measure, which he saw as a product of southern influence. The author, who chose to remain anonymous, thought Ohioans were appeasing white southerners who had moved to the state but disliked seeing black people thriving as "husbandmen, mechanics, and labourers." The law had been unenforced so long, he wrote, precisely because it reflected the concerns of a prejudiced minority. African Americans had cleared and cultivated the Ohio territory on which white southerners settled, but once the landscape was tamed, state officials were happy to exclude black people. Ohio's law seemed to reflect federal policies of Indian removal, and the Pittsburgh writer encouraged policymakers to reconsider enforcing a measure that would "tarnish the fair-escutcheon of our national character."[50] Like Cornish, the anonymous author worried about black people having access to a physical place in the United States, and he made clear that in both past and present, black people had done essential work in building American communities. The letter, written in Pennsylvania about an Ohio law and then printed in New York, asserted black people's Americanness, reflecting their political community that spanned the free states. Black northerners recognized that an exclusionary law in Ohio could set a dangerous legal precedent for the free states. They developed shared political approaches to confront their common concerns.

For instance, a group of African Americans met in Pittsburgh in 1831 to protest colonization, passing a series of resolutions that reflected their concerns about wider legal developments across the North. They declared themselves citizens because they had been born in the United States. "We are just as much natives here as the members of the Colonization Society," they announced. Bonds of affection tied them to their state and nation. "Here we were born—here bred—here are our earliest and most pleasant associations— here is all that binds man to earth, and makes life valuable." They had met to denounce the ACS and to solidify their claims to political rights. As "freemen . . . brethren . . . countrymen and fellow-citizens," they were "as fully entitled to the free exercise of the elective franchise as any men who breathe."[51] These activists worried about Pennsylvania lawmakers' attempts to ban black migration into the state. But they also worried that legislators might take inspiration from other northern states and enact further restrictions of black freedom. Black men in Pennsylvania had the right to vote in 1831, but these activists felt the need to defend their access to the polls. They saw legal developments in New York and Ohio in the 1820s and anticipated that black disfranchisement might sweep across the free states. The Pennsylvanians invoked the nation's founding in their resolutions, pledging "to each other our lives, our fortunes, and our sacred honor," asserting the national significance of their local politics. Black people across the United States were entitled to rights because of their personal histories in the nation, they argued. Black disfranchisement in New York, like proposed residency restrictions in Ohio and Pennsylvania, unjustly excluded black people from American communities. Activists challenged those exclusions together, simultaneously claiming that as citizens, they were entitled to physical communities and a role in governing structures through the right to vote.[52]

In 1837, state lawmakers realized black Pennsylvanians' fears by taking steps to disfranchise black men. Together, legislators and judges outlawed black voting in the state. While Pittsburgh activists had hoped their protest statements would have meaning across state borders, the process of their disfranchisement reflected the locality of much of antebellum law and the ways the lawmakers could use the vagueness of citizenship to further black exclusion. That process began in 1837 in Bucks County, about forty miles north of Philadelphia, after close races for county auditor and commissioner. The defeated candidates contested the results, claiming that the victors had received "between 30 and 40 votes" from black county residents "who, it is believed, had no legal right to vote." Two angry white men sparked the process of statewide disfranchisement in their effort to suppress a few dozen black people's votes. Judge John Fox presided over the suit and agreed with their complaint, ruling that black suffrage required the support of positive law. The state constitution held that "in elections *by the citizens*, every *freeman*" over age twenty-one who had resided in the state at least two years and paid taxes could vote. Fox said those provisions did not include black people.[53] While Fox heard that case, state lawmakers met to consider updating the 1790 constitution. During a convention lasting ten months, delegates agreed to insert the word "white" into the list of voter qualifications. They added an additional qualifier to deny black suffrage, skirting the thorny question of black people's legal status that Judge Fox had raised. The proposal passed with a decisive majority of votes, 77–45, and the legislators inserted the racial qualifier into the amended constitution sent to voters in February 1838.[54]

Black activists focused their protest on the proposed constitutional change. Hoping to influence the vote, a group of Philadelphians met on March 14 in a South Philadelphia Presbyterian church, where they chose Robert Purvis to present their criticism. Purvis had been born free in South Carolina in 1810 and moved to Philadelphia as a child. His father worked in antislavery politics, which likely influenced Purvis, who by the early 1830s worked closely with the radical white abolitionist William Lloyd Garrison. Purvis had also resisted colonization programs in the state.[55] He and his fellow committee members worried that in addition to losing the vote, disfranchisement might encourage efforts to force black people out of Pennsylvania. They cherished voting as a "check upon oppression," without which they would be "thrown upon the mercy of a despotic majority." "Our expatriation has come to be a darling project with many of our fellow citizens," they noted. Voting would ensure black people had a formal political voice as they struggled to secure a physical place in the United States. "We assert our right to vote at the polls as a shield against that strange species of benevolence which seeks legislative aid to banish us."[56] The activists invoked an earlier meeting when hundreds gathered in Philadelphia to protest the ACS. Their address, they said, "was adopted with a unanimity and spirit equaled only by the memorable meeting of 1817."[57] Anxious about the ramifications of disfranchisement, they took the opportunity to make larger arguments about connected injustices and in pursuit of a clearer set of legal protections.

Activists built their challenges to disfranchisement and colonization around claims to citizen status. They reminded white voters "in almost every State we have been spoken of, either expressly or by implication, as citizens." In 1790, Benjamin Franklin, then president of the Pennsylvania Abolition Society, said the organization was designed to prepare freed people "for the exercise and enjoyment of CIVIL LIBERTY." "Are we now to be told," Purvis asked, "that BENJAMIN FRANKLIN did not know what he was about, forasmuch as it was impossible for a colored man to become a citizen of the commonwealth?"[58] Purvis argued that "civil liberty" was equivalent to citizenship and that it must include suffrage. He and his colleagues exploited gaps in the law, crevices into which they could insert their voices and ideas, spaces to make arguments through citizenship. While citizen status did not have a specific meaning, it had been key to the ways lawmakers framed the relationship between individuals and governments as early as the nation's founding. Precisely because of its vagueness, black activists could open discussions about rights by using the language of citizenship.[59]

Like their colleagues in other states, Pennsylvanians emphasized the ways they contributed to their communities as a foundation for their claims to citizen status and formal political rights. They were "tax-paying colored men" and their ancestors had "bled to unite . . . TAXATION and REPRESENTATION." They used ideas about personal uplift to dispute the claims of people like Judge John Fox, who said that black people had been historically and must remain "a degraded caste." Like Judge Fox, the black Pennsylvanians invoked a broad range of legal precedents that further emphasized their contributions. For instance, a New York legislator had opposed suffrage restrictions in his state because black soldiers had fought in American wars. They offered a litany of contributions they felt entitled them to citizen status and political rights. "The very fact that we are deeply interested for our kindred in bonds," they proclaimed, "shows that we are the right sort of stuff to make good citizens of." And by working so diligently to hold onto the franchise, black activists were defending the United States as a republic. "When you have taken from an individual his right to vote, you have made the government, in regard to him, a mere despotism." The threat reached beyond a concern with black voting; disfranchising some was "a step towards making it a despotism to all."[60]

At heart, Purvis and his colleagues urged white Americans to see black people as citizens and treat them as people deserving legal protections. They reached back to the Articles of Confederation, which had denied only "paupers, vagabonds, and fugitives from justice . . . all privileges and immunities of free *citizens*." Significantly, the Continental Congress had rejected a proposed racial qualifier for that article. And on the adoption of the U.S. Constitution, "no change was made as to the rights of citizenship"—the status was no more exclusive than it had been under the Articles. Black politics thrived on formal legal statements that presented citizenship as a significant legal status with uncertain terms. State and federal authorities connected citizen status to rights without narrowing or specifying them and made them available to individuals, with few explicit limits on access. The citizenship that existed in formal law offered room for black people's political maneuvering. Despite their forceful arguments, however, Pennsylvania voters approved the new constitution by a narrow margin in October 1838.[61]

*   *   *

In the early antebellum period, black northerners experimented with a range of arguments, demanding that lawmakers see black people as essential to American communities and, therefore, entitled to rights as citizens. For instance, some activists insisted that if racist laws pushed black people out of the country, Americans would lose valuable members of their communities. Black Ohioans, facing a bond requirement to live in their state, wrote to Samuel Cornish in 1829 that they had begun to consider abandoning the country and settling in Canada. Cornish helped explain their feelings to readers. "If the general government will see with indifference the rights of any part of her citizens so trampled upon," he argued, "I see no reason why, the injured party should not in disgust, forsake the land of their birth and nativity." If they were pushed to emigrate, black Ohioans would "give their strength and influence to a more righteous power."[62] The potential of voluntary black emigration here became a threat about the costs of black exclusion.

At other times, Cornish said black exclusion would tarnish the nation's reputation and limit the republic's radical egalitarian potential. Exclusionary laws would "trifle with the guarantees of our excellent constitution." Black equality was essential to the United States' survival and prosperity as a republic, he argued. Black protest was thus critical for all Americans. The young nation was fragile, he wrote ominously, and it was "threatened with internal national feuds." State laws that flouted constitutional principles might shred the delicate national fabric. "If the proper authorities do not check this evil disposition," Cornish declared, "while in embryo we soon shall have 21 Independant Republicks or petty Kingdoms."[63] Ohio's proposed residency restriction might be a step toward national dissolution. Cornish and the black Ohioans expanded arguments about how black people contributed to their communities. By this logic, when they confronted racially biased laws, black activists were defusing threats to the nation. Cornish's paper displayed black people's contributions in action, spurring the effort to help the republic fulfill its destiny as a beacon of representative government for the world.

Cornish had to shutter the *Rights of All* in late 1829 due to financial difficulties, a common challenge black editors faced. For much of the next decade, he focused on the ministry, only occasionally writing to other newspapers about legal and political matters he felt were urgent. But in 1837, he reentered the publishing world, still convinced that a newspaper was a valuable way to highlight black people's contributions and to claim rights through citizenship. On March 4 of that year, he printed the first issue of the *Colored American*. The black proprietors of the *Weekly Advocate* had decided to change their paper's name and invited Cornish to lead it because of his editorial experience. With the new title, they declared the foundation of their politics: "we are Americans,—*colored* Americans, brethren."[64] They claimed a place in the nation while acknowledging that blackness made their experiences distinct; it was an argument about the essential complexity of the United States. Cornish and his colleagues challenged their legal exclusion by normalizing blackness in the nation.

Under the title, the paper bore the familiar masthead "Righteousness Exalteth a Nation." Cornish planned to continue the work he had done at the *Rights of All*. The paper's offices stood on Frankfort Street, near the recently constructed New York City Hall, and across the street from the Democratic Party's political machine at Tammany Hall. Perhaps Cornish sat at a desk there and thought about the pernicious influence the party of slaveowners bore in northern state lawmaking. In the paper's first issue, he called on Democrats to think in new ways about the terms of American citizenship, invoking the nation's past to support his claims.[65] He printed two messages in which Andrew Jackson called on free black men to defend New Orleans during the War of 1812. Jackson, then a U.S. Army general, asked African Americans to join hands with their "white fellow-citizens" and spoke to concerns that crossed the lines of color. His words refuted claims that black people did not belong in the United States. Cornish continued his history lesson with extracts from the debates at New York's 1821 Constitutional Convention, during which a number of lawmakers suggested that black Americans were citizens and therefore entitled to equal access to the polls.[66] Those items filled the paper's front page, offering prominent endorsements for black citizenship politics.

As he had in the *Rights of All*, Cornish suggested to black readers ways to prove their value to American communities, emphasizing in particular that agricultural work could be a foundation of claims to citizenship and rights. He had written that "every constituent must become perfect, as far as human perfectibility goes, before the body politic can be made perfect," and in the 1830s, he continued to advocate personal improvement as a means to broader societal progress.[67] He again urged black people to turn to agriculture in order to secure legal rights as citizens. In April 1837, for instance, he noted the unmatched fertility of American soil; any "sober and industrious" person could reap a rich harvest. "Morally culpable is he who can 'eat the bread of idleness'" while living so close to such potential, Cornish wrote. "In our large cities, we are passed by as not at all incorporated in the body politic." As they left crowded cites and took up farming, black people would "exert a powerful influence in different communities." With only a small financial stake and "fixed determination," black farmers would become "lords of the soil." African American farmers would exhibit their self-sufficiency in a new realm by cultivating America's "fertile garden," enabling them to "gain some influence in [their] own country."[68]

Again and again, Cornish insisted that black people remake their legal lives through agriculture.[69] In June 1838, he reprinted the message from the *Rights of All* in which he had offered farmland for sale in western New York and urged readers to move and help make their children "useful and virtuous citizens."[70] He then copied an item from a newspaper called the *Buckeye Ploughboy* that said farmers possessed unique virtues, including the intelligence to "discharge in a proper manner the duties of a citizen."[71] Cornish's correspondents also endorsed black agrarianism. A reader who called himself "Franklin" offered specific instructions for black people looking to become independent farmers. Traveling through western territories, Franklin had seen a number of European immigrants returning east from Kentucky and Ohio. Having discovered cheap land in those states, those immigrants had decided to work menial jobs in eastern cities until they saved enough money to buy property in the West. Franklin calculated that if a black man earned $25 each month as a porter and spent $100 per year on room, board, and clothing, he could save enough in one year to buy good western agricultural land. That man's diligence and self-control would secure "the respect and confidence of the best part of the community," while others remained trapped in a cycle of grueling work, extravagant spending, and debt. Franklin imagined a future in which thousands of old, black farmers relaxed in their comfortable homes and regaled their children with fireside tales of the thrift and industry that had allowed them to own the land on which they sat.[72]

By January 1839, Cornish appeared to grow frustrated with the long and as yet fruitless struggle for political rights. He seemed anxious and exasperated as he noted that black northerners bore the burden of defending the nation's principles. "On that portion of us, nominally free, is flung the necessity of battling for freedom." African Americans felt "a love of home which is stronger than death," and their emotional ties spurred their protest. "If we falter, or yield, or basely desert our home in its peril," Cornish continued, "not only will republicanism cease in this Union, but God-like principle will be checked in mid-career." He concluded by explaining why black people remained so dedicated to reforming the nation's laws: "We are not temporary sojourners in a foreign land, nor aliens seeking citizenship, nor slaves begging for liberty—no! we are an integral portion of this Republic, bred and born with it, a portion too on whom rests the onus of proving that this as well as any other form of government, in having the power of adjusting its radical defects, contains the elements of its own duration."[73] The nation's laws were damaged but not beyond repair. Enacting a vision of citizenship that included black people and entailed political rights was critical for the republic because African Americans had done so much to preserve the nation's ideals. They were citizens because they were born in the nation, because they had helped to build it, and because they insisted on improving it. If state lawmakers continued to deny black suffrage, they would chip away at the fragile foundations of republicanism as a form of government. Black people were integral to the nation in part because their legal status would embody either the fundamental flaws or the highest ideals of the republic.

Black activists continued to declare that they could be citizens by proclaiming themselves integral to the United States and seeking new ways to contribute to American communities. They exhibited their value in their states and in the nation and at the same time argued for specific legal protections. Their claims gave substance to the idea of the citizen, which they said entailed the obligations to work and to defend the nation's ideals as well as rights of formal political access. The citizen status they constructed was available to black Americans. They made these claims at an urgent moment, as westward expansion, Indian removal, and the entrenchment of slavery threatened to make the United States an exclusionary empire in which power was reserved to white men. Black activists suggested that national progress need not be defined by slavery and racial exclusion, that African Americans could play a critical role in fostering the growth of the United States.[74]

Those activists were locked in struggle with a vocal faction of white writers who continued working to remove black people from the United States. In 1836, Pennsylvania lawyer John Denny published *An Essay on the Political Grade of the Free Coloured Population*, using law and history to argue that black people did not belong in the United States. John Marshall, the long-serving chief justice of the U.S. Supreme Court, reviewed Denny's manuscript and wrote, "The sentiment it conveys, appears to me, to be perfectly sound"; that endorsement served as the book's preface. With Marshall's support, Denny proceeded to examine African Americans' rights before and after the ratification of the Constitution, a thin legalistic veil for what was in essence a colonizationist tract. He offered his own definition of citizenship to exclude African Americans. Black activists sometimes claimed rights through a constitutional clause declaring citizens of one state must have "all privileges and immunities of citizens" in any other, but "the term citizen is no where defined in the Constitution," Denny noted. Given the legal restrictions black people faced, "it would certainly be a perversion" to call them citizens, he argued. "It appears not a little strange" that more black people had not emigrated to Liberia.[75] "He is tempted there by all the high privileges of political and civil liberty." Black politics was high-stakes work because people like Denny were pushing for their legal exclusion and ultimate removal from the country, and legal authorities like John Marshall endorsed those projects. Colonizationists used the vagueness of the law to justify black removal, demanding that activists resist an American citizenship defined by whiteness.

But in the ways they challenged colonization and disfranchisement, black activists built their own racialized version of citizenship. They endorsed a restrictive standard of conduct in order to secure black legal belonging. People would earn citizen status by performing a set of behaviors dictated by uplift ideology. African Americans had to allay racist anxieties about black freedom to prove themselves worthy of citizen status in order to secure legal protections. For instance, Purvis and his fellow Pennsylvanians called for a single standard of conduct to determine black and white suffrage. But they accepted the idea that lawmakers could limit suffrage based on personal conduct. "We do not ask the right of suffrage for the inmates of our jails . . . but for those who honestly and industriously contribute to bear the burdens of the State."[76] Accused or convicted criminals were far from the only people who might justifiably be denied rights. "We would have the right of suffrage only as the reward of industry and worth. We care not how high the qualification may be placed. All we ask is that no man shall be excluded on account of his color."[77] Black activists in New York and Pennsylvania confronted voting restrictions by arguing that citizenship must secure political rights and economic opportunity. They built a narrow path for black people to secure rights. Their arguments helped perpetuate stereotypes that African Americans were predisposed to poverty or crime. Making personal conduct a barrier to the franchise echoed the belief that African Americans had to be prepared for freedom and legal protection. Activists' arguments about how African Americans should work to earn citizen status perpetuated the ideas that had produced the extant, unequal racial order. The citizenship activists built remained qualified because it required qualification.

*   *   *

A number of black people heeded the calls for uplift and agrarianism in order to confront disfranchisement and change their legal status. Those changes took concrete form in upstate New York on land belonging to the wealthy white abolitionist Gerrit Smith. In 1846, Smith chose to give 3,000 black New Yorkers land to settle in the Adirondacks. He hoped to create an agrarian community in which African American men would attain the $250 of real property necessary to vote. Smith was an abolitionist at heart, and he believed the settlement would help "loosen the b[o]nds of the enslaved." Black activists Theodore S. Wright, Charles B. Ray, and James McCune Smith agreed to work as agents to recruit settlers. Any black person between the ages of twenty-one and sixty who did not already own land and was not a "drunkard" would be eligible for a 40- to 60-acre plot.[78] Gerrit Smith expressed serious concerns about drinking among black New Yorkers. "I am grieved to learn, that intemperance has made such havoc among the colored people of this State," he wrote. "Vain, and worse than vain, will be my grant of land to a drunkard." He asked his agents to send a message to the settlers that would "inculcate the deepest abhorrence of intoxicating drinks." Smith and his agents made absolute temperance a prerequisite for pursuing political rights in the Adirondacks.[79]

Wright, Ray, and McCune Smith included their patron's remarks in their message recruiting potential settlers. They urged applicants to see the Smith Lands as an opportunity to improve "the heart of an almost free state" and to amend its "nearly equal laws." Once the settlers began to till the soil, the inherent nobility of farming combined with the creation of interracial agrarian communities would elevate black New Yorkers in the minds of white observers. The land grants were an opportunity for a "practical vindication of our claims to manhood."[80] By cutting timber, building homes, and clearing land, taking on all of "the labour and privations incident to pioneer cultivators," black people could embody a masculine American ideal and assert their place in a community of self-sufficient landowners.[81] Black New

Yorkers would enter the formal political community by owning land, and they would claim a place in an American cultural community by moving west and conquering the wilderness. That process demanded "the labour of self-denial"—thrifty habits to sustain new rural communities—including above all "TOTAL ABSTINENCE FROM ALL INTOXICATING DRINKS." "The grant to you is free, untrammelled, unconditional," the agents lied.[82] Wright, Ray, and McCune Smith sought a specific type of person for the settlement, crafting a citizenship that included the vote and mapping a path to that status on the narrow route of thrift, industry, manliness, and temperance.

Willis Augustus Hodges was among those who heeded the call to the Smith Lands, continuing his lifetime of movement in search of opportunity. Hodges was born in 1815 to free parents in the Tidewater region of southeastern Virginia. As a child, his family endured a series of violent attacks by armed bandits. "No free person of color . . . was safe in person or property," he wrote.[83] Hodges said that "the friends of the American Colonization Society" had perpetrated those attacks in order to compel black Americans to emigrate. He felt connected to his "native land" and refused to leave the United States, but he did want to escape the South. Hodges moved to Manhattan in 1833, where he was disappointed to find so many black people struggling to support themselves with work in menial service occupations. He quickly recognized how difficult it was to find more gainful employment. One afternoon, he lost his job as a laborer on a ship, but being too embarrassed to go home in the middle of the day, he volunteered to shovel fertilizer with a group of cartmen, a decision that brought him a bit of good fortune. The head cartman noticed Hodges at work and helped him find a steady job as a porter, a position he held for five years.[84]

"I had never been able to read much," Hodges declared, but he was inspired by abolitionist lectures he heard in New York, and he subscribed to three newspapers, including the *Colored American*.[85] He also organized African Americans in the developing community of Williamsburg, Brooklyn, to take part in black state conventions held in the early 1840s. Hodges spoke at the 1841 convention in Troy, where he praised the virtues of agrarian life in contrast to the limited opportunity available in the cities. That same year, he helped organize the Williamsburg Union Temperance Benevolent Society and served as its first president.[86]

Hodges plunged into political work in the 1840s, deciding to publish a newspaper of his own to claim an independent public voice. In 1846, New

York voters faced a referendum on the property qualification for black suffrage, and Hodges joined the struggle against disfranchisement. A white editor of the *New York Sun* urged readers to reject any change, arguing that black men's voting would be a step toward racial intermarriage. Hodges responded to the editor, but the *Sun* charged $15 to print his argument, then placed it in a corner of the paper reserved for advertisements. "The Sun shines for all white men, not black men," the editor explained. Hodges connected with Thomas Van Renesslear, a black activist who had previously worked on antislavery newspapers, and together they launched the *Ram's Horn* on January 1, 1847.[87] Only one issue of the paper survives, and it includes an announcement signed "W. A. H." for a meeting of the New York Emigration Association, intended to organize black settlement on the Smith Lands. Hodges believed the land grants "must eventually prove a blessing or a curse," though he leaned toward the former. Once they moved upstate, settlers would contribute "timber, leather, iron, furniture and clothing" to markets for trade. "There too," he added, "our young men and women who are now the victims of vice and idleness, would have regular employment under those who have an interest in their future happiness."[88] Hodges preached the virtue of rural life, encouraging people to leave cities like New York and even smaller towns like Utica and Troy. He became "convinced that something besides 'speechifying' . . . had to be done if we wanted our rights." After a series of meetings, Hodges forged a "little band" with eight black families, left Williamsburg, and settled on a 40-acre tract in the Adirondacks.[89]

Hodges made his home in Franklin County and later reported that while living there, he was elected to the position of town collector. A New York law of 1845 prohibited any property qualification for officeholding. Owning land might have allowed Hodges to vote for himself and some of his fellow black settlers to cast ballots as well. But his election points to the odd legal reality that it was easier for a black man to hold office in 1840s New York than it was for him to vote.[90] Hodges's election provided a direct form of political engagement and affirmed his legal position in the state and the nation. Settling on the Smith Lands allowed him to secure that place.

Willis Hodges's story brings together histories of black agrarianism, anticolonization, uplift, and the pursuit of formal political rights. His life stands at the nexus of those critical aspects of black citizenship politics in the early antebellum period. Hodges illuminates the legal possibilities of black life in the mid-nineteenth century. Activists made potent arguments about

FIGURE 1. Willis Augustus Hodges, from I. Garland Penn, ed., *The Black Press and Its Editors* (1891). Hodges earned a place in this collection because of his work as a newspaper editor. But his life also reflects the many other avenues for black citizenship politics that people pursued outside of the realm of print culture.

WILLIS A. HODGES.

citizenship and took action that secured political rights. But his experience was peculiar in many respects. Rare fortune opened the door for his achievements: his free parents helped him secure a formal education, he had disposable income that allowed him to relocate to and move within New York, and he had a helpful white man recommend him for a job as a porter. Only through those opportunities did Hodges achieve something like the citizenship that people like Samuel Cornish had so long tried to build. Leaving the city allowed him to own land, contribute his labor to a community, and find an avenue to formal political participation. But what Hodges secured was a contingent citizenship; it was not a status available equally to African Americans.[91] Black people crafted citizenship through a struggle for specific rights based on the terms that had conferred those rights on narrow a subset of white men. Hodges's achievements, particularly his election to local office, could obscure the exclusion that characterized black people's lives. Surpassing the state's legal standard for black suffrage did not directly confront the inequality at the heart of the state's law. Instead, Hodges assumed the burden of his blackness and asked other African Americans to do the same, to navigate the world under the legal weight of their race. The citizenship that activists constructed and the legal rights Hodges attained involved adopting a specific, regimented way of life, embracing a set of restrictions that might, in return, produce certain privileges and protections.

Hodges's outstanding accomplishments emphasize the challenges African Americans faced as they sought legal protections in American communities. His experiences reveal the boundaries of a citizen status that black people had to earn through contributions that white Americans only reluctantly permitted or acknowledged. Citizenship was useful to black people because it was being constructed in public debate, but existing legal structures constrained the terms of that debate. Given the barriers that stood between black people and the legal lives they imagined, it is worth reflecting again on John Russwurm and the way he explained his move to Liberia. Black people might achieve a great deal in the United States, as Willis Hodges had. Individuals could experience a meaningful kind of legal belonging. But given the constant hurdling, given the terms under which they may be grudgingly admitted into the political community, perhaps John Russwurm was right to say black Americans could never truly enjoy their citizenship. As African Americans fought against racial exclusion, they built their own set of barriers to membership, crafting a citizenship that was less than freedom and that reproduced inequalities. Those restrictive arguments continued to shape black protest in the years to come.

CHAPTER 2

"Union Is Strength":
Building an American Citizenship

Temperance Hall was an odd name for a former tavern. Briefly in the 1830s, the three-story building in Philadelphia's Northern Liberties, a few blocks from the Delaware River and a short stroll from Independence Hall, was a fashionable place to have a drink and see a concert or play. But the Northern Exchange, as it was then known, went out of fashion, and when the business failed, a group of teetotalers purchased it to serve as a meetinghouse. The building embodied the evils the temperance advocates looked to reform, and its new name gave their program a constant voice. Presumably, they would have held their major gatherings in the second-floor theater, meetings that likely attracted some of the city's 10,000 free black residents, among the largest such populations in the antebellum North.[1]

Whether or not they joined the teetotal crusade, black Philadelphians certainly knew about and had access to the building. For four days in August 1845, activists reserved Temperance Hall to hold what they later called rather simply a "Convention of Colored People." Unlike other antebellum conventions, little evidence remains regarding the substance of the event. No surviving list records the names of attendees or officers. No minutes indicate who addressed the gathering or what issues the delegates debated. That the convention lasted four days might suggest that it included a large group of attendees and participants; it could also mean that a handful of delegates disagreed for days about strategy. And it is frustratingly unclear whether the event's organizers planned it as a state or national convention. Despite those gaps in the record, when delegates closed the meeting with an "Address to the Free Colored People," they made clear their central political goals. They wanted to confront legal exclusion, and they described the convention as part of a project "to unite the whole family of free colored people in interest and feelings" in that pursuit. In this way, activists looked to make the project of building American citizenship a collective black project. The convention could bring together a broad body of politically engaged people. Perhaps a large gathering could show the American public that black activists were invested in democracy and fit to take part in the nation's formal political processes. The Philadelphia convention was part of a string of such meetings held across the Northeast and Midwest in the early 1840s designed to foster a cohesive activist community and present collective arguments on black Americans' rights.[2]

What we know about this meeting comes from a statement of its "views and object," bearing the names of Jehu Jones, Nathan W. Depee, Benjamin Pascal, Jonathan C. Miller, and Leonard Collins. "Union is Strength," they proclaimed, and their present circumstances demanded "unanimity of action." They looked to continue the work of their activist predecessors by denouncing the American Colonization Society's removal program, and they warned of persistent, intense efforts at black removal that were taking place in "a neighboring state."[3] They might have been thinking of the aggressive and organized Maryland colonizationists, who separated from the national body of the ACS in the late 1830s and established a shipping company to link them with their colonial settlement in Liberia.[4] For the Philadelphia delegates, colonization was an attack on black people's belonging in the United States, a project that could prevent African Americans from claiming citizenship by denying them physical space in the country. In response, they urged black people to pursue "our national rights, as they are secured to all citizens, in the Constitution."[5] The delegates' speech raises important questions about black politics in the 1840s and African Americans' developing arguments about citizenship. Why did those men place so much emphasis on black unity in that particular historical moment? And what did it mean for them to envision citizenship as a protection of "national rights" under the federal Constitution?

Those Philadelphia delegates, along with their counterparts in other locations throughout the early 1840s, made the transformative claim that citizenship should be a national status connecting individuals to the federal government. In the early nineteenth century, few American people felt that the national government should play an important role in their lives, and many worried that centralizing legal authority might tread dangerously close to monarchy or tyranny. Not only had the nation's founders refused to define citizenship in its founding documents, but also in the antebellum period, individual Americans typically did not see the federal government as an important force for shaping their legal lives.[6] The framers of the Constitution left unsettled the question of whether ultimate sovereignty resided in the states or the federal government. By extension, it was unclear where a person should turn in seeking an authority to secure and protect his rights. The precise terms of both state and national citizenship and the specific ways those separate legal identities related to one another were uncertain. The legal structures under which American people lived were defined most robustly at the state level. But the program of colonization compelled black people to argue that they belonged in the nation, and as they did so, black activists put forward new ideas about citizenship as a relationship between individuals and the federal government.[7] The activists in Philadelphia therefore called for fundamental legal change that would expand the reach of the federal government, bind individuals more firmly to its power, and yield a unifying legal status under which American people would live.

In the early 1840s, faced with state laws limiting their rights and denying them protections, black activists sought a relationship with the federal government that would make real the egalitarian language of the nation's founding documents. They reimagined the relationship between individuals and American governments, both state and national. Activists made claims on different governments based on the specific concerns they faced at particular political moments. While they issued strategic appeals to state governments, black northerners also saw legislators and judges on the state level constructing specific barriers to black rights, defining state citizenship in ways that were often built around racial exclusion. Given the specificity of some state-level restrictions, activists appealed to a national citizenship because of the broad, soaring, egalitarian language in the nation's founding documents. In so doing, black people answered questions about who had access to the law and made claims that framed the federal government as the chief arbiter of individuals' rights and protections.[8]

Black activists' calls for a unifying citizen status both mirrored and influenced their desire for a political community knit together by shared concerns. They worked to revive the national convention movement, presenting themselves as a "family of free colored people," in order to seize the power of numbers to promote their political aims. Activists thus linked their investment in a national community of citizens to their desire for a unified community of African Americans. But in that project, they experienced the challenges of ideological conflict over both the past and future of black people in the United States. Their work to craft a national citizen status emerged amid arguments over the geographic expansion of the nation and the future of slavery and freedom in the country. Most critically, black activists argued among themselves about the best approach for the fight against slavery, an internal struggle that limited their efforts to make collective claims about citizen status.

*   *   *

Black men took to the sea in large numbers in the antebellum period. The ocean, they felt, could be a means to economic security as well as a place of physical and psychological liberation, and African Americans came to comprise about one-fifth of the people who worked for northern merchants in the burgeoning shipping industry. That the sea provided black men with so much freedom alarmed white southerners already on edge due to rebellion among the enslaved. In 1822, Denmark Vesey's planned revolt sparked anxieties and led to a wave of prosecutions and executions in South Carolina. That same year, state lawmakers adopted the Negro Seamen Act, requiring that when vessels made port, black sailors had to disembark and be detained in jail.[9] From the 1820s through the outbreak of the Civil War, seven southern states would follow South Carolina and pass laws restricting black seamen.[10] Southerners passed these laws because they wanted to use the power of their state governments to protect their enslaved property and their own lives, but the laws generated intense opposition among northern lawmakers, abolitionists, and black Americans. The ensuing debate touched on crucial questions about the nature of citizenship and the relationships between individuals and American governments, and these arguments represent the range of ideas lawmakers held about federalism, citizenship, and black people's legal status.

In 1824, a man of color named Amos Daley was jailed when his ship made port in Charleston. Daley, with his captain's support, claimed that he had been born free in Rhode Island and was a citizen of the state. He said that because of the Constitution's Privileges and Immunities Clause, he was entitled to move freely in South Carolina as in any other state. That provision, also known as the Comity Clause, was one of the central tools that black activists used to make arguments about the content of citizenship. "The citizens of each state," the clause read, "shall be entitled to all privileges and immunities of citizens in the several states." Its wording created an opportunity for black activist work because it connected citizenship to a set of legal protections but remained vague about who state citizens were or what privileges and immunities they should possess. When they invoked the clause, Daley and his attorneys presented a richly textured argument about what citizenship was—a legal status that accrued to a person based on birth in the nation, one that should protect an individual throughout the United States and, in particular, should offer free mobility within the nation's borders. South Carolina authorities were unimpressed by that specificity. Denying Daley's claims to citizenship and the support his captain offered, officials bound him to a whipping post and delivered thirteen lashes, punishment, perhaps, for having the gall to make radical arguments about his legal status in the heart of American slavery.[11]

The Negro Seamen Acts roused opposition far beyond southern ports. In the late 1830s, a group of Massachusetts merchants brought their concerns about the laws to their state legislature, which appointed a special committee on the issue in January 1839. Although powerful commercial interests opposed the laws, the legislative committee refused to act, calling it "inexpedient" to intervene. That ruling provoked an impassioned response from the committee's minority, led by George Bradburn, a Unitarian minister and budding antislavery advocate.[12] Bradburn, like Amos Daley, invoked the Comity Clause to argue that because black sailors moved freely in Massachusetts, they ought to be able to do the same in South Carolina, Louisiana, or any other state, regardless of slaveholders' political dominance. Bradburn argued that black men were citizens in a way that suggested the matter was not debatable. But that confidence belied his own uncertainty regarding how exactly citizenship connected individuals to the governments that comprised a federal system. Black sailors, he claimed, were "freeborn citizens of this State, and consequently of the United States also," and were therefore protected by the Privileges and Immunities Clause.[13] He said South Carolina's Negro Seamen Act was an unjust state denial of black rights. And yet the root of Bradburn's argument was that black sailors were connected to another state, that they were citizens of Massachusetts. Would the prerogatives of Massachusetts lawmakers override those of South Carolinians?

Bradburn reasoned that the U.S. Constitution protected black sailors because they were citizens of Massachusetts, but he buried contested assumptions about sovereignty and citizenship in his constitutional claims. Indeed, he spoke as part of a minority in opposition to South Carolina's Negro

The Sailor's description of a Chase & Capture.—

"Why d'ye see 'twas blowing strong, & we were lapping it in forecastle under in Portland roads, when a sail hove in sight in the offing; we saw with half an eye, she was an enemy's cruiser.— Standing over from Cherbourg, better she could'nt come, so we turned the hands up to draw the splice of the best bower but she not liking the cut of our jib hove in stays; all hands take sail away; away flew the cable end for end & before you could say peas we had her under double reef'd top sails & top gallant-sails, my eyes how she walked, licking it in whole green-seas at the weather chefs tree & canting it over the lee yeard-arm pigs & live lumber afloat in the lee scuppers but just as we opened the hill standing through the tail of the race, by the holy! I thought she'd have lift us all the nines but she stood well up under canvass while Johnny Crapaud was grabbing to it nigh on his beam ends so my boys we bowsed in the lee guns, gave her a Mizzen reef & found she had as much sail as she could stagger under, we came up with her hand over fist & about seven bells she began to play long balls with her stern chasers, but over board went her fore top mast- her sails took aback & she fain would be off, but we twigging her drift let run the clew garnets ranged up to windward & gain her a broadside twixt wind & water as hand as she could suck it, that dose was a sukner d—n the shot did she fire afterwards hard a Starboard flew our helm & whash went our cathead into her quarter gallery with a hell of surge over board went her mizzen mast in dashed our boarders & down came her Colours to the Glory of Old England & the flying Saucy with three hearty cheers !!!!"

London Published by G.Humphrey, 27 St James's Street January the 7th 1822.

FIGURE 2. "The sailor's description of a chase & capture," George Cruikshank (1822). Black men found gainful employment at sea, and many also enjoyed feelings of freedom and a sense of community among fellow sailors. As southern state lawmakers worked to protect slavery, the mobility of black sailors raised important questions about sovereignty and citizenship. Rare Book and Special Collections Division, Library of Congress.

Seamen Act because so many disagreed that black people were entitled to legal protections as citizens. And although he invoked federal authority, Bradburn declared it "a paramount duty of the state, to protect its citizens."[14] He argued around unresolved constitutional questions about the relationship between state and federal governments and state and national citizenship. Still, it is clear that Bradburn understood that citizen status was an important legal concept and that claiming the status could be a productive strategy for protecting black Americans. He read the Constitution in the same ways that many black activists did, using its ambiguities to secure legal protections for black people. His arguments convey the uncertainty surrounding the precise relationship between a citizen and different American governments, a question that black activists would work to resolve in the coming years.

Amos Daley and his counsel as well as George Bradburn made arguments with transformative potential for American law. In the antebellum period, lawmakers generally agreed that citizenship indicated a person's connection to a place, but they held varying ideas about the bonds of sovereignty and allegiance that would link individual citizens and various levels of American government. In fact, segments of the American population showed little concern with the content of citizen status, emphasizing instead their connections to community organizations to secure political and social powers. Few agreed whether local, state, or federal authorities should determine the content of citizenship or even that the content of citizen status should be important for their lives.[15]

At the same time that George Bradburn issued his minority report, another group of lawmakers from his state argued in favor of federal sovereignty yet denied that it would secure black rights. In February 1839, a group of women delivered a petition to the Massachusetts House that 1,400 other women had signed, calling for "the immediate repeal of all laws of the State which make any distinction among its inhabitants on account of color." The petitioners cited a law that excluded black men from state militias, but the Committee on the Judiciary appointed to handle the petitions denied that this exclusion was unjust. Massachusetts law called for only white men to serve in militias, which was "but the recital, in terms, of the act of Congress, the supreme law of the land." As for the exclusion, they called it a "silent exemption" through which "the colored citizen" had been relieved of the obligation of militia service. Even if they wished otherwise, they could not act, for the petition asked legislators to "cut the knot which cannot be untied." "The power of enrolling the citizens in the militia belongs to the

United States," they concluded, "and not to the state sovereignty."[16] It is unclear how they arrived at that decision, but committee members stated that federal authority should determine at least one aspect of citizenship. In the process, Massachusetts legislators highlighted what was, for black Americans, the vexing problem of citizenship's uncertain meaning. Although the lawmakers described black men as "colored citizens," they did not feel that that status should allow them to form or serve in state militias. Instead, they presented a citizen status that was not necessarily connected to rights. Black activists could use citizenship in their work, but those who opposed them could also deploy the same tool to constrict black freedom.

The response to the women's petition also points to the ways federal authority as established was potentially oppressive for black Americans. While Bradburn invoked both federal law and state birthright to claim citizenship for black people, his colleagues covered themselves in the same constitutional authority to deny responsibility for a specific exclusionary legal act. Perhaps this explains the approaches that Bradburn and Amos Daley took in challenging the Negro Seamen Act. They may have argued that black people were citizens based on their status in New England states because they were uncertain that federal authorities would agree with their claims. The way they used the Privileges and Immunities Clause—claiming a federal citizen status based on its conferral at the state level—could empower antislavery or antiracist northern lawmakers to deem black people citizens and could skirt potential opposition by a larger national government that included dozens of proslavery and racist lawmakers. They looked to exploit the particular opening that interstate comity provided to begin building a federal legal status for black Americans.

State judges similarly delivered a range of opinions on the way citizenship should function in a federal system. Judicial disagreements about sovereignty and black rights in Pennsylvania were central to the process of disfranchising black men in the state. As with the denial of black militia access in Massachusetts, the fact that citizenship was so vague made it possible for judges to construct the status in ways that both secured and denied specific rights to black Americans. For example, on October 13, 1835, William Fogg, a free black man living in Luzerne County in northeastern Pennsylvania, traveled to the polls to vote in races for governor and other state and local positions. Fogg met all of the state qualifications for a voter: he was over twenty-one years old, had lived in the county for at least two years, and had paid taxes to the county government at least six months before the election date. But when he presented his ballot and qualifications to Hiram Hobbs, who served as inspector for the election, Hobbs "refused to receive his vote." Fogg sought legal redress and gained a favorable hearing from Judge David Scott, who instructed the jury that the election official Hobbs had unjustly abridged Fogg's rights. Hobbs's attorneys argued that because of his race, Fogg "was not a citizen within the meaning of the constitution," but Judge Scott said that argument imposed an additional, extralegal qualification for suffrage. Further, Scott said, Pennsylvania's gradual abolition law, passed in 1780, suggested that state lawmakers had wanted "to make the man of colour a freeman." He claimed that the state's founding generation had been looking to allow black men access to the legal status of freeman, which had traditionally been linked to voting.[17] There was nothing explicit in state law that excluded black people from voting, and so, Scott ruled, William Fogg ought to have the right to vote.[18]

Judge Scott's instructions compelled the jury to agree that Fogg had been unjustly disfranchised, but his forceful directions would become the foundation for Hiram Hobbs's appeal. In the state supreme court, Chief Justice John Bannister Gibson found, or perhaps created, a legal basis to disfranchise black people. He mentioned a 1795 decision in a state appellate court that prohibited black suffrage, and although he produced no written record of that case, through word of mouth and memory, Gibson ruled that it was valid precedent. He proceeded to dismiss Scott's arguments by crafting a history in which Pennsylvanians had tacitly acknowledged that black people should not participate in formal political processes. While the state enfranchised "every FREEMAN" who met particular qualifications, it did not necessarily include African American men, such as William Fogg, who happened to have been free. When Pennsylvania adopted her constitution, "the term freeman had a peculiar and specific sense, being used like the term citizen, which supplanted it, to denote one who had a voice in public affairs." In 1682, Gibson noted, English law had detailed the terms of the status of "freeman," which included the franchise. Because being a freeman meant far more than simply being free, Gibson argued, "it is difficult to discover how the word freeman . . . could have been meant to comprehend a coloured race." In a twist on Corey's and Bradburn's arguments, Gibson also invoked U.S. law in support of his opinion, arguing that the Privileges and Immunities Clause was an insurmountable obstacle to black suffrage in the state. To claim that William Fogg was a citizen of Pennsylvania or was entitled to political rights would "overbear the laws imposing countless disabilities on him in other states." Gibson closed with a sympathetic air. Whatever lawmakers may desire, they were obligated to look beyond "considerations of mere humanity" to recognize that state laws had been crafted by people who opposed black rights. He declared himself "bound to pronounce that men of colour are destitute of title to the elective franchise."[19]

Gibson invoked multiple levels and generations of government to bolster his argument, and perhaps most strikingly, he interpreted a federal restriction of state laws through measures that state lawmakers had passed. He claimed that popular concerns and the mandates of state legislatures limited the ability of the U.S. Constitution to confer legal protections on a marginalized group. Society, he suggested, bound law on both the federal and state levels. Gibson thus defined citizenship in a way that excluded free African Americans and allowed him to deny that they could vote in Pennsylvania. But he did so without clarifying what level of government had the power to define and regulate citizen status.

As John Gibson declared that William Fogg should not have voted, his colleague John Fox, a Pennsylvania district judge, issued a similar ruling against black suffrage. Fox decided that a few dozen black men who voted in Bucks County should not have been permitted to do so. He concluded that slavery in the past and legal restrictions in the present meant that no free black person should be recognized as either "a *citizen* [or] a *freeman*" according to the state constitution. The 1790 state constitution had equated the terms, setting out qualifications for "elections by the citizens," in which "every freeman" who met the bar could vote. Fox decided to exclude African Americans from both statuses, covering all bases in his quest to disfranchise black men. Like Gibson, he invoked restrictions from other states. As early as 1829, he noted, Illinois and Massachusetts had prohibited interracial marriage. More telling, Fox thought, was Ohio's legislative effort to forbid black people from taking up new residence in the state. Those and other measures indicated that African Americans, although free, remained "an inferior and degraded caste."[20] One could not reasonably conclude that any member of that group should be allowed to hold office, and because the Pennsylvania constitution linked citizenship to officeholding, one must recognize that black people were not citizens.[21] Fox's ruling expanded a narrow question of black suffrage in a local election to make a broad argument that denied the possibility of African American citizenship.

Both of these decisions indicate that Americans saw the imprecise definition of citizenship as an important legal tool for their efforts to align their society with their racial ideas. What is striking is that this imprecision was as important to people like Amos Daley and George Bradburn, who sought physical protection for black sailors, as it was to Judges Fox and Gibson, who wanted to legalize black exclusion. More than an uncertainty, more than a problem, the ambiguous concept of citizenship could be a cudgel that lawmakers wielded against black Americans. The same uncertainty that made particular kinds of black politics possible enabled white supremacist lawmaking and urged black activists to use citizenship to challenge their exclusion.

Still, the law in the antebellum period was not simply a force that acted against black people's interests. Judges like Gibson and Fox denied black people legal protections in part because African Americans were working so ardently to secure them and because, in some cases, they succeeded. In the early nineteenth century, for instance, hundreds of enslaved people sued for freedom in Missouri courts. As in the later case of Dred Scott, slaveowners in the state often traveled and brought their human property beyond Missouri borders, sometimes sojourning for months in free territories. Enslaved people in the Midwest had opportunities to learn the legal culture of the region and could find ways to move themselves closer to freedom. African Americans filed nearly 300 freedom suits in the St. Louis County Circuit Court in the fifty years before Dred Scott's case, and more than one-third of those suits resulted in emancipation. These were moments when black people acted in formal legal spaces and secured recognition of legal personhood, when the law declared individuals to be entitled to basic protections, including control over their own bodies.[22] These cases mark the opportunities black people had to use the law, but what these claimants secured was neither equality nor a formal citizen status. Although the many freedom suits reveal that black exclusion was not absolute in the antebellum period, the possibility of a legal hearing would not satisfy free black Americans. They were working to establish a clear standard of access and an equal set of protections, rights, and privileges through citizenship.

Legal decisions like those of Fox and Gibson that denied black suffrage and the possibility of black citizenship pushed activists to pursue a legal relationship with the federal government as a way to potentially supersede state legal restrictions. When Fox invoked laws in Illinois, Massachusetts, and Ohio, he encouraged black people to seek change beyond a state judge's authority. His decision pushed black activists to challenge a patchwork of state-level exclusion with a higher legal power. Most important, Fox and Gibson bolstered black activists' efforts to use citizenship in their work. In their decisions, judges like Fox and Gibson confirmed that black citizenship politics was potent, that citizen status was key to how governments conferred and protected individual rights, and that the terms of citizenship were unstable and therefore contestable. Judges and lawmakers embodied the oppressive force of state governments in the period but at the same time revealed the potential for influencing the meaning of citizenship that could include ideas from both white lawmakers and black activists.

Black activists, though, had their own disagreements about the nature of citizenship in a federal system, and the complexities of African American identity in a slaveholding nation shaped their discussions about political strategy. In August 1838, for example, a debate between Samuel Cornish and the black minister and educator Lewis Woodson connected tensions over identity to ideas about government power. In their discussion, printed in Cornish's *Colored American*, the men agreed that free black people were too concentrated in cities. But while Cornish encouraged people to move west and integrate rural communities, Woodson (writing under the pseudonym "Augustine") called on African Americans to build their own society in the hinterlands. Woodson had been born free in Virginia in 1806, and his experiences in that slave state might have shaped his program of black separatism and self-sufficiency.[23] Writing to Cornish, Woodson declared that he intended to purchase lands "from the Congress of our native country" to use for separate black settlements. He scoffed at Cornish's rebuttal that the plan amounted to "colonization magnified." Woodson agreed with Cornish that black people should strive to "possess the inalienable rights of American citizens"—he saw citizenship as an important aim because it could be connected to a broad set of legal protections. But Woodson argued citizenship should be just that, a legal relationship, while Cornish felt that it ought to entail emotional bonds, "an identity of interest" among individuals. Woodson pointed out that people in different states or regions often felt little connection to their neighbors, and he argued that black people might embrace a separate racial identity that would not amount to a rejection of a place in the United States. "Men may be American citizens without having any *intercourse* with each other," Woodson wrote. Neither residency nor race could exclude black Americans from citizen status, which he said should be a simple result of their birth in the nation and the fact that they had "contributed to the general welfare."[24] Both Cornish and Woodson embraced the possibility of a citizen status that would connect black Americans and the federal government. But Woodson was not concerned with a status that would represent bonds of identity or love, which Cornish suggested were essential to gaining federal protection.

These debates among black activists and white lawmakers were particularly urgent in the early 1840s, as Texas moved to the center of American political discussions. Debates over Texas annexation raised questions about the very shape of the nation and what geographic change might mean for national principles. In 1838, John Quincy Adams, then a Massachusetts congressman, spoke against Texas annexation, arguing that the "gag rule" that blocked discussion of slavery had silenced significant opposition to proposals to add Texas to the union. Adams felt that the principle of the nation as "a compact of the People" might crumble if Congress voted to annex Texas without representing the breadth of American opinion on the issue.[25] Meanwhile, President John Tyler laid the groundwork for Texas annexation as early as 1841, and by 1843, cabinet officials publicly promoted annexation as a way to defend the country against antislavery British influence. By alleging British conspiracy, they framed expansion south and west as essential to national interests and identity, not simply a concern of southern states.[26] Other northerners echoed Adams's concerns, as in a Massachusetts meeting in which people argued that annexation endangered the republic. " 'Domestic tranquility,' " they said, "will not be promoted by the increased strength of its great disturbing cause." Texas seemed poised to determine whether the country would remain half slave and half free, to make a definitive statement on "what the country itself shall be."[27]

The extent to which the physical shape of the nation and its defining characteristics were up for debate in the late 1830s and early 1840s gave particular currency to black people's arguments that citizenship should first and foremost connect individuals to the federal government. When activists called themselves citizens of the United States or appealed to federal authority, they made themselves part of urgent conversations about what constituted the United States, who belonged in the country, and how its government should relate to individual Americans. Black activists spoke a language that was familiar and important to lawmakers and others when they made their arguments about the terms and content of citizenship in a dramatically changing nation.[28]

*   *   *

As they argued that citizenship should connect them to the federal government, African Americans worked to build a broad political community that transcended state and local boundaries. They worked simultaneously to forge a black American community and an American citizen status. Beginning in the late 1820s, a handful of New Yorkers sought to represent the free black populace, hoping to unite African American voices and address their shared concerns. Understanding that their arguments about citizenship could affect all free black Americans, they wanted their statements to emanate from a coalition that crossed state borders. Unity was a central idea in their politics, but activists disagreed about the form a coalition should take and the ideas that should motivate its work.

Black newspapers and national conventions were two of the most powerful tools activists used to create a black American political community. Cornish's work at the *Rights of All* emphasized the power of political unity. Faced with the financial challenges of sustaining a newspaper in the early antebellum period, Cornish's investors called for support from a broad community of "people of colour" who might fill their subscription rolls. Encouraging people to feel connected to one another could make the paper financially stable and further black protest by tapping the energies and ideas of a larger body of potential activists. In 1829, Cornish and his colleagues argued that the *Rights of All* was "the only channel of communication which we have with the whites—the only voice by which we can speak to our brethren at a distance." They understood that newspapers were crucial political tools for uniting people and amplifying their statements to lawmakers and the voting public.[29]

Calls for a wider black political coalition seemed especially urgent in response to the American Colonization Society's alarming vision of forced removal. Activists had launched the national convention movement in 1830, and delegates to that first meeting made clear the ties that bound them to the nation. They denounced the ACS as the "African Colonization Society," denying its organizers' claims to represent black Americans. They also established their own "American Society" of free black people and announced its chief goal as "improving their condition in the United States." They undercut the push for emigration to Liberia by calling for a black settlement in Upper Canada—present-day Ontario—not as a permanent home for African Americans but as a means to alleviate the prejudice and economic inequality that resulted from overcrowding in northeastern urban centers.[30]

The ACS's removal programs, which were organized at the state level, gave rise to shared concerns that brought free black people together across state borders. African Americans recognized that ACS supporters would not be satisfied with simply removing black people from Maryland or Ohio. Activists identified black American political concerns and worked beyond state borders by traveling and exchanging information. These were central political tactics in demanding a national citizen status that would offer legal protection from injustices like forced removal. In 1833, Nathaniel Paul, a black minister based in Albany, New York, leaned on an image of unified protest in his anticolonization work. "The coloured people are unanimous in their detestation of, and opposition to, this Society," he noted, "and if they go to Africa, it will be because they are compelled."[31] The ACS pushed activists to assert a connection to the soil on which they stood, and that rhetoric claimed a physical space and forged bonds among black Americans.

Opposing colonization thus united black Americans in a broad political community and encouraged activists' investment in unity as a tool to secure rights through citizenship. After holding national conventions each year from 1831 to 1835, black activists did not gather in the latter half of the decade, but they looked to revive the event in the summer of 1840 when Maryland lawmakers proposed state-funded black removal. On June 16, a group of activists meeting in New York called for a national convention, declaring that "the existence of the late Maryland *Black Law* should arouse every colored inhabitant of this Nation to a proper sense of his endangered condition." The organizers hoped the convention would bring together an impressive number of black Americans, enabling "*simultaneous* action" against the ACS. They chose New Haven as the site for their proposed meeting, perhaps to convey the power the movement had outside of larger urban centers. In a nod to the geographical breadth in which black politics flourished, the several dozen signers of the document identified themselves by their home cities, including Brooklyn, Poughkeepsie, Nantucket, Worcester, Hartford, Newark, Princeton, Pittsburgh, and Cincinnati.[32] They used the call to show that they had united a dispersed community and bypassed allegiance to states, conveying a wider opposition to the Maryland proposal. But in the coming years, internal strategic differences led black northerners to struggle to revive the national convention.

Over several weeks before the 1840 convention call went out, free black Americans discussed its possible revival in the pages of the *Colored American*. Charles B. Ray, then editor of the paper, wrote in early May that he supported a national convention as a means to deal with "American caste" and to enable black people to "take a higher and firmer stand for our rights as American citizens." In soliciting responses on the subject, Ray opened a debate on the function of a broad-based black American politics. Some of the correspondents agreed with Ray that a national convention could unite the scattered populace of "disfranchised American citizens." But Ray wondered aloud whether or not such a plan truly represented black people broadly. Noting a series of upcoming political events, including meetings of the American Moral Reform Society in Philadelphia, a New York state convention in Albany, the Ohio School Fund Society, and various New England temperance groups, Ray suggested that the black men in attendance should dedicate portions of those meetings to planning what might be a truly national convention. He hoped that working through those meetings might produce a new call that would capture "the voice of the people."[33]

In using his newspaper as a venue to debate the merits of a national convention, Ray imagined that print culture was a way to construct political unity. While a handful of Ohioans might visit New York's convention, or teetotaling Pennsylvanians could trek to a New England temperance meeting, Ray saw more potential in the spread of the written word. He understood the coalition-building power of print, that given time and republication, a call originating at any local gathering could garner support from across the free states. As editor and sole proprietor of a well-established black newspaper, that concept served Ray's interests, but it also argued for wider opportunity by imagining a political community that was open to any person with access to the printed word and a desire to claim a voice in political debates.

That Ray's newspaper effectively served this purpose is borne out by the responses he received, which suggest that people relished the opportunity for conversation without the hardships of travel.[34] For example, African Americans who met in Worcester and Pittsburgh in June 1840 sent records of their proceedings to Ray's newspaper. Black Pittsburghers found the original call for the New Haven convention too hasty and argued that a national convention should be held no sooner than the spring of 1841 in order to achieve "a union of the whole." Meanwhile, those gathered in Worcester thought a convention that would promote "united action in our cause" could not be held before September 1841.[35] As the meeting date for the New Haven convention approached, a number of black people gathered in the city to protest the gathering. They called themselves "citizens of New Haven," though some had traveled from Hartford and New York City to express their concerns. They denounced the proposed convention as "inexpedient, and uncalled for," and noted that organizers had failed to consult residents of their intended host city. These critics declared that the convention call represented only "a meagre proportion of our people." If the call did lead to an assembly, they argued that it should not be called a national convention, a title they saw as too important to be claimed prematurely by a political minority.[36]

Although Ray and others agreed with the New Haven convention organizers that it was critical to oppose colonization, the convention's critics were also deeply concerned with organizing a geographically diverse political community. Indeed, their desire for such a coalition was so powerful that concerns about unity at times seemed as though they might distract activists from the project of claiming legal protection through citizenship. Beyond the reality that no single free black person or group of people could truly speak for all African Americans, free and enslaved, the desire for unity produced tensions among activists and, at times, efforts to silence alternative viewpoints.

In the end, the New Haven convention failed rather spectacularly. Ten days before it was to begin, some of those who had signed the call publicly withdrew their support.[37] On September 7, the appointed opening date, one man arrived in New Haven to sit as a delegate. The next day, the gathering grew to five, two of whom lived in the city, and they met at a private residence on the edge of town. Upon hearing this news, Charles Ray gleefully reported that the convention had been "almost a total failure," satisfied, perhaps, that his paper had led people to reject the meeting. "The Convention did not come off quite so well as we expected," Ray quipped. "We thought there would have been two or three others in attendance."[38] Much of his satisfaction arose from evidence (at least in his own newspaper) that black people placed such significance on broad political engagement. They appeared to agree with him that, if a national convention was to be part of black citizenship politics, it should not be planned hastily or called for trivial matters and that it ought to be organized by a representative body and held in a location convenient for people across the free states. Nonetheless, Ray's humor must have been as bitter as it was biting, given his expressed interest in constructing a citizen status connected to rights and his sense of the value of a national convention for that pursuit.[39]

In addition to internal strategic differences, racist mob violence presented a serious challenge to reviving the national convention.[40] After the New Haven fiasco, for example, black Philadelphians began planning a national gathering in their city to be held in the summer of 1842, but hostile white observers organized to prevent the meeting. In their convention call,

activists cited the U.S. Constitution and claimed "the privileges and immunities of citizens."[41] Even in their early planning stages, meetings intensified
white opposition. One observer noted that, because of ACS doctrine and
black disfranchisement, white Philadelphians were conditioned to believe
that their black counterparts were not entitled to any legal protections. He
reported that white youths would "justify outrages on the colored children,
by [saying] 'they have no rights.' "[42] Many people had no context in which
they could comprehend the idea of black equality and viewed any work to
that end as a destabilizing attack on society.

In the summer of 1842, as black activists planned and white Philadelphians simmered, black people paraded through Philadelphia to celebrate
West Indian Emancipation Day. On the morning of August 1, 1842, nearly
1,200 people came together for a celebratory march across the Schuylkill
River in the western part of the city.[43] One of their banners depicted a black
man pointing with one hand to his broken chains and with the other to the
word "LIBERTY" writ large in gilded letters above his head. Later, white
rioters would claim that the banner bore the more dangerous slogan "Liberty
or Death." Sometime before eleven o'clock, a handful of young white men
contrived to block the parade; black marchers at the head of the procession
"removed" them, and in the process, one of the white men fell to the ground.
"The word was passed round that a white boy had been thrown down by
'the niggers.' "[44] A larger crowd gathered, and a street fight ensued. Black and
white Philadelphians traded blows for an hour, hurling stones and chunks of
bricks and causing severe injuries on both sides. The white mob claimed the
streets as their own, scattering the marchers and destroying the offending
banners, thus denying that black politics had a place in their community.[45]

Suppressing the Emancipation Day parade only spurred the mob to further violence. Through the evening and all of the next day, bands of white
rowdies roved South Philadelphia, an area with a large African American
population, attacking people on streets, smashing windows, barging through
locked doors, and setting fire to private homes and public buildings. They
threatened firemen with similar brutality, leading those volunteers to stand
idly by as flames engulfed a black church and meeting house.[46] Finally, on
the evening of August 2, the city council and mayor agreed to fund a special
police force that patrolled the streets "armed with heavy maces" to suppress
the violence. All told, about twenty people were hospitalized with serious
injuries as a result of the riots. Perhaps more important, hundreds of black

Philadelphians abandoned their homes to mob violence, compelled to seek refuge "in the woods and swamps of New Jersey."[47]

That mob was outraged over a specific celebration of black freedom as well as the general prospect of organized African American politics and activists' claims to rights as citizens. A Philadelphia correspondent to the *New-York Daily Tribune* blamed the victims in his account of the violence. He argued that protest intensified prejudice because of what he called "the insolent bearing and unbecoming airs" of vocal black activists. That activist minority had pursued "obnoxious measures . . . indicated most unequivocally in the 'National Convention,' which was about to assemble in this city, and to which the late unfortunate procession was probably a preliminary step." The correspondent quoted the call for the convention, in which organizers denounced colonization and claimed legal protections as citizens, a political project that the correspondent termed "ill-advised." His account of the riot criminalized black politics, declaring that people who did not engage in activism would remain "entitled to the ample protection of the laws" but that all others were subject to extralegal violence.[48] Here again, a white observer promoted a hollow kind of legal belonging that African Americans were working to redefine.

The activist claim that black Philadelphians were American citizens and were entitled to federal protection particularly galled white supremacists. The violent response and its justifications reveal that the choices to pursue national black political organization and claim an American citizen status were distinctly radical and palpably dangerous. The Philadelphia correspondent for the *Tribune* obscured the reality that black people were protesting precisely because they did not have the protection of the laws, that their "ill-advised" convention call was part of a search for the privileges and immunities his account falsely claimed were already available. The white reporter's response to the convention highlights the importance of tangible legal change. African Americans needed a fundamentally restructured set of laws that would make real the legal order under which white northerners claimed they lived. The planned 1842 convention did not come to fruition, but its claims regarding federal authority, black American identity, and national citizen status permeated later convention efforts.

*   *   *

The violence in Philadelphia did not quell black Americans' desires to hold a national convention or their arguments that citizenship should be a legal relationship with the federal government. Many black activists understood themselves as Americans and wanted to access federal power to challenge state-level legal restrictions.[49] Black protest operated in dialogue with formal law and politics in the United States, and the democratic principle of strength in numbers was a key part of their shared language. African Americans had seen the value of collective resistance to colonization, and they worked to expand on that accomplishment. After more than a decade of exchanging information, concerns, and protest strategies across state boundaries through print and in person, they had extensive experience working in broad activist communities. Black activist unity was not natural or inevitable, but long-standing circumstances and the exigencies of the moment made it especially important during the early 1840s. And so, after the failed New Haven convention and the violent suppression of the Philadelphia gathering, African Americans looked again to hold a convention in Buffalo, New York, in the summer of 1843. In that meeting, they argued for an American citizenship and experienced the ways ideology hindered the project of building that status.

In the spring of 1843, several dozen men from Massachusetts, Connecticut, New York, New Jersey, Pennsylvania, and Ohio signed a convention call arguing that collective work was essential to black politics. They described themselves as descendants of a common set of black political forefathers and stated that their goal was to bring together "the oppressed citizens of the United States." "In a great degree," they said, "we have become divided" due to the long gap between national conventions. A gathering of activists would promote collective political work and enable them "to secure the enjoyment of their inalienable rights." They called black people from across the country to "come and rally under the banner of freedom," invoking the American flag as a symbol of national unity and the government's expressed ideals. The phrase also pointed to the activists' goal, an enrichment of freedom, which they hoped to realize by building a tangible connection between black Americans and the federal government. To stand under the banner of freedom would mean that the government had embraced black people as part of the nation and that they might be protected as members of the American community.[50]

The convention succeeded in connecting black people from across the country, with fifty-seven men attending from seven states, as far west as Michigan and as far south as Georgia. In a nod to their host city, delegates named Buffalo resident Samuel H. Davis convention chair and invited him to deliver opening remarks. Davis had been born free in Maine in 1810 and educated at Oberlin College, later moving to Buffalo, where he taught and served as principal at the Buffalo African School.[51] Davis focused convention delegates on the work of constructing citizenship as a legal relationship. He recognized that free black people faced a variety of legal restrictions that typically differed in each state. But he encouraged them to see their shared desire "to secure for ourselves, in common with other citizens, the privilege of seeking our own happiness in any part of the country we may choose." State laws violated the most important elements of the U.S. Constitution, which guaranteed "freedom and equal rights to every citizen." This was a remarkable interpretive move, one with which Pennsylvania judge John Gibson and others would have disagreed. But the vagueness of citizenship as established in the Constitution made Davis's argument possible. The document suggested that citizenship was an important legal status, connected it to individual rights, and at no point said that certain people, particularly on the basis of race, were to be excluded from the status. Davis thus felt assured in describing racial oppression as a "cankerworm in the root of the tree of liberty," a disease that ought to alarm the country as a whole. Black activists needed to alert white Americans to the problems of their racialized legal system, to "change the thoughts, feelings, and actions towards us as men and citizens of this land." And black unity was an essential part of that process. Quoting from an 1824 history of the United States, Davis invoked the founding fathers as a model for collective action, men who revealed in their revolution "that a people, united in the cause of liberty, are invincible to those who would enslave them."[52] Davis guided delegates in their work at the meeting and at the same time ensured that black and white listeners understood activists' dedication to defining the content of citizen status.

The convention was an opportunity for black people to demonstrate that they were capable participants in a democracy and to knit together a political body that might collectively present arguments about citizenship. But among the challenges delegates encountered in the search for unity, they found themselves without a familiar and productive means of communication: the *Colored American* had published its last issue in December 1841. Convinced of the political value of print, they organized a committee on the press and called for the establishment of a new weekly paper "devoted impartially to the welfare of our whole people." African Americans wanted to reclaim the power of print media to shape public opinion and to unite behind a single, explicitly political publication in order to do so.[53]

Delegates also appointed a committee on agriculture, which delivered a message stressing the virtues of agrarian life in the abundant space available in the United States. The Buffalo convention encouraged African Americans to embrace the colonialist impulse and take ownership of the nation's physical landscape. Working collectively in rural communities, black people could leverage their economic stability and demographic strength to shape legal structures in new states and territories. For evidence of that path to influence, David Jenkins, a committee member from Ohio, presented a letter from black farmers who had settled in Mercer County, on that state's far western border. Taking "the advice of our abolition friends," several hundred African Americans had moved there in 1837 and settled into productive, comfortable lives. They purchased land, tamed the wilderness, built farms, and lived among white neighbors. The Mercer County settlers called on other black people to join them. Beyond what the settlers saw as the intrinsic value of economic productivity, they noted that work would allow black people to show their usefulness to society and counter the influence of prejudice. They suggested that any black person could go west and flourish, noting that they had built their new lives using only the funds they would otherwise have devoted to rent in a city. The committee in Buffalo cited similar farming communities in other Ohio counties and credited black movement to rural areas with decreasing prejudice in the developing West. And they encouraged migration to Michigan, Indiana, Illinois, and then-territories Wisconsin and Iowa. Moving to some of those places might have been "objectionable on account of their laws"—Illinois in particular had a set of harsh, exclusionary black laws—but people could potentially change legislation, particularly in territories and newer states.[54]

That call for black emigration constituted a radical protest against state proposals to exclude black people from their borders. Black identity in relation to the United States was fraught given the realities of slavery and legal exclusion. But activists were vocal about how important it was that they had been born in the nation.[55] The call to move west and shape American development politicized nativity as a path to changing the nation's laws. It was a declaration that black people identified as Americans, that they should be connected to the national government and should thus be entitled to all the space that the nation claimed. Connection to the United States, they suggested, superseded any state efforts to bar them. The Mercer County farmers and the committee members disregarded the idea that black people could be outlawed from any part of the country. Their call for people from eastern cities to move to the old Northwest framed black identity as a bond with the nation. Black people moving to the West were not abandoning their home states but were instead populating their native country, claiming their place in American social, economic, and political communities.

Holding the 1843 convention in upstate New York embodied this westward push of blackness. These ideas of a black American identity and the potential to change legal restrictions through broad collective action were central to the Buffalo convention. Meeting in upstate New York might have insulated the activists from urban racial violence, but it was also a conscious choice to look beyond the traditional gathering place of Philadelphia. It was another way of presenting black people as Americans, conveying the reality that their political communities existed beyond East Coast cities and the argument that people ought to be connected across the free states. Those present at the convention expressed a desire to examine and redefine their "moral and political condition as American citizens," to discuss the reality of their status and convey their ideas about their proper position in the country. During the convention, delegates engaged extensively with Buffalonians, delivering speeches in the evenings at meetings in local churches that were "largely attended by the citizens generally." Those orators included established figures such as Charles B. Ray, as well as a number of young men already celebrated for their oratory, most notably Henry Highland Garnet and Frederick Douglass.[56]

Amid those imposing personalities and the wide-ranging issues that delegates presented, one person with little experience claimed a central role at the convention by making a direct argument about the nature of citizenship. William C. Munroe traveled to Buffalo from his hometown of Detroit, where he worked as a teacher and minister and had emerged as an important figure in activism around the Great Lakes.[57] Munroe had previously served as president of Buffalo's Union Moral and Mental Improvement Society, and so he must have crossed Lake Erie with some frequency.[58] In Detroit, he had led the expansive work of the Colored Vigilant Committee, which encouraged education and uplift among free African Americans in addition to securing their physical freedom.[59] And he had joined other activists in pursuing equal suffrage in Michigan.[60] While Munroe had not previously attended national conventions, he was experienced with the forms of collective black politics and had been working toward substantive change in African Americans' legal lives by the time he arrived in Buffalo.

Perhaps because of his reputation in the city, Munroe sat on the convention's business committee, a group of nine men who drafted resolutions for the delegation's approval. Typically, conventions centered on those resolutions, deciding which of them should be published and in what language in order to broadcast a protest ideology, condemn specific injustices, and recommend avenues for change. At times, black and white newspapers printed only these resolutions in lieu of other records from conventions.[61] Munroe and his fellow committee members directed the 1843 convention through more than thirty proposals, a position from which they shaped the convention's message to the public and its legacy for free black people's lives.

On the afternoon of August 16, Munroe stood before his colleagues and presented Resolution No. 10, which was brief and direct: "by the second section of the fourth article of the Constitution of the U.S., we [are] citizens."[62] In so doing, he asked delegates to endorse an explicit claim to national citizen status under the Constitution. As had so many before him, Munroe invoked the Privileges and Immunities Clause, arguing for federal supremacy over restrictive state policy and calling for a legal relationship with the U.S. government. Munroe delivered "a flaming speech" in support of the resolution, rejecting rulings from "inferior courts" that black men were not citizens. "Mr. Munro[e] thought it high time for us to speak out upon this subject, and that the present was this time."[63]

Munroe's language helps explain why so many black activists were invested in the idea of a national citizen status under the auspices of the federal government. Black activists paid close attention to developing legal exclusions and opportunities; they understood that laws influenced their daily experiences as much as social and economic circumstances. Indeed, it is not difficult to imagine that some delegates had in mind the disfranchised black Pennsylvanian William Fogg during Munroe's impassioned speech. African Americans appealed to federal authority because northern lawmakers were finding ever more sophisticated ways to restrict their rights. Wielding the same power through which they had begun the long emancipation in the early nineteenth century, state lawmakers built structures of racial exclusion that were not necessarily bound to the peculiar institution or to federal authority. States disfranchised black people, imposed residency restrictions, and funded colonization, all representing the increasingly oppressive tendency of state law toward African Americans.[64] Faced with this legal reality, black people like William Munroe looked to the federal government as an alternative authority that might remove those constraints. They had no real evidence to support the theory that federal authority might operate in their favor, but black activists did have ample experience with state lawmakers who opposed black equality. Most importantly, they had the opportunity to construct a legal relationship under which federal power would work for them. The vagueness of the Constitution and the uncertainties surrounding citizenship provided a space for Munroe and others to define the federal government as an authority that could secure black rights. Munroe could make a sensible legal argument that African Americans were citizens, that they were entitled to privileges and immunities. That the precise content of citizenship was a question made it a useful tool for black Americans.[65]

Munroe and his colleagues turned to the federal government because of the language of the nation's founding documents. Nothing in state law could match the broad power and interpretive flexibility of the Declaration of Independence or the Constitution's Comity Clause. And while northern state constitutions often echoed the rhetoric of national founding documents, black activists took legislators to task for measures that contradicted that language. In August 1843, for example, while protesting disfranchisement in their state, a group of black Ohioans called on the legislature "to repeal such laws as deprive us of those rights which pertain to citizenship." The activists believed "in the philanthropy of the founders of this republic" and announced that their goal was "to be true and faithful supporters of the same when we are recognized as citizens."[66] State laws oppressed them, and while they wanted state authorities to effect legal change, they based that argument upon ideas expressed in national founding texts. Ultimately, they sought a legal status that superseded state authority and through that status the rights they felt state governments had unjustly restricted.

William Munroe and the Buffalo delegates help us understand more fully the project of building a black political community that emerged in the early 1840s, culminating in the address issued from the 1845 Convention of Colored People that opened this chapter. When those activists in Philadelphia declared "Union is Strength," they positioned themselves within a pattern of black politics focused on collective action to build an American citizen status. As they closed that 1845 convention, they explained that their chief goal, like that of other national meetings, had been "to unite the whole family of free colored people." Once united, they could petition the "authorities of our country . . . for the repeal of every law injurious to us [as] native born Americans." Eliminating restrictive state laws would move them toward their goal of a national citizen status that secured legal protections by linking individuals with the federal government. They also called for a standing organization to arrange petitioning efforts and maintain a network of traveling lecturers who would inform black people in various communities of the importance of collective political engagement. Disunity presented a number of threats, as it had since the origins of the ACS. If they remained divided, the delegates worried, black Americans "must submit to be driven out of the country, where we were born." These activists suggested that black political unity would be key to achieving national unity. In order to show that they were Americans who deserved a place in the country, they first had to join together as African Americans to issue a strong statement representing a broad population. Unity had a practical political value, enhancing activist voices as they reached out to the federal government. Presenting a united front would enable black people to speak with "the voice of one man making respectful, but strong demand on the constituted authority of the country for JUSTICE."[67]

*   *   *

The reverberations of the 1845 speech suggest not only the power of the national convention movement but also the shortcomings of its revival as a way to produce collective claims about national citizenship. Although the Buffalo and Philadelphia conventions reflected a desire to establish a unified political community, they revealed deep fissures in African American activist communities. None of the men who signed the 1845 address appear to have attended the 1843 convention. In fact, the Buffalo meeting did not feature a single delegate from Pennsylvania, a state with nearly 50,000 free black residents.[68] Convention organizers in the early 1840s cherished the idea of a body that would effectively gather and represent people from across the free states, but the variety of black people's social circumstances and protest ideologies hindered the effort to forge a unified African American political community. African Americans arrived in Buffalo in 1843 with conflicting antislavery ideologies that stood in the way of their stated goal of changing and specifying their legal status. Those tensions hindered the project of presenting a clear set of terms for American citizenship. Black activists did not share a sense of the extent to which the nation must change, the degree to which its laws needed to be rewritten in order to secure rights and protections for black people.

Perhaps the most significant outcome of the 1843 Buffalo convention was Henry Highland Garnet's "Address to the Slaves of the United States of America." That speech became a major point of conflict and highlights the major barriers to black political unity. Garnet was born a slave in Maryland in 1815, but he and his family escaped during his youth, resettling in New York City, where he attended the African Free School. Despite his youth, Garnet's colleagues chose him to chair the Business Committee at Buffalo, perhaps in recognition of his oratorical reputation. Garnet, likely in conjunction with his wife and fellow activist Julia Williams Garnet, wrote a radical speech in advance of the meeting and, with the power of his position, delivered it before the assembled delegates and proposed that it be included in the printed convention record. The address brought enslaved people into the political community that activists so desired, but its content revealed the distance between free black northerners and their counterparts in bondage. Garnet embraced all African Americans as "Fellow-Citizens," announcing that through nativity, both free and enslaved were "justly entitled to all the rights that are granted to the freest." He urged resistance through self-defense, admonishing enslaved people to protect themselves and their families from abuses at the hands of their owners. "To such degradation," he proclaimed, "it is sinful in the Extreme for you to make voluntary Submission." But Garnet offered a remarkably simple solution: "go to your lordly enslavers, and tell them plainly, *that you are determined to be free.*"[69] It is hard to know precisely what Garnet expected from the address. If he had intended for enslaved people to follow his advice, he ignored the challenges of circulating abolitionist ideas in the South, the limits of slaves' literacy, and the real peril of revolt. If he sought simply to rouse abolitionists to action, he succeeded, although in so doing, he showed little regard for the real challenges of slave revolt.[70]

Garnet's speech caused an uproar at the convention, especially when he declared that enslaved people "had far better all die—*die immediately*, than live slaves."[71] Many delegates were unhappy with Garnet's tone; Charles B. Ray, ever mindful of the public sphere, proposed that a committee edit the message to temper passages that "might in print appear objectionable." Garnet responded with another speech of more than an hour, detailing the horrors of slavery and arguing that his address to the slaves offered an ideal path to self-emancipation. The published proceedings note that this second speech left "the whole Convention . . . literally infused with tears" and met thunderous applause from the assembly. Frederick Douglass might also have shed a tear, himself less than five years removed from bondage, but still he expressed serious reservations about Garnet's vision of resistance. Douglass heard "too much physical force" in the speech, and while he doubted that it would reach the slaves, he remained concerned that the convention would be at fault if the address somehow sparked an insurrection. He encouraged black abolitionists to "[try] the moral means a little longer."[72]

In the early 1840s, Douglass supported a pacifist antislavery approach that stemmed from William Lloyd Garrison's ideas about justice and power. Garrison had helped introduce Douglass to public antislavery work and the strategy of moral suasion—discouraging violence and using rhetoric to convince white Americans of the evils of slavery. In his response to Garnet's address, Douglass argued that all black activists should pursue that approach, that the Buffalo delegates "were called upon to avoid" slave rebellion. Douglass "wanted emancipation in a better way."[73] He continued to hope that a broad emotional and ideological shift would lead Americans to acknowledge the sins of their institutions.

With their ideological fervor and oratorical skill, Douglass and Garnet intensified divisions among the delegates and shifted the convention's focus away from the terms of citizenship to a debate over antislavery philosophies. For two days, delegates discussed the merits and implications of Garnet's address, and twice they voted narrowly to exclude it from the printed convention record.[74] The delegates argued so intensely over Garnet's speech because they wanted so much to fight slavery and also to encourage the public to embrace black people as Americans. The possibility of publishing a common agenda was enticing, but it also aroused ideological passions and highlighted the challenges of bringing dozens of people into agreement on how best to both fight slavery and build legal equality.[75] Douglass argued that the Constitution was a proslavery document and that change must come from outside by remaking the nation's legal structures. Garnet in the early 1840s supported the Liberty Party, a formal political group with ambitions to bring antislavery politics into Congress and fight bondage from within the bounds of the current Constitution. These black activists were engaged in the same debate that occupied federal lawmakers regarding Texas—a dispute over whether the nation was properly defined by slavery or freedom. That disagreement over abolitionist tactics absorbed the delegates through the oratorical force of two of the rising stars of black politics.[76]

Intense antislavery tensions thus presented a fundamental challenge to other political goals in the early 1840s. It is instructive to return here to

William C. Munroe's resolution, a forceful argument on black Americans' legal status rooted in the U.S. Constitution. When he invoked the Privileges and Immunities Clause to declare black people citizens, Munroe made the significant claims that the status was a product of federal authority and that it was available to African Americans through nativity. Both of these claims were increasingly central to black activist work in the early 1840s. But convention delegates responded to Munroe's resolution through their ideas about antislavery strategy. Abolitionist factions limited opportunities for thoughtful discussion of Munroe's resolution on its own merits. By positioning black Americans under the protection of the Comity Clause, Munroe essentially argued that the Constitution was an antislavery document, that its text contained a statement of African Americans' rights. Douglass objected, as would any Garrisonian, and denounced the Constitution as "a slaveholding instrument [that] denied *all* rights to the colored man." Even before he faced off with Garrison's camp, Munroe had to step outside the bounds of the Business Committee to present his resolution "in a very forcible manner." Garnet and his allies had tried to push Munroe's measure out of the convention's resolutions, perhaps aware that it would give Douglass a chance to make his arguments about the Constitution. Rather than debating visions of the content of citizen status, delegates discussed Munroe's resolution through their ideas about the best approach in the fight against slavery. In a remarkable sequence, the debate over Munroe's resolution ended when the committee to revise Garnet's "Address to the Slaves" returned with their report. One delegate suggested discussing Garnet's address the following day, but his colleagues denied the proposal. Munroe saw his statement on citizenship and federal authority cast aside for an important speech but one that bore little relation to the convention's stated goals of reconsidering black Americans' legal status.

In the brief moments when delegates did take up Munroe's claim to citizenship, some opposed it because they felt that it was too obvious to merit restatement. "Nothing could be plainer," one man declared, "than that native free born men must be citizens, and . . . the converse of this was palpably absurd." His opposition reflected a complex politics, superficially embracing Munroe's claim but at the same time stifling it. Perhaps Munroe's opponents recognized the importance of citizen status but worried that if black activists began to make arguments to claim citizenship, they would encourage white Americans to challenge them. That may explain why in one of the convention's final acts, Alphonso Sumner of Ohio called for Munroe's resolution to be "expunged from the minutes," and a majority of the remaining delegates agreed. It seems that to those men, the fact of black citizenship ought to be accepted without question or justification. But when the delegates silenced legal reasoning on their own behalf, they prevented the convention from issuing a statement that might define citizen status. Munroe's resolution was potentially far more than a claim that African Americans were citizens. It could serve as the beginning of a move toward crafting the specific terms of that status, building it around a set of legal protections and using it to connect individual black people to the federal government. Despite that potential, the resolution has survived in the record only because Garrison's *Liberator* reprinted Douglass's criticism of it, including a full quotation of Munroe's proposal.

But perhaps Alphonso Sumner and others who opposed Munroe's resolution felt it did too little. Sumner may have agreed about the importance of citizenship but felt Munroe had failed to specify the privileges and immunities they wanted the status to secure. Munroe said that citizenship should connect individual black Americans to the federal government as a result of their birth in the United States. He embraced a broad, accessible status, sketching out a legal claim that he might then use in pursuit of a set of rights. But Alphonso Sumner may have been distinctly concerned with making an argument about that set of rights. In the early 1840s, Sumner established the *Disfranchised American*, a newspaper based in Cincinnati with a title that pointed to his political concerns. As a result of Ohio's Black Laws, Sumner could not vote. He had no access to a jury trial if someone claimed him as a fugitive. If he had family living in another state, whether free or enslaved, they could join him in Ohio only after posting the required $500 bond as surety for their good conduct.[77] Sumner may have wanted to erase Munroe's resolution from the record because he believed it would fail to change black people's legal lives. Sumner and Munroe, then, might point to the challenges of building black citizenship, the force of divergent ideas about how exactly activists should deploy a particular type of language in pursuit of concrete change.

Or, perhaps, not all black activists were as interested as Munroe in claiming or defining citizenship. For many of those who were, their ideas about the status were filtered through their particular approaches to the problem of slavery. These were black abolitionists, and while their politics encompassed far more than antislavery, that fight was critical to their ideas about the shape of the nation, as much as it was for congressmen debating the meaning of the Negro Seamen Acts or Texas annexation. Still, in the early 1840s, black activists became convinced of the importance of claiming a place as part of an American community. State lawmakers had begun to exercise their authority to exclude African Americans. And free black people recognized that if Ohio, Pennsylvania, or Maryland imposed restrictions, then any other state could and likely would do the same. The Declaration of Independence, the U.S. Constitution, and even the Articles of Confederation provided valuable tools in the struggle for equality, including a vague, yet powerful, limitation of states' power over citizens. Black people used the Privileges and Immunities Clause because it fit so neatly with their goals; it established the power of citizen status but left open to interpretation the specific rights the status entailed. And so they continued striving to be recognized as citizens, a status they defined as national and administered by the federal government. Black activist work pushed lawmakers and other Americans to consider the possibility that the federal government should be an active force in shaping individuals' legal lives. Through the revival of the national convention, the call for federal support for racial equality, and the invocation of federal law in opposition to specific state restrictions, black protest from the early 1840s laid important foundations for protest that would continue through the mid-nineteenth century. But African Americans' reliance on federal protection and the nation's founding documents would be sorely tested by restrictive legal developments in the coming decades.

CHAPTER 3

Nations, Revolutions, and the Borders of Citizenship

The summer of 1845 found Frederick Douglass aboard the steamship *Cambria*, bound for Liverpool, England. Douglass's public profile skyrocketed after the Buffalo convention of 1843. He had traveled to Buffalo during a nearly two-year lecture tour across the Midwest and Northeast, developing a repertoire of emotional abolitionist appeals and compelling stories about his life in bondage. Douglass's storytelling culminated in 1845 with the publication of the *Narrative of the Life of Frederick Douglass: An American Slave*. The *Narrative* made him perhaps the best-known black person in the United States, but fame required Douglass to acknowledge publicly that he was a fugitive slave. Douglass sought refuge that summer, boarding the *Cambria* to begin a lecture tour of the British Isles.

The nineteen months he spent in Europe transformed Douglass's activist work. On the voyage to Liverpool, he befriended the ship's British captain, who invited Douglass to tell his story on the deck. But a group of white Americans refused to allow Douglass to lecture on slavery and threatened to throw him overboard if he tried to do so. That was the first of many incidents Douglass would use to contrast the welcome he experienced in Europe with the pervasive prejudice of his native country. Touring the British Isles changed his ideas about his relationship to the United States.[1] In 1846, during a stop in Belfast, Douglass wrote to William Lloyd Garrison "as to nation, I belong to none." Slavery and legalized racial exclusion made him feel alienated him from his homeland. "I am an outcast from the society of my childhood," he continued with a characteristic flourish, "and an outlaw in the land of my birth. . . . If ever I had any patriotism, or any

capacity for the feeling, it was whipt out of me long since by the lash of the
American soul-drivers."[2]

Douglass used his sadness to advance the project of changing African
Americans' legal lives. He felt like an outcast because slavery had corrupted
his native country, robbing the United States of its potential to be an inclusive republic. Traveling to Europe elevated Douglass's international profile,
exposed him to the possibilities of black life beyond U.S. borders, and helped
him articulate complicated feelings about the United States. The journey
armed him with ideas and experiences he used in his activism in the United
States. For years after he returned from the British Isles in 1847, Douglass
would write about the distance between such people as the welcoming British
captain and the racist American mob on the *Cambria*, using Europe to pro-
voke change in the country he wanted to call his home.

Douglass also made wealthy friends in Britain, and when he returned to
the United States in late 1847, he used some of their money to purchase his
freedom for $711. Those friends also gave Douglass funds to launch his own
newspaper, the *North Star*, in Rochester, New York, in December 1847.[3]
Within a few months, Douglass would fill the paper with coverage of revolutions that began in Europe in the late winter of 1848. He looked on with
pleasure as radical political work tore down monarchies and built European
republics, and he was eager to report on and celebrate the revolutions.

Beyond Douglass, across African American communities, activists said a
great deal about Europe and Europeans in their political work during the late
1840s. Even black people who did not travel overseas saw the value of European events for their protest statements. The revolutionary creation of European republics showed that radical politics could reorder power structures
and redefine relationships between individuals and the state. Leaders of the
1848 revolutions reimagined citizenship when they demanded new, mutual
obligations between governments and the governed. In the 1840s, black people continued to wrestle with their feelings about the United States and to
question whether they could build a real legal connection with the government. Activists reflected on European politics and European people as they
imagined their ideal community and fought for legal change in the United
States.[4]

"We live in stirring times, and amid thrilling events," Douglass declared
in the *North Star* in August 1848. "Our brave old earth rocks with mighty
agitation."[5] European rebels connected across national borders, and people
like Douglass thought and wrote about the potential of a community of

citizens that was not defined by the limits of any particular nation.[6] During the late 1840s, African Americans reconsidered the kind of community in which they wanted to belong. They felt connections to an international group of people united in reform work and made arguments for a citizen status that did not tie individuals to a specific physical place.[7] Ultimately, activists remained invested in securing legal rights through their connections to the United States, and they emphasized nativity in contrast to the foreignness of European immigrants in their calls for legal protections. Black activists thus used Europe and Europeans in complex ways in their protest during the late 1840s. The continent transformed their claims about the nature of citizenship and offered activists a new set of tools to pursue change. They claimed legal protections through a series of arguments about others who should be excluded. As they responded to revolution in Europe, African Americans considered the potential of a citizen status that might be free from national borders but remained focused on building a legal connection to the U.S. government based on their birth in the nation.

*   *   *

In the late winter of 1848, political demonstrations in Europe turned violent, initiating a new Age of Revolutions.[8] Mass protest turned into riots in the streets of Paris, Munich, Vienna, Budapest, Krakow, Berlin, and other urban centers of power. Revolutionary turmoil expanded beyond the cities as artisans and rural peasants protested their political marginalization. Shared concerns about political and economic inequality linked rebels across the continent, and geographic boundaries seemed to crumble in the face of a European revolution. When French rebels declared their nation a republic in February, they fostered a "springtime of the people," characterized by popular opposition to monarchy, celebrations of uprisings in distant countries, and cries of unity in rebellion.[9] After dethroning monarchs (many of whom, like France's Louis-Philippe, simply fled from growing mobs), rebels typically held popular elections for new governments. Large numbers of Europeans participated in the revolutions through voting as well as informal political forums such as community associations, street demonstrations, and newspapers. People seemed to have liberated themselves from oppressive hierarchies through a combination of peaceful protest and violent uprisings. Few Americans ignored the drama, largely because newspapers had proliferated in the United States, fostering public awareness of national and international events.[10] Free black people, like their white American counterparts, created and participated in that extensively informed community.

As early as the 1830s, significant numbers of black activists cultivated their political consciousness by looking beyond the borders of the United States, in part through celebrations of British West Indian emancipation each year on the first of August.[11] Emancipation Day celebrations in the late 1840s allowed activists to integrate revolutionary Europe into their politics. On August 1, 1849, Frederick Douglass opened a speech in Rochester by reading British and French emancipation acts and applauding the events of the revolutionary spring. "We live in times which have no parallel in the history of the world," he reminded what was likely an already well-informed audience. "Kingdoms, realms, empires, and republics roll to and fro like ships upon a stormy sea."[12] The Atlantic Ocean bridged the gap between American people and Europe's rebels. "Steam, skill and lightning, have brought the ends of the earth together."[13] Douglass's poetic phrasing added color to real technological change. In early 1848, the *Cambria*, the ship on which Douglass had sailed to Britain, brought news from Liverpool to New York in only fifteen days, spreading information that connected people in distant places.[14] Editors like Douglass enhanced popular awareness of foreign events and created a context in which people could feel connected to others an ocean away. Discussions of the 1848 revolutions fit within a tradition of celebrating the first of August, part of an Atlantic political outlook black and white activists had long worked to cultivate.

Beyond antislavery communities, many in the United States saw 1848 as an opportunity to celebrate the American Revolution, believing their country had inspired Europeans to reject tyranny and choose freedom. The 1848 revolutions seemed to present the United States as the cornerstone of a republican Atlantic world. News from Europe covered the front page of the *New-York Daily Tribune* on March 20, 1848, with a headline trumpeting the "ABDICATION OF LOUIS PHILIPPE!" The paper compiled coverage from across the continent but focused chiefly on events in France. French people had taken the first step in "the Emancipation of Europe," editors wrote, conferring a continental significance on one country's revolution.[15]

Some white Americans worried European countries might surpass the United States in terms of the liberties and protections they offered residents. In the early 1840s, Rhode Island men rebelled in pursuit of universal white men's suffrage in the state. One of the rebels, a man named Martin Luther, sued state authorities on the grounds they had entered his home illegally. Luther's case went to the Supreme Court in 1848, where his lawyers linked his plight to rebellion overseas and argued the United States would lag behind the new republics of Europe if states continued to deny white men's voting rights. This was the context in which black activists invoked Europe. Their arguments about the relative rights and freedoms available in their country would have sounded familiar to many white Americans.[16] African Americans worked to instill in the public a nuanced sense of the meanings of Europe's revolutions for the United States. Activists used Europe to convince people of the extent of unfreedom and inequality in the United States. For black northerners, as for Martin Luther in Rhode Island, the revolutions demanded that people acknowledge the gap between America's founding legal language and the realities of life in their own country.

For instance, in December 1848, black Pennsylvanians met for a state convention where they cited European events in their pursuit of equal suffrage. They spoke to white Pennsylvanians, seeking support for their campaign to have the word "white" removed from the state constitutional clause on voting rights.[17] Pennsylvania lawmakers had disfranchised black men in the late 1830s. But the state held yearly meetings at which voters could present grievances to their representatives, and delegates to the black convention hoped white voters would raise the issue of black disfranchisement. White Pennsylvanians would thereby serve as "the representatives of the Coloured Citizens of this Commonwealth."[18] The activists noted celebrations of the news from Europe. Pennsylvanians had "hailed with joyful acclamation the accession of liberal France to the great family of republics, because it thrust the keystone from the arch of monarchical governments throughout Europe." But people in the United States should not celebrate republicanism abroad when its principles were so deeply flawed at home. "However much you may admire and extol the progress of free principles in other states," they wrote, "that of your own dearest Pennsylvania must occupy the highest seat in your affections."[19]

The delegates appealed to voters' pride in their home state as a way to condemn white hypocrisy. White Pennsylvanians clearly did not cherish "free principles" if a black convention was necessary to confront disfranchisement. Black activists questioned whether a state that excluded from formal politics so many of the people it governed could be called a republic. Calling themselves "coloured citizens" made a multilayered argument about the terms of citizenship. They asserted their place in the political community and claimed the moral high ground, a position from which they shamed their white counterparts. Citizenship must entail suffrage, they argued. Black Pennsylvanians urged white voters to think critically about the transformative meanings of European revolutions and to push for legal change in the United States as vigorously as they celebrated foreign news.

Europe and its revolutions enriched black politics in 1848 and well after the first flush of revolution faded. On May 31, 1849, Douglass spoke at the New England Antislavery Convention about the gap between European freedom and American slavery. The U.S. Constitution empowered Congress to raise a militia to "suppress insurrections," Douglass noted, reminding his audience that even professed abolitionists might be obligated to protect slavery.[20] "You, the citizens of Boston, have sworn, before God, that three millions of slaves shall be slaves or die," he announced. He charged all in his hearing with the crime of human bondage because those three million enslaved people were in fact "held by the U.S. Government."[21] White abolitionists had failed to dedicate themselves fully to support a revolutionary upheaval of the legal structures of American slavery. To reinforce his point, Douglass cited joyous reactions to the recent French Revolution:

> You welcomed the intelligence from France, that Louis Philippe had been barricaded in Paris—you threw up your caps in honor of the victory achieved by Republicanism over Royalty—you shouted aloud "Long live the republic!"—and joined heartily in the watchword of "Liberty, Equality, Fraternity"—and should you not hail, with equal pleasure, the tidings from the South, that the slave had risen, and achieved for himself, against the iron-hearted slaveholder, what the republicans of France achieved against the royalists of France?[22]

Douglass expressed similar ideas in his most famous speech, delivered July 5, 1852, in which he wondered aloud what Independence Day could mean to African Americans. In the 1852 speech, he described feeling distant from white Americans and charged all American people with the national sins of slavery and racism. He was building those arguments in 1849 in Boston by reflecting on the meanings of European events for his political concerns.

In the 1849 speech, Douglass made arguments about the content of citizenship by criticizing a large proportion of white Americans. When he denounced "citizens of Boston" as supporters of slavery, he implicitly attacked their claim to the status because they condoned their nation's slaveholding government. A person should be invested in work toward human freedom and equality in order to be regarded as a citizen, he argued. Douglass defined citizenship by excluding people he believed were unworthy of the status; he thus used the concept in an effort to purge racism from American communities. Douglass and other black activists criticized white Americans who took European events as a cause to celebrate their republic. Black people noted that the American Revolution had failed to produce a nation that offered freedom or legal protections to large segments of its population. They used European events alongside the language of citizenship to demand legal change in the United States.

*   *   *

When black activists talked about Europe and used citizenship language in the late 1840s, they imagined new kinds of communities with new criteria for belonging. They thought in new ways about what the legal status of citizenship could be.[23] African Americans envisioned a citizenship defined by an individual's work toward human liberation, one that was not determined by a person's place in a particular nation. Such a citizenry could reach beyond national boundaries and theoretically offer people the opportunity to choose to belong through their behavior.[24]

American people tended to see Europe as a continent united in rebellion, which helped encourage black activists to consider connecting with rebels in distant nations. During their uprisings, Europeans did reach out to people in other nations, building what appeared to be a continental movement with common ideological roots. "All the European states share in the excitement" of France's new republic, one newspaper editor declared. People across Ireland celebrated France's rebellion with "bonfires, and rejoicings." In Switzerland, people were "in ecstasy at the late events in France." Some leading Swiss government officers resigned and provisional officials quickly voted to recognize the French Republic. Rebels in France returned these gestures of support. In late March, Alphonse de Lamartine, who had formally declared the Second French Republic, encouraged a group of Irish visitors in their struggles for religious and political liberty, saying their work had "at all times moved the heart of Europe."[25]

Further, nobles in Europe worried that figures like Lamartine and the revolution in France would spark uprisings across the continent. A French count serving as ambassador in Austria fainted when he learned of Louis

Phillipe's abdication; when he regained consciousness, he fled for the monarchal safety of England. In Spain, "Queen Christina was so much effected [*sic*] by the news from Paris, that it was found necessary to bleed her twice."[26] Rebel leaders like Lamartine produced such anxiety because they called for a continental community of freedom fighters. It seemed the oppressed people of Europe had risen together to remove tyrants. Lamartine also appealed to black Americans because he suggested they might find a home in a broad new community composed of people dedicated to fighting oppression. Some black Americans began to envision themselves as members of such a community and to make arguments about who did and did not belong.

Surveying Europe's political landscape, Frederick Douglass agreed with many that France had sparked the "more substantial fires" raging around the continent. "The French metropolis is in direct communication with all the great cities of Europe," he said, and anxiety spread from imperial Austria to czarist Russia.[27] Douglass, like other observers, exaggerated the extent of real cooperation in Europe.[28] But the vision of a collective revolution had a strong emotional and intellectual appeal to American people. In March 1848, nearly 300 Americans marched to the Hôtel de Ville, the traditional center of Paris's municipal government. There, they presented officials of the new French Republic with an American flag and the French Tricolor linked together on a single pole. The flag was an "eternal emblem of the alliance between France and the United States," conveying a powerful desire to connect with continental revolutionaries.[29]

For years before the 1848 revolutions, black activists had practiced their politics beyond national borders through their work in Anglo-Atlantic abolitionism. African Americans worked alongside the British and Foreign Antislavery Society and had organized first of August celebrations for Britain's abolition of slavery in its West Indian colonies. Black people had long used Europe in their politics. In September 1838, just after Britain abolished slavery in its colonies, Samuel Cornish's *Colored American* questioned how any person in the slaveholding United States could "compare himself with the least and lowest of the European nations." African Americans connected with British abolitionists for help publishing narratives of their lives in slavery. For many black Americans, Britain and, by extension, Europe could help them articulate the injustices of their native country and feel a powerful sense of belonging in political communities.[30]

The radical abolitionist William Lloyd Garrison joined black Americans in seeking political ties beyond the United States, publishing his newspaper

FIGURE 3. Garrison antislavery banner. Cotton, paint, by unknown, Boston (1843).
This sign might have hung on the walls during an antislavery meeting, reminding
abolitionists of the insufficiencies of the American republic and pointing them toward
a way they might criticize the United States in contrast with the politics of Europe's
monarchies. Collection of the Massachusetts Historical Society.

the *Liberator* under the masthead "Our Country is the World, Our Countrymen are all Mankind." At a celebration of Garrison's work in July 1849, black
Bostonians presented him with a silver pitcher inscribed with that motto in
appreciation of "his undeviating devotion to the cause of Universal Emancipation."[31] The celebration was also an occasion to bid farewell to William
Wells Brown, a fugitive slave and abolitionist who had been invited to participate in the World's Peace Convention scheduled for late August in Paris. The
Peace Convention wed antislavery and nonviolence advocacy, and it offered
Brown a formal voice in Atlantic reform conversations as an acknowledged
representative of a broad African American public.[32]

Voyagers like Brown further highlighted the political value of Europe for
black Americans, even those who did not leave the United States. Thomas
Paul Smith, a young black activist tasked with introducing Brown at the July
1849 farewell, said Brown's travels had the potential to strengthen bonds
among scattered reformers. Smith was proud of "the brother we are to send

to represent us in Europe" and also envious that Brown would be working directly with Europe's revolutionaries. "Tell European freemen . . . that the great heart of American philanthropy beats in unison with theirs," Smith announced, "and that we entreat them to take courage, and never despair— for the triumph of the right is sure." The crowd applauded Smith's senti- ment, convinced of the potential of Brown's voyage.[33] Smith and other free black people embraced European revolutions in some of the same ways as their white American counterparts, claiming U.S. support would help bring about "the triumph of the right" abroad. But these black Bostonians also saw Brown as their representative in a continuing fight to change the United States, a person who would travel to Europe in pursuit of justice for black Americans at home. When Brown joined the Peace Convention, he claimed a voice for black Americans in an activist community that reached far beyond the borders of the United States.

The Boston celebration reflected some of the ideas Frederick Douglass expressed in the late 1840s, both at a commemoration of the first of August in 1848 and at the New England Antislavery Convention in July 1849. Black people looked to join a community engaged in fighting oppression. Ameri- cans who claimed citizen status were responsible for working toward justice in their country, Douglass argued. There was a silent "so-called" in his remarks as he charged "every American citizen" with the sin of slavery. A citizen had the power to effect change in pursuit of human liberation, and if Americans rejected the constitutional compromises that upheld slavery, "the slave [could] instantly assert and maintain his rights."[34] Douglass, Thomas Paul Smith, and the audience of black Bostonians united in arguing that belonging should be defined by a person's work on behalf of the oppressed. These activists extended earlier claims that a person's belonging should be determined by their contributions to a community. They developed these ideas in the midst of turmoil in Europe, reflecting on people like Lamartine, who envisioned a broad community composed of those who challenged repressive power structures.[35]

While black Americans across the North celebrated Emancipation Day and the possibilities of Europe's revolutions, some believed black activists were too invested in uprisings on that distant continent. A group of black New Yorkers began publishing the *Hyperion* in August 1849, and in their newspaper, they challenged black activists who sought political connections with Europeans. Like other antebellum newspapers, the *Hyperion*'s short life span raises more questions than it answers. The editors' personal histories, their financial circumstances, and their daily work to manage the newspaper are uncertain. Indeed, much of what we know about the *Hyperion* comes from the *North Star*. Douglass announced the beginning and the end of its publication and printed the *Hyperion*'s introductory letter to the public.[36] The editors launched their paper with a statement on protest movements connected across national borders. They criticized Douglass and other editors for overlooking the ways race created a "common bond of fraternity and interest" between black people in the United States and the West Indies. "We wish to cultivate the broadest identification of each member of the race with the whole," they noted.[37] At a time of enduring public interest in the 1848 revolutions, they spurned Europe and embraced a community defined by blackness in the Americas.

The *Hyperion*'s editors did join other activists in looking beyond U.S. borders to try to change the terms of their legal lives. People of African descent had been "denationalized when they were torn from their native shores," they argued, and since then, black Americans had only begun to "[acquire] the powers and the rights of a new nationality." To the editors, nationality meant "equal civil and political rights in a government." Black people should make their home in any nation "which protects us in all the rights of citizenship." They would not be moved by loyalty to the United States when the country continued to exclude them. While the editors did not specify the rights they desired, they made clear their interest in securing tangible legal protections. By privileging rights, the *Hyperion*'s editors imagined a citizenship that was not predicated on nativity, suggesting that black Americans might secure legal protections outside of the United States. In fact, they agreed that Europe's revolutions had encouraged wider reform even as they criticized the "employment of physical force" in those uprisings. In the late 1840s, black activists were thinking in various ways about the boundaries of a community of citizens and the possibilities of connecting with distant people and places in pursuit of rights.

Legal exclusion had emotional consequences that helped push black Americans to look beyond U.S. borders as they developed their political claims. Many African Americans shared the feelings of disconnection from their native country that Frederick Douglass expressed during his travels in Britain. Those feelings encouraged activists to seek out different kinds of communities. John Russwurm's decision to leave the country in 1829 reflected the same doubts Douglass expressed, a common anxiety among black people that they might never truly be equal members in an American community.[38]

In the 1840s, white Americans continued to pursue black removal, and a number of states debated measures to exclude black people from settling within their borders. It is not difficult to imagine the emotional effects of those laws, discouraging black Americans from feeling connected to the United States and pushing them to seek community elsewhere. In 1849, when William Wells Brown was in England, he wrote a letter to the man who had once owned him in which he described his alienation from the United States. Brown loved the United States, but he also felt "driven from his own country." He took solace in the fact that in England, he was "regarded as a man."[39] Brown and Douglass explored the politics of sentiment, expressing personal sorrow over their marginalization and using their feelings to craft a specific critique of the oppression all black Americans faced. Legal and social forces at home pushed black people out of the United States at the same time that external freedom fights cultivated their desires to connect to a different community. It was in this context that black activists imagined new geographic possibilities for citizenship.

The idea of a citizen status linking people across national borders had tremendous potential because so much seemed likely to change in the late 1840s. Centuries-old power structures in Europe crumbled under the weight of popular opposition. Conflict over slavery in the United States threatened to split the nation in two. It appeared that the governments on which individuals had long based their identities might be nearing their ends.[40] People anxious about the turmoil of unstable governments might be drawn to a community that was not bound to a nation with unjust laws. Although monarchies were restored in much of Europe by the end of 1848, black activists continued to invoke the rebels who had tried to change the continent. The links black Americans forged with those rebels might have been hardened by the realization that they shared an experience of struggle against a stronger, unrighteous power. Black Americans continued to relish the possibility of an Atlantic activist community, and in so doing, they rethought the shape of citizenship, questioning understandings of it that linked a person to a physical place.

*   *   *

Against the backdrop of Europe's revolutions, black activists constructed a community that was necessarily exclusive. Imagining a citizen status that linked freedom fighters around the Atlantic Ocean left no room for people who did not challenge slavery and prejudice. The idea of a community of activists appealed to black northerners in part because it gave them power to determine the nature and shape of their own citizenry.

When black activists criticized American hypocrisy, they distanced themselves from the national majority and lent greater weight to their work of envisioning a community beyond the nation. Martin Delany, in his role as coeditor of the *North Star* from 1847 to 1849, urged black people to look beyond the borders of the United States in their political work. His writing expanded on ideas that were central to the editors of the *Hyperion*. He saw African American oppression as part of a shared experience for black people around the world and advocated for racial unity in the struggle against injustice. "Let the colored races look well to their own interests," Delany demanded, "let them act for themselves." He called on enslaved Cubans to "hoist the flag and draw the sword of revolution." Because white people had celebrated rebellion in Poland, Greece, France, and Italy, they should also approve of a slave revolt in Cuba.[41] To Delany, slavery and prejudice highlighted the critical gap between black and white Americans' interests. He wanted African Americans to embrace that distance and focus on improving their collective black lives.

While black activists questioned whether they could belong in the United States, many continued to seek tangible benefits of an American legal status, including passports for travel abroad. In the early nineteenth century, a passport was a simple piece of paper identifying an individual as a citizen and entitling him or her to protection of the laws as that person traveled abroad.[42] As they struggled to secure passports, black people used their experiences to further their criticisms of the United States. In 1849, Secretary of State John Clayton rejected a black man's passport application, claiming that African Americans only received the documentation when they traveled as servants to diplomats.[43] Black activists were outraged, especially because a passport could be an important acknowledgment of their legal position in the United States. William Wells Brown wrote from London, "I have felt ashamed that I had the misfortune to be born in such a country." Before he departed for Europe, Brown had his passport request denied. But significantly, he had traveled beyond the borders of his native country, where he used his place in an international activist community to reinforce his arguments. "We will not write our wishes upon the stone walls in America," he declared, "but we will write them upon the hearts of the people of the entire world, until we shame the Americans into good manners."[44] Those walls at

once represented the denial of black Americans' legal claims, the social barriers to black membership in an American community, and state and federal
restrictions on black people's movement and residency. Brown and his colleagues sought an alternative community and gathered evidence from abroad
to criticize the legal results of prejudice in the United States.[45] Writing from
Europe, Brown represented the emancipatory possibilities of the world
beyond the United States. He had physically separated himself from the
nation in a way that symbolized the marginal legal position of all black people
in the country. Embedded in an Atlantic activist community, Brown shamed
white Americans and reimagined them as the outsiders, excluded from an
international citizenry in which he had claimed a place.

Antislavery white American and European observers encouraged Brown
and his colleagues in their work to exclude the supporters of slavery from
their newly imagined community. At an 1848 Whig Party convention, Judge
Stephen C. Phillips asked delegates to reject the slave-owning Virginian
Zachary Taylor as a presidential candidate because both England and France
had abolished human bondage.[46] Douglass's *North Star* reprinted a series of
critiques of the persistence of American slavery. The editor of the Richmond
Southerner worried Americans would find "the entire civilized world . . .
arrayed against us," if slavery endured.[47] Editors of the London *Times* read
celebratory coverage of the 1848 revolutions in New York newspapers and
joked that the typical American seemed to hold "in one hand a red banner,
inscribed with the words, 'Death to Tyrants,' and in the other, a cat o'-nine-
tails." American newsmen, the *Times* pronounced, seemed to court Russian
despots at one moment and French revolutionaries the next.[48] These critics'
opinions reflected the minority in the United States but suggested that slavery
isolated Americans from a community of Atlantic popular opinion. Douglass
urged American people to see that they held the power to regulate slavery
and to change their relationship to critical observers overseas.[49]

Douglass's *North Star* employed a white Briton named John Dick, who
helped make the paper a textual space for an interracial, international community that criticized slavery and racism in the United States. In July 1849,
he published "A Column of Atrocities," newspaper descriptions of the brutal
corporal punishment meted out to enslaved people in the United States for
relatively minor offenses. "It is a disgraceful catalogue," Dick wrote, and
showed that no American should "talk of sympathising with the oppressed
in other lands."[50] In another article, he called it "a mockery . . . for a people
who have just elevated a slaveholder [Zachary Taylor] to the office of chief

magistrate . . . to talk of 'advancing the hopes and interests of European democracy.'" He quoted antislavery poet John Greenleaf Whittier, who rendered the critique of the slaveholding republic in verse:

And shall we scoff at Europe's kings,
When Freedom's fire is dim with us,
And round our country's altar clings
The damning shade of Slavery's curse?[51]

John Dick, along with most of his black and white activist colleagues, saw the federal response to the *Pearl* incident in 1848 as an especially damning indicator of the limits of American republicanism. That April, a group of seventy-seven enslaved people finalized their plans to escape slavery in Washington, D.C. They recruited two white men, Edward Sayres and Daniel Drayton, to aid their flight. Sayres owned the schooner *Pearl*, a two-masted sailboat with space for the runaways belowdecks. On April 15, the black Americans crowded onto the ship and their white collaborators let the *Pearl* drift down the Potomac, hoping to cross the Chesapeake Bay, then turn north toward freedom along the Atlantic Coast. Unfortunately for the voyagers, tides and wind did not cooperate. Late on April 16, the steamship *Salem*, property of a man who owned some of the fugitives, apprehended the passengers and crew aboard the *Pearl*.[52]

Federal officials fined Drayton and Sayres $140 for each enslaved person on board the ship, and the two men languished in prison for four years, unable to gather the funds necessary to purchase their own liberty. John Dick found this to be the height of injustice. People could not be made into property, he argued, and therefore the *Pearl*'s black passengers "had a perfect right to leave Washington city." The hefty fines levied on Drayton and Sayres showed the nation's government to be "more unjust than the rule of the Czar of Russia—more tyrannical than that of Rome, in the balmiest days of inquisitorial priestcraft." Dick condemned all who consented to the two men's punishment. He questioned whether Americans were "true lovers of liberty," embedding in Douglass's paper a European endorsement of black activist efforts to marginalize the slaveholding republic.[53]

Martin Delany, William Wells Brown, and John Dick together argued that America's ideals were hollow. They imagined a community dedicated to human liberation and denied access to all those who did not rebuke racist policy and practice. Europe's revolutions offered a new tool for American activists to criticize the United States and encouraged black people to think in new ways about the kind of community to which they hoped to belong. They also pursued a significant experiment in thinking about how one might belong, the path by which one could attain citizen status. The U.S. Constitution suggested nativity was a foundation for the status, and African Americans had long sought legal protections based on their birth in the United States. Their claims had long been denied. Now, free African Americans envisioned an alternative community in which behavior, rather than birth, would define their status. That was an appealing idea for people born with skin that marked them as subordinate members of an American caste system. In rethinking the possible shape of their communities and arguing about the terms of membership, black people put forth new ideas about the nature of citizenship as a connection between individuals and governments.

*   *   *

As black activists looked across the ocean and considered alternative communities, most continued to hope they could secure legal protections based on their status as native-born Americans. Their chief interest in Europe was as a tool to change their legal position in the United States. Through news from Europe, activists highlighted the United States' distance from its expressed ideals in the hope of pushing lawmakers toward change. Black Americans were interested in Europe's revolutions in part because the toppling of monarchies encouraged activists to believe they might transform the unjust government of their country. While they repeatedly glanced and grasped across the Atlantic, free black northerners focused on changing their legal lives in the United States, using distant rebellion to secure rights at home.

Delegates to the state convention held in Pennsylvania in December 1848 hoped European revolutions might spark change in their home state. They seemed optimistic as they called on white voters to support equal suffrage. "We shall live and labour in the glorious anticipation of success," delegates proclaimed.[54] Perhaps they felt encouraged because they had "been witnesses to these soul-stirring appeals to Republicanism in foreign nations." They drew a favorable comparison between revolutionary Europe and their own state's long history of freedom. But the delegates also demanded changes in black people's legal lives. Pennsylvania's history had "placed her on an eminence to give laws to the world," but state lawmakers had neglected their duty to uphold republican government by disfranchising black men.[55] News of the Revolutionary Spring helped black people present a compelling set of arguments to white voters as they worked toward equal suffrage.

Delegates also issued an "Appeal to the Colored Citizens of Pennsylvania" that criticized black residents of the state for apparently neglecting their duty to protest. Their complacence was especially conspicuous in contrast with the revolutionary energy of Europeans. It is difficult to know whether delegates had observed any real apathy. They claimed most black Pennsylvanians did not grasp the significance of European events, which seems odd given the proliferation of news in print.[56] "Now, fellow citizens," delegates chided readers, "we should feel a deep interest" in the energy and objectives of Europe's revolutions. "Shall the spirit of liberty continue to inspire every nation," they asked, "rock every government, and freight every breeze, and leave us like some unnatural excrescence, or motionless adamant unmoved by its power [?]" Events in Europe presented an important moment for African Americans to seek legal change. Delegates called on black Pennsylvanians to pursue a meaningful citizenship, a status they described as a constitutional guarantee of "full, civil, and political liberty."[57] European revolutions signaled the potential to change relationships between individuals and governments and led vocal activists to encourage others to seize the same opportunity at home.

Across the free states, news of Europe's rebels energized black protest. At the conclusion of the 1848 Colored National Convention in Cleveland, delegates echoed France's revolutionary creed, offering "three cheers for Elevation—Liberty—Equality, and Fraternity." Delegates issued an address to the African American population, citing "the spirit of the age" and "the upward tendency of the oppressed throughout the world" as encouraging evidence of the imminent end of government oppression. Human bondage and nominal freedom had rendered black Americans "the most oppressed people in the world." Because free black people and their enslaved brethren were "chained together," the struggle for liberation in the United States would be more arduous than any that took place in Europe. But delegates looked overseas for encouragement, urging their "fellow-countrymen" on "to still higher attainments" and to more ardent protest work.[58] Their identity as black Americans took precedence over the kinship they might have felt with European rebels. They demanded that free black people take on the twin responsibilities of fighting legal exclusion in the North and slavery in the South.

Even after monarchs returned to power across much of Europe, black Americans continued to reflect fondly on the 1848 revolutions. Jermain

Loguen looked back on the brief republican moment in his call for a New York state convention in 1850. Loguen, a black abolitionist and minister, had escaped slavery in the 1830s and lived briefly in Canada before taking up residence in New York. In his position as president of the state's convention board, he called people to meet and rally against "the old systems of slavery that have too long afflicted the world." "The thrones of tyrants are falling," he proclaimed, and the oppressed should be inspired to further resistance. Loguen asked his black "Fellow Citizens" to gather for a convention in order to "strengthen the bonds of union among us," to support activist publications, and to establish more opportunities for technical and liberal arts education. He planned the convention to coincide with the first of August celebrations, maintaining links between black American protest and a wider activist community.[59] Loguen invoked European uprisings as he sought to bring black Americans together to pursue an array of transformative causes in their home country.[60]

Reflecting on the 1848 revolutions helped black people think critically about the terms and the nature of the relationship they wanted with the U.S. government. Their troubled feelings about their native country complicated the work of using European events to change the United States. Appeals to an international community were more than simply political strategy because black travelers felt so much freedom and opportunity overseas. They thought seriously about whether they had a future in the United States. Given their legal marginalization, many black people wavered between enthusiasm about the nation's possibilities and disdain for its people and policies. The speeches and writings of people like Douglass, Brown, and others convey their ambivalence. For instance, speaking in Syracuse at an 1849 celebration of the first of August, Samuel Ringgold Ward, another fugitive slave and abolitionist, claimed a place within the nation he recognized was defined by its racism. Americans had been loath to abolish slavery, he said, because "we are so abominable a set of negro-despisers, that we cannot possibly see anything to admire in the negro character, nor anything commendable in the doing of justice to negroes."[61] Ward's language points to his complex black American identity. He took ownership of American prejudice because he wanted so much to secure a place in the United States even as he recognized it as a nation of "negro-despisers." Similarly, William Cooper Nell hoped black people would be inspired by "the fires of liberty now gleaming on the vine-clad hills of France." Those flames, he hoped, "will not only shed light, but heat, o'er the frozen surface of American pro-slavery." Black people had "ever been ready to worship at Freedom's shrine," and he hoped African Americans would persist in their work to crack the hardened surface of their oppression in the United States. Finding the path to real freedom was a "problem for nations to solve," and he urged black Americans to lead that struggle.[62]

In November 1849, Douglass looked back on the past eighteen months and contemplated the meanings of European events for black Americans. He had seen monarchs fall and then rise again through a violent counterrevolution. He and his colleagues were surely discouraged by the dismantling of Europe's short-lived republics. Still, laws in the United States left him to question the possibilities of black life in his home country. "To make us detest the land of our birth," Douglass wrote, "to abhor the government under which we live . . . would seem to be the animating spirit and purpose of all the legislative enactments of the country with respect to us." He used the 1848 revolutions to warn the U.S. government against alienating black people. "America cannot always sit, as a queen, in peace and repose." He added, "prouder and stronger governments had been shattered by the bolts of the wrath of a just God."[63] Douglass called for racial justice in American law and hinted that continued oppression might bring divine intervention. He was a devout Protestant and a dogged believer in the egalitarian potential of the United States; there was no neat division between his faith in God's power and in America's laws. Divine justice could help black people achieve their natural rights to freedom and equality by forcing changes in American policy.

Douglass pointedly criticized the government's decision to deny William Wells Brown's passport application. Before black Americans could travel abroad for their own purposes, Douglass said, they would be required to "[forfeit] all the immunities of an American citizen." American policies gave him the sense that "the highest crime we could commit is that of patriotism."[64] As black people used revolutionary Europe to criticize the United States, they might have become increasingly sensitive to their marginal status. Douglass felt homeless; he was unable to identify with postrevolutionary Europe, but he had been spurned repeatedly by his native country. Europe's revolutions intensified the emotional struggle through American prejudice.

Black activists also contrasted themselves with European immigrants in the United States as they argued for rights as citizens. Black Americans used foreign-born people to highlight the effects of racism and claim rights based on their birth in the country. In so doing, they promoted their own variety of exclusionary nationalism, suggesting that nativity should be the foundation of individual rights and citizen status.

Douglass explained his feelings of alienation in part through the legal opportunities available to European immigrants. Black northerners were often excluded from schools, public accommodations, and the electoral franchise, but he argued that newly arrived white immigrants met an enthusiastic reception and were granted those and other rights upon their arrival in the United States. Legal protections were "free to English, Irish, Dutch, [and] Scotch" immigrants while native-born black people remained excluded.[65] The presence of immigrants in the free states profoundly influenced black Americans' arguments about citizenship.[66]

The privileges afforded European immigrants reflected the power of race in determining a person's relationship with American governments. Black activists called for change in the racial order by contrasting their native birth with the foreignness of immigrants. Black northerners used people from distant places in an effort to embed themselves more firmly in their native soil. In 1849, a number of black Bostonians protested the all-black Smith School because they felt segregated education would encourage racial exclusion in other aspects of society. Opponents of the Smith School were particularly resistant to it because European immigrants attended the city's common schools while African Americans were prohibited. "It is rather annoying to our feelings," they wrote to city officials, "when we perceive not only all other citizens in enjoyment of the right of common schools, but foreigners of all kinds, too, who are *white*, are not rejected."[67] Those Bostonians claimed a citizen status based on nativity and denied it to "foreigners." They defined citizenship as the purview of people born in a country. As they pursued racially inclusive public education, African Americans used national borders to limit the concept of citizenship they promoted.[68]

Since the 1830s, activists had used their native birth to claim rights as citizens, and it remained an essential tool in succeeding decades. At the New England Antislavery Convention held in Boston in May 1849, Frederick Douglass protested colonization because it denied the power of black nativity. Black people should be "regarded and treated as American citizens" because their earliest ancestors had arrived in Virginia in 1619, "the same year that the pilgrims were landing in this State." African American history was long, but "Irishmen, newly landed on our soil . . . have the audacity to propose our removal from this, the land of our birth."[69] Invoking the colonial past raised the specter of the long history of black bondage in the Americas. As Douglass framed it here, citizenship was thrust upon a person at birth, leaving an individual no choice in the matter. When he invoked the twenty African captives sold in Virginia in 1619, he implied that citizenship need not entail legal protections or even free status. Opponents of black rights could seize on his claim to argue black people belonged in the United States only in servile roles. But Douglass believed black people's historic presence was critical, that it underlined the injustice of offering rights to immigrants before African Americans. The sheer scope of African American history meant black Americans were entitled to at least the same legal protections available to recent arrivals.

At times, black activists echoed stereotypes about immigrants to make their political arguments, although in other cases, they challenged nativist tropes. Black northerners argued for a citizenship that would exclude nonnative-born people but did not entirely oppose the presence of European immigrants in the United States.[70] In May 1848, Douglass expressed anger and sadness at the fortunes of Irish people in their home country and as immigrants to the United States. Famine ravaged Ireland, and priests expelled the destitute to seek work in America. Douglass also described or perhaps simply invented an accident at a construction site in which two Irish immigrant workers were killed. Despite the array of misfortunes they encountered, Irish people had made themselves an indispensable part of the nation's labor force, helping build the Erie Canal and sustain maritime commerce in New York Harbor.[71] Perhaps Douglass and other black people felt a kind of kinship with these immigrants, as both groups were associated with labor and were sometimes linked in discussions about who should comprise the American working class. In April 1849, Douglass reprinted an article from a Kentucky newspaper suggesting southerners might be freed from their reliance on enslaved black people if they would "invite intelligent citizens to come here and settle," building a productive labor force comprising European immigrants and white emigrants from other states.[72] While he sympathized with Irish people's suffering, Douglass must have chafed at the suggestion that African Americans were unintelligent and immigrants might be deemed citizens on their arrival in Kentucky.

When activists invoked stereotypes of people like immigrants from Ireland, they protested the nation's embrace of immigrants and presented themselves as better Americans. Activists had long said citizenship required a person to make useful contributions to society, but in the 1840s, Douglass suggested Irish immigrants must meet further important qualifications, however useful they might be. "If their children are educated and brought up in temperance," Douglass wrote, "as an affirmative precept they will prove the most useful and valuable body of citizens that our republic can boast of."[73] Temperance was an important virtue among black and white reformers, but it had a distinctive resonance when discussing Irish people, often mocked as irredeemable drunkards in antebellum popular culture. Douglass reworked the concern white northerners had over whether free black people were prepared for rights. His rhetoric was hypocritical yet strategic. Douglass claimed the power to confer citizen status, then withheld it from Irish people because they were intemperate, illiterate, and most importantly immigrant. If he could deny a group a place in the body of American citizens, then surely Douglass and other native-born black people were part of that body. At the same time, he suggested others did not respect Irish workers' contributions and presented himself as the moral conscience of the citizenry. Douglass may have introduced the trope of Irish intemperance in order to denigrate immigrants and elevate the implicitly more restrained free black population by contrast. In so doing, he claimed a firm place in the nation for African Americans. But in a way, Douglass's use of the stereotype might suggest that he did belong; perhaps rather than strategy, his language showed that he had inherited American prejudices about particular immigrant groups.

It is more than simply ironic that free black people challenged their marginal status by defining citizenship in exclusionary ways. Exclusion was central to the process of making claims through citizenship.[74] As African Americans used citizen status and imagined different kinds of communities, they constructed substantial populations of noncitizens in an effort to solidify their claims to a place in those communities. Because the terms of citizenship were so uncertain, lawmakers and other people could often define a person as a citizen only by showing they were different from groups identified as noncitizens. For instance, lawmakers sometimes described minorities and women as noncitizens in order to argue citizenship was available equally to white men of all classes. Black people made European immigrants noncitizens in their work to change the structures of American law.[75]

Black activists might also have wanted to push some people out of the formal political community. In the antebellum period, Garrisonian abolitionists struggled with the fact that democracy had allowed slavery to flourish in the United States. They believed in the righteousness of democratic government in principle but worried about the potential for immoral actors to corrupt such a government.[76] Black activists wrestled with similar concerns, recognizing in the political power of the slaveholding states a barrier to their pursuit of rights through a relationship with the federal government. Because the majority in the United States seemed to support slavery and racial exclusion, activists must have understood that disempowering slaveowners, among others, might clear a path for them to secure rights and protections through the federal government. Black northerners might have looked to profit from the exclusionary implications of their arguments about the terms of citizenship.

Black people called for the exclusion of slaveowners and immigrants, as well as those they deemed intemperate, those whose antislavery principles were not sufficiently pure, and myriad others, because they were invested in building a specific, robust legal relationship with the U.S. government. When they talked about Europeans and citizenship, black people were not concerned with the ways their work might produce or prevent equality. They aimed to make more people free and to secure political power and legal protections to more black Americans. They reimagined communities in an effort to open legal structures to black people in the United States. Activists saw the challenges of creating racial justice and focused not on supporting American democracy as it existed but on making the United States a place where black people had formal legal access and influence.

*   *   *

Free African Americans had ample opportunities to think and talk about Europe as a distant continent in a state of upheaval and Europeans as people with a growing presence in the United States. When they talked about Europe in the late 1840s, they understood their words could be read by a larger audience than when they spoke on other political concerns or at other times. Black activists embraced the freedom struggle at the heart of Europe's revolutions and bristled at the ways European immigrants secured legal protections in the United States. The multiple presences of Europe in America further complicated black people's ideas about their relationship to their native country. Black northerners experimented with the idea of joining an international community in the late 1840s, but they remained invested in claiming rights as citizens based on their birth within the nation, advocating for a status that was exclusive and limited by established borders.

In April 1848, with Europe's revolutions in full flush, Frederick Douglass captured the complex issues surrounding African American identity and the potential of an international citizenry. In an editorial published under the simple title "France," Douglass explored the reasons black people felt pulled toward different places and the sources of their ideas about different kinds of communities. Print culture and steam travel together had effectively narrowed the Atlantic Ocean and made possible political movements of unprecedented geographic scope. News of revolutionary political action traveled "with lightning speed from heart to heart, from land to land" and required immediate judgment from "all members of our common brotherhood." Douglass believed an essential human unity connected people across national borders, and at the same time, that technology and political enthusiasm fostered the creation of new, broader communities. As rebels and activists connected, shock, confusion, and terror bound together "the despots of Europe [,] the Tories of England, and the slaveholders of America." The actions of "the oppressed and plundered" throughout the world produced those anxieties. Marginalized people savored the news of revolt in France and anticipated a future when they might echo those events in their own countries.[77]

But Douglass also emphasized the barriers to American connections with Europe's rebels. "It would be unbecoming us to extend, and France to accept our Sympathy," he argued. Among those in the United States, only "negroes and Abolitionists" could truly sympathize with oppressed Frenchmen. "The fact is, while Europe is becoming republican, we are becoming despotic; while France is contending for freedom, we are extending slavery." His choice to use the possessive "we" was significant. As both a black person and an abolitionist, Douglass could sympathize with French rebels, and he did in various ways during the late 1840s. Yet he was also part of the United States and wanted others to view him in the same way. "There is no sympathy that can be called national, for France, and we ought to be ashamed to affect it," he declared.[78] While his rhetoric might have been an attempt to shame proslavery Americans, it also suggested the depth of his desire to belong in the United States. He took ownership of the nation's most troubling sins.[79] At the same time, he seemed to feel further shame precisely because he was so dedicated to a nation that refused to accept him. As much as he wished for a secure place in a community and saw opportunities to belong elsewhere, Douglass could not reject the United States. He felt an emotional bond to his home and hoped his native birth might prove strong enough to provide him and other black people with a real legal connection to the republic.

As they deployed the politics of shame in the antebellum period, black activists tended to stop short of suggesting that the United States was irredeemable. An international community of activists could help black Americans experience a sense of belonging, but it would not provide them with the legal relationship they desired. The ways activists talked about Europe's revolutions and immigrants underlines the broadest goals of their citizenship politics. African Americans wanted to feel bonds of brotherhood in a community, but most importantly, they wanted legal protections, including formal voice in a government. The U.S. Constitution made possible precisely that kind of legal relationship, provided lawmakers would agree black people were entitled to its safeguards. An international citizenry was a powerful dream, but a citizen status that tied black people to the United States not only could change black Americans' legal lives but also would transform the nation of their birth.[80]

Frederick Douglass's experience in Europe began when he fled from that slaveholding and slave-catching republic in 1845. Throughout the 1840s, as activists made public arguments about the precise ways governments should relate to individuals in the United States, they did so with an awareness of the urgent need to connect with a government that would protect their lives as free people. In the 1830s and 1840s, African Americans struggled to help liberate fugitive slaves and to protect free people who were alleged to have fled bondage. Black and white abolitionists increasingly organized to defend people from slavery, while white southerners and lawmakers began arguing for and building structures to expand slaveowners' reach and secure their grasp on human property. Perhaps fugitives and activists like Frederick Douglass, William Wells Brown, and Samuel Ringgold Ward recognized the limits of a connection to Europe's rebels because they saw how urgently black people needed legal protections of their personal security. Imagining a different kind of citizenry might do little to defend black people from bondage, although black activists tackled those projects simultaneously. In the 1830s and 1840s, black men and women insisted that citizenship entailed a right to personal security, and they practiced a range of political tactics to compel American governments to take steps to defend black freedom.

CHAPTER 4

Runaways, or Citizens Claimed as Such

William Dixon did not want to spend another night in a dank, crumbling cell in Bridewell Prison. But on the afternoon of April 12, 1837, inside a courtroom at New York City Hall, Judge Richard Riker announced that he had not yet decided whether Dixon was free, as the prisoner so vehemently maintained. Two sheriffs approached the African American defendant and prepared to escort him to the nearby jail. Dixon had been seized on his way to work the previous week by a group of slavecatchers who claimed that he was a fugitive from Maryland. As the sheriffs led Dixon downstairs, he could see through the city hall's large front windows, offering a clear view of the massive crowd waiting outside.[1]

New York's city hall stands, as it did on that spring afternoon, in the middle of an eight-acre park carved out of lower Manhattan's irregular blocks. On April 12, as Dixon stood accused in the courtroom, more than one thousand African Americans had congregated in that park. The sheriffs escorting Dixon were apparently unconcerned about the crowd. Just after three o'clock, they led Dixon through the front doors, and the people in the park surged toward the captive. Several attacked the sheriffs with wooden clubs, causing the besieged guards to release the captive from their grasp. One woman pulled a knife from beneath her dress and passed it to Dixon, who, in his surprise, stood by for a few moments while a thousand strangers fought to seize his freedom. When he overcame his shock, Dixon fled toward Broadway to seek shelter in the busy city streets. The crowd continued to struggle with authorities. Judge John Bloodgood, who to that point had not been involved in the case, ran outside to support the sheriffs. When he reached the plaza, "a strapping negro wench" grabbed Bloodgood in a chokehold and a group of young black men "pretty well pummeled him, and tore the coat completely off his back." (An antislavery newspaper reported that the judge later wished that he had brought along his pistols, regretting a missed opportunity "to send a few of the damned niggers to hell."[2]) Meanwhile, Dixon ran north along Broadway. A man on horseback tried to stop him, but Dixon's new escort—several black men armed with clubs—protected the fleeing prisoner. Reaching Duane Street, just a few blocks from the city hall, Dixon opted to take cover, ducking into a coal cellar and hoping to wait out his pursuers. His protectors dispersed, and his freedom was short lived. A few hours later, authorities, tipped off by a witness, stormed into the cellar, seized William Dixon, and carted him back to Bridewell.[3]

Efforts to rescue William Dixon and other alleged fugitives were an important part of African Americans' pursuits of legal protections in the antebellum North. Dixon was held captive in a nation with a legal system designed to preserve black slavery. Measures like the federal Fugitive Slave Act of 1793 empowered slaveowners to cross state lines to pursue runaway property, placating southerners who worried that northern law and politics threatened the institution of slavery.[4] That legal system, combined with the value of enslaved people, meant that black northerners lived in a precarious freedom; they might be seized mistakenly by slave catchers or with malice by unscrupulous kidnappers.[5] But while black people gathered in crowds to resist arrest, many also continued working through the law to safeguard their freedom. Activists denounced the injustices of slavery in public in multiple ways, demanding legal changes to solidify their fragile freedom. Dixon's rescue was one such public statement. The men and women who broke the law to liberate him declared that they would not comply with governing structures designed to preserve slavery.[6]

That rescue was one of many public incidents in which black people defended alleged fugitives in ways that made claims about the terms of citizenship. Echoes of William Dixon's claims to freedom and of his rescuers' footsteps could be heard in the case of Adam Crosswhite, a fugitive slave who black activists liberated in two mob actions in Michigan in 1848. Separated by a decade, these incidents come together as collective claims for legal protections of black freedom. Dixon, Crosswhite, and the dozens of women and men who came to their aid were parts of the larger story of African Americans challenging existing laws in their work to claim rights through citizenship.

Free African Americans framed personal security as a key aspect of citizenship. Antebellum black activists repeatedly, brazenly broke the law in efforts to protect real and alleged fugitives, making violent public demands for personal protection as citizens.[7] Rescues of real and alleged fugitive slaves reveal the ways black people who were not vocal public figures thought about their legal status and practiced citizenship politics. Black northerners took to the streets en masse, demanding protections against slave catchers. They participated in rescues, offered financial support for vigilance committees, and organized informally for community self-defense. Their actions called for change in a legal order that privileged slaveowners' interests over those of black people. Large numbers of black northerners together acted in ways that reflected their desires for protections of their personal security. Through these actions, black people made arguments about the terms of citizenship as they called for a new legal relationship with state and federal governments based on the nation's expressed interest in promoting freedom. William Dixon's rescue and his simultaneous defense in court illuminate the multifaceted politics of seeking personal security. Both legal and extralegal acts pushed toward change in fugitive slave legislation.[8] Activists recognized the legal potential of fugitive rescues, understanding that physical confrontations with authorities could do important work toward securing legal change.[9]

Congress enacted a restrictive Fugitive Slave Act in 1850 that expanded the reach and enhanced the power of the slave-catching infrastructure. "The only way to make the [law] a dead letter," Frederick Douglass declared in 1852, "is to make half a dozen or more dead kidnappers."[10] Rescues and attempts to free black people, including those of Anthony Burns and Shadrach Minkins, dominated national headlines in the 1850s. But William Dixon and Adam Crosswhite highlight the extent of extralegal resistance before the passage of the strict Fugitive Slave Act. By the time Douglass issued his bold threat, thousands of lesser-known black people had long promoted violent extralegal politics and had brought those ideas to bear in northern communities. The Fugitive Slave Act was a direct response to the destabilizing force of popular black protest of the 1830s and 1840s.

In confronting fugitive controversies, activists raised essential questions about the nature of citizenship—the ways individuals would relate to state and federal legal structures. To what extent was formal law a viable avenue for African Americans to protect themselves and their families? Was American law at heart a liberating or oppressive force for black people? Fugitive slave legislation and the demand for personal protection complicated the work of using citizenship to secure legal change. As black people challenged established legal authority, their tactics suggested they were uninterested in securing freedom through the law. But their lawbreaking was strategic, resisting particular manifestations of a legal system designed to preserve racial slavery and outlining new terms for citizenship as a status that would protect freedom. William Dixon, Adam Crosswhite, and their rescuers represent black thought in radical practice, deployed in ways that could redefine legal relationships between individuals and governments throughout the country.

*   *   *

Article IV, Section 2 of the U.S. Constitution embodied the possibilities and challenges of black people's efforts to use citizenship in pursuit of legal protections. The first of that section's three clauses contained one of the Constitution's few references to citizen status, requiring that each state provide equal "Privileges and Immunities" to citizens from other states. That was valuable for black activists looking to use citizenship as a path to rights.[11] But the third clause offered federal protection of slaveowners' property rights, ordering that fugitive slaves "shall be delivered up" to their owner if they ran across state lines. The Constitution made possible black citizenship politics in the same breath that it gave white Americans the broad power to seize black people as fugitives. Black politics presented to the public a critical tension in the foundations of the law. Activists urged people to consider whether their legal system could support both racial slavery and black freedom. By making claims as citizens, black northerners worked toward legal protections that could destabilize slavery while broadening and solidifying black freedom.

William Dixon was first arrested near his home on the Bowery in Lower Manhattan on April 4, 1837. Dr. Walter Allender of Baltimore had hired the slavecatcher A. G. Ridgeley to pursue a fugitive slave he called Jacob Ellis, or "Allender's Jake," who had run away in 1832. Ridgeley brought the man he claimed was "Jake" before New York City judge Richard Riker as the token of a successful manhunt. But the black man protested, "calling himself Wm. Dixon" and insisting on his freedom. Riker had to decide whether to grant Ridgeley a writ to remove the alleged fugitive from New York, and Dixon worked to convince the magistrate of the injustice of that choice. "It is hard, your honor, to be thus treated in this land of liberty," Dixon told Riker. Beyond that critique of the slaveholding republic, Dixon denied that he should ever have been arrested on such a charge. "I am an innocent man," he said plainly. "I am a freeman." It was after Dixon's testimony on April 12,

FIGURE 4. Front view of New York City Hall, author's photograph (2014). While
William Dixon sat in a courtroom facing Judge Richard Riker, an estimated 1,000
African Americans came together on this plaza in front of the city hall, waiting for a
chance to set him free.

the second day of his hearing, that black New Yorkers liberated him from
City Hall Park.[12]

Kidnapping posed a persistent threat to black northerners, but it is difficult to know precisely why so many gathered to liberate William Dixon on
the afternoon of April 12, 1837. In 1840, more than 16,000 black people lived
in New York City, so a crowd of a few thousand freedom fighters was certainly possible.[13] The New York Committee of Vigilance (NYCV) reflected
black New Yorkers' history of organizing to defend their freedom. Founded
in 1835 by an interracial group of antislavery advocates, the committee
engaged in work they called "practical abolition."[14] They sought legal protections against kidnapping and aided people they knew had fled slavery. Vigilance work took multiple forms, all of which demanded a legal relationship
between individuals and governments in which the latter would protect black

freedom.[15] Black people rescued William Dixon, as they had organized the NYCV, understanding that they might fight kidnapping and slavery with public demands for legal change.[16]

Black activist and newspaper editor Samuel Cornish debuted the *Colored American* just a few weeks before Dixon's arrest, and he covered the case in many of its early issues. The arrest of a black man who claimed he was free was a central concern for Cornish and his politically minded readers. In coverage of Dixon's hearings, Cornish called for changes in state laws that empowered a single magistrate to decide questions of personal freedom.[17] "Every thinking, intelligent mind," he said, should see a jury trial as the most just way to decide such cases. He doubted New York judges could provide a fair hearing and cited Justice Bloodgood's violent wishes in the aftermath of the city hall mob as evidence of the extensive racism among local legal officials.[18]

But as Cornish denounced the legal structures that allowed Dixon's arrest, he also criticized the mob for liberating him. Cornish described the crowd as "a multitude of illiterate people, white or colored," who, rather than practicing calculated politics, had "become mere subjects of passion."[19] Although he stood among the leaders of the NYCV, he denied responsibility for the mob action. Instead, he blamed a "brother Editor" for "well meant, yet . . . injudicious remarks" that sparked the riot. Cornish did not name that editor or his newspaper, but he reprinted portions of a call for public displays of outrage after Dixon's arrest. The nameless editor had dreamed of "twenty, nay fifty thousand persons present" to witness or perhaps to oversee hearings of alleged fugitives. "This business of gentleman kidnapping ought to rouse the entire city," the editor continued.[20]

The mob action was a popular protest of the legal order that made black freedom perilous, a call for new protections for black Americans. But Cornish distanced the rioters from readers of his paper when he presumed that many of Dixon's rescuers were illiterate. His critique pointed to the many ways black northerners engaged with print culture. Through word of mouth, his "brother Editor" had spoken to a community large enough to organize more than a thousand protestors. Cornish surely hoped his own newspaper could carry such weight. His critique of the mob touted the power of the black press to shape and reflect the concerns of a broad African American community. Dixon's arrest sparked black outrage in print and on the streets, though Cornish seemed to favor a more controlled public response.

Cornish was particularly unhappy that women had played prominent roles in the rescue. Those activist women had "degraded themselves," he wrote. "We beg their husbands to keep them at home for the time to come, and find some better occupation for them." For black women, whose voices were often marginalized in newspapers and public meetings, street politics offered the appealing opportunity to assert their political positions in public. The woman who stood at the front of the crowd and handed Dixon a knife was concerned about securing his freedom. She might have relished the opportunity to step outside the bounds of respectable women's work and aid an alleged fugitive. Or perhaps she was an experienced practitioner of community vigilance, a person who led the charge against the sheriffs and had little concern for Cornish's gendered ideas. Whatever her history might have been, on that April afternoon, she embraced a critical role in Dixon's rescue, and the people who joined her did not stand in the way of her radical political statement.[21]

Although Cornish decried the mob as a disorganized crowd, the people who freed Dixon shared many of the editor's political convictions and concerns about the existing legal order. They did not believe Judge Riker would provide a fair hearing or offer real protections for a black person's freedom. The black women and men who gathered at city hall protested Dixon's arrest, the pervasive danger of kidnapping, and the ideologies and legal structures that threatened black Americans with bondage. William Dixon's case and his rescue had significant implications for all black New Yorkers.

But Cornish and his colleague David Ruggles worried that the mob might hinder the legal possibilities of Dixon's case, which could offer an avenue to secure legal protections for black freedom. Ruggles, in his role as secretary of the NYCV, wrote in early 1838 about free black people's perilous legal position. "We have no protection," he said. "Captivity is inevitable . . . unless the laws protect us." Dixon's case was a fight "for the right of trial by jury for himself, and for all persons claimed by man as fugitive slaves in the state of New York."[22] Cornish shared that sense of the case's legal potential. New York offered a few narrow avenues for alleged fugitives to secure jury trials. In the late 1820s, state lawmakers revised statutes regarding alleged fugitives in an effort to find a middle ground between upholding the 1793 Fugitive Slave Act and protecting the state's free black residents. Under the law they created, a slavecatcher had to offer sufficient evidence to a judge before he could arrest an alleged fugitive. The person seized would then have a hearing before the judge to determine his or her status, during which the accused could seek the writ of *homine replegiando* to initiate a jury trial to decide the case. While trial by jury was a possibility under New York law, judges including Richard Riker had been reluctant to grant the writ of *homine replegiando*.[23] In September 1836, black New Yorkers protested Riker, who had recently allowed a number of black people to be seized and removed south. "The people of color can expect no protection from the laws as at present administered," they proclaimed.[24] Dixon's case was another opportunity to seek the writ of *homine replegiando* and perhaps to change the treatment of alleged fugitives. NYCV lawyers wanted Dixon to have a jury trial and all other rights of due process that protected any white person charged with a crime. They presented their argument as a simple request but hoped it might establish a transformative precedent. Securing a judge's support for a jury trial law could protect people from kidnapping and make possible a legal defense for actual fugitive slaves. With Dixon's impassioned pleas and with a well-organized defense, the lawyers might establish a firmer precedent for *homine replegiando* and jury proceedings in subsequent cases by securing the writ from the notoriously pro-slaveowner Judge Riker.

Cornish published his harsh critique of the city hall protestors because he thought they had limited the case's potential to secure black people rights as citizens. He denounced the mob as "the Thoughtless part of our Colored Citizens," condemning them for placing a new obstacle in the path of Dixon's counsel. He wrote directly to black New Yorkers and also hoped to speak to white readers and lawmakers. He distanced himself from the rioters who showed a flagrant disregard for the law. In contrast to the mob, Cornish and other black New Yorkers were thoughtful, considerate black citizens, interested in working within established legal parameters to build a relationship with the government that could protect black freedom. Still, it was critical to Cornish that black people who did seek legal redress for their grievances did so in a legal system that would hear and respond to their concerns. Denouncing the mob was not only an argument that citizens should obey laws but also a claim that citizenship should connect individuals to governments that were concerned about their safety. Such a connection would necessarily defend black people's freedom. Thoughtful black citizens chose not to riot because—or perhaps only so long as—they could realistically hope for government protection. Cornish suggested that an ideal black citizen understood the law and sought security through available legal channels, even in the face of imminent threats to their freedom.

Cornish's criticism of the city hall mob points to the decisions black activists made about protest strategies. Black Americans, he wrote, were confronting a "REPUBLICAN *Slave* system" and therefore needed to change the law that upheld that system in order to secure black freedom. He felt it best if the people who liberated Dixon would leave that work to the New York Committee of Vigilance and the "eminent lawyers" they employed. He encouraged respectable public behavior as part of a strategy to work in court toward the radical project of making the law protect black freedom. In truth, Dixon's rescuers, in their violent protest, did work that called for legal reform. But Cornish worried that a forcible liberation would not change the systemic problems that constantly threatened black northerners.[25]

Vigilance workers had proven their ability to free some people. But Cornish wanted a firm legal foundation for black personal security. His statement on the mob closed with a deft rhetorical move calling for a new legal relationship between black people and the state government. He asked white lawmakers to offer "pardon and clemency . . . in behalf of the ignorant part of our colored citizens."[26] Dixon's African American rescuers were part of a community of citizens even though they had openly broken the law, he argued. To Cornish, the mob action resulted from black Americans' doubts that the law would secure their freedom. No citizen should harbor such doubts. While he hoped the court would offer a path to secure black personal security, he implied that white New Yorkers might continue to see mobs so long as African Americans were denied substantive legal protections of their freedom.[27] Lawbreaking was the consequence of a broken justice system; that argument enhanced his demands for legal protections for African Americans as citizens. Black people broke the law because they were ignored when they spoke to authorities in other ways.

William Dixon's hearings resumed after his attempted rescue, and his reliance on courts and lawyers proved fruitful. After weeks of deliberating, Judge Richard Riker granted William Dixon the writ of *homine replegiando* in July 1837. Releasing Dixon on bail with the possibility of a future jury trial was a surprising turn for Judge Riker. But the magistrate heard from several witnesses who testified to Dixon's freedom and decided he lacked sufficient evidence to send the prisoner south. Dixon returned to life in New York in a freedom made tenuous by the possibility of future legal proceedings but all the same a life outside of southern bondage. It seemed Samuel Cornish and William Dixon and his representatives in the NYCV had been right to use the law in pursuit of protections for black freedom.[28] Judge Riker heard Dixon's arguments and responded favorably. The NYCV had laid foundations for a changed legal position for black people, a citizen status that would ensure authorities defended the freedom of individual African Americans.

*   *   *

Dixon's case was in some ways profoundly local. A crowd of black New Yorkers angry about kidnappings in their city rescued him; city residents led his legal struggle against a city official known to be a friend to slaveowners' interests. But NYCV advocates believed Dixon's case held meaning for broader struggles to protect alleged fugitives. Coverage in the Philadelphia *National Enquirer*, edited by the white abolitionist Benjamin Lundy, suggested interest in Dixon's case beyond Manhattan. On April 29, 1837, the *Enquirer* ran an article titled "Trial by Jury," noting that Massachusetts lawmakers had proposed to "restore the trial by jury, on questions of personal freedom." Directly below that news, Lundy printed an item titled "Kidnapping in New York," updating readers on William Dixon's hearing.[29] A New York City arrest and a legislative debate in Boston were both newsworthy for a Philadelphia editor. Black and white activists understood that state laws emerged in and were shaped by an interconnected national geography.

Black personal security became an increasingly urgent issue for lawmakers and activists across the free states in the late 1830s, and claims for legal protections spurred debates about sovereignty and the nature of citizenship. Massachusetts abolished the writ of *homine replegiando* in 1835 during a backlash against radical abolitionism in the state. State legislators reflected on New York's laws and said they wanted a simpler process for adjudicating fugitive cases. *Habeas corpus*, which provided only a hearing before a judge, was sufficient protection against "unlawful imprisonment and restraint," they argued. Then, in 1836 and 1837, the state's substantial, impassioned antislavery community organized a petitioning drive that culminated in the enactment of a law restoring *homine replegiando*; this was the change the *Enquirer* celebrated in April 1837. Advocates of the new Massachusetts law hoped it would allow any alleged fugitive to have a jury trial on demand.[30]

Lawmakers in free states further south took steps to confront the more visceral threat of slavecatchers invading their territory. New Jersey legislators passed a jury trial law in the spring of 1837. In late 1836, a man who had fled slavery nine years before was arrested and brought to trial in New Jersey. Members of the Pennsylvania Abolition Society, one of the nation's oldest antislavery organizations, traveled to their neighboring state to represent the fugitive, arguing the case up to the New Jersey Supreme Court. There, Chief Justice Joseph Hornblower ruled that no single judge should decide questions of personal freedom and that alleged fugitives were entitled to due process.

His ruling helped to produce a state law requiring a panel of judges to preside in fugitive cases and allowing either party in such cases to request a jury. In June, the *National Enquirer* printed the text of New Jersey's law, announcing that "friends of humanity will be highly gratified" with a law that helped solidify the presumption of freedom for black people in the North.[31]

Pennsylvanians petitioned their state legislature in late 1836 as their New Jersey neighbors had, but in the winter of 1836 and 1837, lawmakers spurned their calls for a new jury trial law. Those representatives were in the midst of a campaign against black rights, revising the state constitution to disfranchise African Americans in 1838. In July 1837, as William Dixon went free in New York, the *Enquirer* reported on the case of another alleged fugitive arrested just outside of Philadelphia. Activists organized quickly to secure a recess in the case, during which they would gather witnesses on behalf of the accused. But the trial was held before a single judge, a man who had previously granted "seven [fugitive] warrants in one day." The *Enquirer*'s correspondent encouraged antislavery Pennsylvanians to form "a large audience" when the trial resumed; with a substantial crowd "to witness these exhibitions, they will not occur very frequently." The paper thus called for extralegal resistance, hoping crowds like William Dixon's rescuers could intimidate slavecatchers and judges in the absence of a jury trial to protect alleged fugitives.[32]

Lawmakers in the 1830s wrestled with questions about interstate comity and the property protections to which slaveowners were entitled, which offered important opportunities for activists to seek legal safeguards for black freedom. As early as the 1820s, some northern state lawmakers sought to limit slaveowners' property rights. They challenged laws that allowed sojourning— the practice of southerners bringing slaves into northern states for up to sixty days at a time—and said their state abolition laws superseded slaveowners' desires to transport freely their human property across the country. Sectional legal structures gradually diverged during the antebellum period, and by the Civil War, most northern state legislatures declined to protect slave property in the ways that were essential to southern state law. This must have encouraged activists who sought a connection with state and federal governments founded on the protection of black freedom. African Americans recognized that William Dixon's case had legal potential because lawmakers in their states seemed increasingly interested in preventing kidnapping and protecting even enslaved people who had fled to the free states.[33]

Black people expressed a shared vision of a citizenship across the free states, claiming the status should offer alleged fugitives legal protections, a relationship in which governments would presume and defend freedom rather than slavery. While people in the Northeast read news in the *National Enquirer* and other papers about emerging protections for alleged fugitives, activists worked for similar change in other states. "Persons claimed as fugitives from Slavery, ought to have the right of trial by Jury before being consigned to hopeless bondage," declared a group of black Michigan residents.[34] Activists' political concerns and strategies developed within the interconnected geography of antebellum black protest. The movement and exchange of people and ideas shaped the daily lives, the political concerns, and the dreams of African Americans in places like New York, Detroit, and Cleveland. Those interactions built a protest community spanning the North and contributed to arguments for a citizen status available to people across state lines.

And so as in other northern states, while black New Yorkers rioted and Ruggles and Cornish wrote, lawmakers moved toward new protections of black freedom. It is difficult to trace direct lines of influence, but black print culture and street politics allowed African Americans to make direct claims in ways that were legible to lawmakers and other white Americans.[35] The forms of black protest demanded discussions about African Americans' legal status. In 1839, members of the New York State Assembly first considered a law to provide all alleged fugitives trial by jury. Opponents said *homine replegiando* offered sufficient protection for the accused and worried that a new measure would violate the Fugitive Slave Act of 1793. One supporter of legal change sketched the limits of the law as it stood, challenging his colleagues to explain "the practical operation of the '*homine* something,'" joking that "he hardly knew what to call it." State senators eventually voted down the proposed jury trial law, but lawmakers presented it again in May 1840, and it passed both houses on the strength of an increased Whig membership.[36] The law was one in a pattern of northern personal liberty laws designed to hinder the work of slavecatchers, protect alleged fugitives, and allow white northerners to wash their hands of slavery's stain.[37] In addition to providing for jury trials, the New York law required a claimant to pay a $1,000 bond before seizing an alleged fugitive. Further, if the court decided against the claimant, he was responsible for court costs and a payment of $100 to the accused.[38]

Activists had used citizenship to seek precisely this kind of legal development, and the *Colored American* portrayed the law as a boon to nearly all New Yorkers. "Hereafter . . . our venerable Judges will be relieved from the necessity of passing sentence upon the poor fugitive, single handed and alone." Further, the measure would "serve as a protection to our brethren throughout the State, against Southern encroachment." Only those who made their living seizing fugitives could oppose the law; "such blustering concerns throughout the state, will find their slave catching attended with something more of difficulty than formerly."[39] The law did not change African Americans' legal status, but activists celebrated the tangible legal protections it offered. Further, black northerners likely hoped the jury trial law symbolized the potential for broader legal changes, believing they might similarly use citizen status to secure other rights they desired.

Still, so long as slavery existed, black freedom remained tenuous. The protections black people secured and the specificity they lent to the concept of citizenship were constrained by the facts that most African Americans were legally enslaved and that the people who owned them held vast political power. Because legal protections of black freedom destabilized slavery, slaveowners organized to fight threats to their economy and social structure.[40] Legal debates regarding alleged fugitives became increasingly contentious after the case of *Prigg v. Pennsylvania* in 1842. Edward Prigg was a Maryland slavecatcher who went in pursuit of Margaret Morgan and her two children, who had fled bondage in the state in 1832. Prigg tracked Morgan to Pennsylvania, where, in 1837, he took steps to arrest her and send his quarry back to Maryland. Prigg followed the provisions of an 1826 Pennsylvania law designed to prevent kidnapping. He needed a local legal official's permission to arrest the alleged fugitives and remove them from the state. He seized Morgan and her two children and brought them before Thomas Henderson, a local justice of the peace. But Henderson, as a low-level court official, did not have the authority to issue a certificate of removal for Morgan; he refused to hear the case. Prigg, likely concerned that Pennsylvania law would hinder his slavecatching work, took Morgan and her children south without legal sanction. Pennsylvania officials charged Prigg with kidnapping, and a jury in York County found him guilty. Prigg appealed to the Supreme Court of Pennsylvania, which agreed with the lower court; that led the slavecatcher to seek his final legal recourse before the U.S. Supreme Court.[41]

The Supreme Court's ruling protected slaveowners' interests but did not resolve questions of comity surrounding fugitive slaves. In the Court's opinion, Justice Joseph Story declared Pennsylvania's 1826 antikidnapping law unconstitutional because it violated the constitutional clause requiring that fugitives be "delivered up" on the claim of a person entitled to their labor.

Story read the Constitution as a bond between property owners and the federal government, and he ruled that states could pass no laws to interfere with the immediate seizure of a runaway slave.[42] The decision was a mandate for the right to recapture alleged fugitives in the free states; it sparked outrage in antislavery communities. Thomas and Robert Hamilton, brother editors of the New York *Weekly Anglo-African*, said the ruling offered slaveowners an "absolute and illimitable" right to arrest alleged fugitives. They believed the decision nullified existing protections for black people. "All laws securing to the citizen of a Free State claimed as a slave a trial by jury," they said, were little more than "a dead letter."[43] The *Prigg* decision endorsed slaveowners' rights to recapture fugitives, but it did not resolve how that process would take place. Story exempted northern state governments from any requirement to assist the process of arresting fugitives or removing them to the South. The justice would later present his opinion as a victory for antislavery interests. He asserted slaveowners' right to seize fugitive property in the North but left open the possibility that northern states could pass personal liberty laws to deny aid to slavecatchers and protect black freedom.[44]

The Hamilton brothers and other black activists denied claims to the antislavery value of the *Prigg* decision. They anticipated a rash of kidnappings in the wake of the case. "We believe there is much danger, and we warn our people to *watch*." They used the problems of *Prigg* to justify lawbreaking, slyly suggesting that readers pursue collective vigilance work. "We are not prepared to advise our people to assemble and organize associations, for the purpose of self-defence. . . . We do not at present consider that the most prudent course to pursue." But they did not need to advise black northerners to create vigilance committees; urging readers "to *watch*" suggested that they continue and expand their existing organizations. Rather than discouraging self-defense, the editors simply asked black people to be discreet as they organized extralegal protections. Look after yourselves, they said; prepare to defend against kidnappers. But avoid publicizing those preparations, hold private meetings, and conceal from lawmakers and others your capabilities. The article might be seen as a warning to slavecatchers that they would meet black resistance if they plied their trade in the North. The Hamiltons called to mind the image of thousands of men and women, organized through mysterious means, fighting to free William Dixon. Black people, fired by "the spirit of freedom which burns within us," would protect one another regardless of judicial mandate or southern aggression.[45]

Vigilance work flourished in the late 1830s alongside the pursuit of legal protections, two prongs in northern resistance to the intrusive slave power.[46] Robert Purvis led black and white abolitionists in establishing the Vigilant Committee of Philadelphia in 1837. Like the New York Committee of Vigilance, the Philadelphia group blended legal and extralegal tactics, financing court proceedings and purchasing fugitives' freedom while also helping runaways escape their pursuers.[47] At a June 1839 meeting, about a dozen men who comprised the committee leadership agreed "that those persons who entertain Strangers of a certain description Shall be compensated therefor[e]."[48] And, in a step with which the Hamiltons might have disagreed, they chose to announce their names "in the public papers."[49] While the committee leadership appears to have been all male, the idea of "entertaining" fugitives points to some of the silent, critical vigilance work of black women. They would likely have been responsible for housing and feeding runaways as they were for activists traveling to a lecture or a public meeting in another town.[50] Publicizing their vigilance work displays a surprising comfort with acknowledging lawbreaking but also suggests the range of people who made the committee's work possible. The Vigilant Committee needed money and may have publicized their names to convey to potential donors that they could be trusted with donations and had done work worth supporting. Black Pennsylvanians offered what they could, contributing to collections at Bethel A. M. E. Church and at a celebration organized by a Presbyterian sabbath school in 1841.[51] As they solicited aid and "entertained" fugitives, the Vigilant Committee included a wide segment of black Philadelphians in negotiations over the legal relationship between black people and Pennsylvania's government.

By breaking the law as they worked to redefine their legal relationship with governments, activists outlined a citizen status defined by people's participation in the process of lawmaking. Governments should hear black people's concerns and respond, even when activists expressed those concerns in direct defiance of established law. Vigilance work conveyed targeted disdain for extant legal realities. Activists wanted state and federal governments to protect black people as part of an investment in people's natural right to freedom. Their work had the potential to secure specific protections for themselves and change the foundations of law in the United States. Claiming jury trial protections through citizen status while breaking laws that did not protect freedom demanded new terms for the relationship between individuals and governments in the United States.[52]

David Ruggles sketched that vision in his response to the *Prigg* case, raising questions about the implications of the struggle for a jury trial law. During William Dixon's legal proceedings, he had advocated forcefully for jury trial legislation. But he came to see that as a flawed step toward remaking the nation's legal order. "The existence of a jury trial law," Ruggles wrote in January 1843, "conceding to slavery the right to incarcerate humanity as a chattel personal, is at variance with my notion of equal rights, the Declaration of American Independence, the laws of Nature, and of the living God." New York's jury trial law made it possible for a black person to be sent into slavery by state authority, a tacit endorsement of slavery's legitimacy. The very notion of a law to prevent unjust enslavement acknowledged that enslavement could be just for certain individuals. Ultimately, protecting people from slavery or kidnapping would not achieve the larger black activist aim of securing legal protections for freedom through citizen status.[53] Ruggles sought a new foundation for the nation's laws, a presumption of freedom and a robust set of protections against human bondage.

In the 1840s, faced with radical black politics and the northern intransigence embodied in the personal liberty laws, federal legislators sought new protections of southerners' rights to runaway property. They said the government's chief responsibility was to protect property owners against demands for legal assurances of black freedom. John C. Calhoun, a leading advocate of the slaveowners' cause, believed personal liberty laws had nullified the slaveowners' right to claim fugitives.[54] In May 1848, South Carolina senator Andrew Butler addressed his colleagues in the interest of reclaiming power, calling slaveowners "a doomed minority" and spurring them to action in defense of their property rights. "The sentiment of the North against the institution of slavery is advancing with the certainty of the malaria," Butler cried.[55] Butler and other southerners focused their politics on demands for federal legal protection of their economic and social system.[56] At the time, Congress did not act on Butler's anxieties, but black activists watched closely, recording in papers like Frederick Douglass's *North Star* southern demands for greater access to fugitives.[57] Black politics pushed people like Butler to make new claims about their legal status and the proper relationship between individuals and governments. Individual black people pursuing freedom and activists publicly seeking legal protections intensified southern lawmakers' work to restrict black people's rights.

Lawmakers like Butler felt justified in their anxieties as they watched northern officials take steps to defend black freedom with decisions that made their states hostile to slaveowners' interests. In 1845, for instance, Kentuckian Robert Mateson purchased a farm in Illinois and began sending his slaves north for a few weeks at a time to work his new landholdings.[58] On one such trip, Jane, an enslaved housekeeper, claimed freedom for herself and her four children. Jane looked to seize the opportunity of her presence in a free state. Mateson's lawyers, including a young Abraham Lincoln, fought Jane's suit up to the Illinois Supreme Court. There, Lincoln argued that Jane and her children were seasonal workers who, in a legal sense, were only transported through, rather than residing in, Illinois. The court rejected Lincoln's legalistic claim; because Illinois's constitution barred slavery and no positive federal law asserted Mateson's right to bring slaves into a free state, Jane and her children were free. Mateson had voluntarily brought his slaves north, so the Fugitive Slave Act of 1793, which pertained only to runaways, did not apply.[59] As in other freedom suits of the period, judges recognized the importance of federal law but ruled on the basis of a state's provision for black freedom, reflecting the limits of interstate comity.[60] That must have encouraged black activists who heard congressional shouts for stricter laws on the recapture of fugitive slaves. Jane's successful freedom suit meant that some American lawmakers would still hear African Americans' concerns and that it remained possible to build a legal relationship that could protect black freedom.

*   *   *

While northern lawmakers seemed increasingly interested in keeping their states free of slavery, many black and white activists believed the possibilities Jane's case represented were insufficient protections of personal security. For every judge willing to decide in favor of black freedom, there was a lawyer like Abraham Lincoln looking to uphold the law of property ownership, a slaveowner interested in defending his profits, and a set of slavecatchers who wanted to make money doing that work. In 1847 and 1848, a fugitive slave named Adam Crosswhite called an antislavery community into action to counter that multifaceted threat to the freedom that he and his family had claimed. The defense of the Crosswhites further challenged the nation's pro-slavery legal infrastructure. In two confrontations, black and white activists showed how invested they were in the struggle for personal security. They sparked chaos in response to an attempted fugitive arrest, and both implicitly and explicitly demanded new terms for a citizen status that would protect them from slavery.

Adam Crosswhite, his wife, and their four children fled slavery in Kentucky in 1843 and made their home in Marshall, Michigan, about 100 miles west of Detroit. Marshall was inviting because it harbored an active abolitionist community; ironically, it is possible that the family's owner tracked them down by targeting antislavery centers in search of the fugitives.[61] By January 1847, Francis Troutman, grandson of the Crosswhites' owner Francis Giltner, had located the family and gone in pursuit with a handful of slavecatchers. On the morning of January 27, the slavecatchers, joined by a local sheriff named Harvey Dickson, approached the Crosswhite home. Adam Crosswhite saw them coming, and he and his eldest son tried to run, but some of Troutman's posse caught them and brought them back to the house. Troutman announced that he and Sheriff Dickson would arrest the family as fugitives, giving Crosswhite the opportunity of a hearing in court. Under an 1827 law, Michigan required anyone claiming a black person as a fugitive to bring the accused before a judge and prove legal ownership.[62] Crosswhite convinced the slavecatchers to allow him to leave the house "to consult counsel" in preparation for a hearing, which he did, escorted by Sheriff Dickson. In their absence, dozens of black and white townspeople materialized in and around the Crosswhite household. When Adam Crosswhite returned, the crowd began threatening the slavecatchers, hoping to frighten them away from the family. James Smith, a black man "with a club raised, approached within five or six feet" of Francis Troutman and "threatened to smash out his brains."

The crowd grew to more than 100, keen to prevent any arrests. William Parker, a black neighbor, declared to all present that he would risk his life to prevent the Crosswhites being taken into custody. Alongside these threats, the antislavery crowd took on some of the more genteel forms of antebellum politics. According to subsequent court records, members of the crowd proposed and adopted resolutions expressing their intent to resist Troutman and Sheriff Dickson. White abolitionists were vocal participants, including Charles Gorham, who resolved "that these Kentuckians shall not take the Crosswhite family by virtue of physical, moral, or legal force." His call met with "general acclamation [and] much noise."

Ultimately, the activists kept the Crosswhite family out of the hands of authorities simply by expressing their willingness and exhibiting their capacity to resist. Sheriff Dickson could not control the crowd. During the confrontation, Troutman produced a signed warrant to arrest the fugitives, but Dickson declined to execute it. Convinced the slavecatchers were no match for the hundred-strong antislavery mob, the sheriff persuaded Troutman that it would be dangerous and fruitless to attempt an arrest. The following day, Charles Gorham encountered Francis Troutman in a Marshall courthouse and informed him simply of the outcome of the confrontation: "Your negroes are gone." Overnight, abolitionists had ushered the Crosswhites east toward the Detroit River, where they crossed the border into a more secure freedom in Canada.

The civil language of the court records surely belies the tension and fear that the Crosswhites felt. But those records do convey the complex political and legal consciousness of black and white residents of Marshall. An inter-racial antislavery coalition broke the law to free the Crosswhite family for a number of reasons, chief among them the simple legal fact that the family members were fugitive slaves. Again, Marshall's abolitionist community and proximity to Canada would have attracted runaways. Perhaps some of the Crosswhite's black defenders had previously freed themselves and felt it was important to show that they would fight for others' liberty. William Parker's claim that he would risk his life to protect the Crosswhites also asserted that he would do so to defend his own freedom as well as that of any of his neighbors.

The crowd at the Crosswhite home seemed convinced of the righteous-ness of their resistance, that they were making just arguments about black people's legal status, even if they were violating specific statues. Charles Gor-ham said Francis Troutman could not seize the Crosswhites, even with the exercise of "legal force." The assembled crowd, composed largely of Cross-white's black neighbors, agreed. According to later testimony, Gorham declared "that public sentiment was above the law." Like the rescue of Wil-liam Dixon, black and white northerners decried the injustice of laws that upheld slavery. Their actions broadcast their concern that even if the Cross-whites were brought to court, the proceedings would not be a fair process to determine their status. In this approach, black activists differed from aboli-tionists like William Lloyd Garrison who rejected the Constitution and the nation's formal politics. These women and men combined their extralegal resistance with calls for government protections of their freedom. They held on to the possibility that they could correct the system's embedded injustices and rebuild the law in a way that would protect black lives.[63]

After the Crosswhites escaped, their owner Francis Giltner filed suit in federal court against Charles Gorham and two other white abolitionists who had aided the fugitive family. The case seemed clear—abolitionists had cele-brated, even gloated, about rescuing the Crosswhites and guiding them to

FIGURE 5. "A Bold Stroke for Freedom," William Still, *The Underground Railroad*
(1872). The armed woman and children depicted here confronting a group of
slavecatchers reflect the broad range of black people who took part in the work of
defending freedom, often through practices of violent self-defense. Prints and
Photographs Division, Library of Congress.

Canada. Defense lawyers argued that Gorham and his colleagues were
involved but had not been active agents of that rescue. They had not physically taken the Crosswhites out of Troutman's hands or led the family out of
the country, the lawyers maintained. Supreme Court Justice John McLean
heard the case in the U.S. circuit court in Detroit. In 1842, McLean had
dissented in *Prigg v. Pennsylvania*, denying that the personal liberty laws,
which protected free black people, contradicted the 1793 Fugitive Slave Act,
designed to secure runaway property. But in *Giltner v. Gorham*, McLean
issued forceful instructions directing the jury to side with the slaveowner.
"There seems to be no doubt of the right of the plaintiff to the services of
the fugitives," McLean said. Aiding the escape was a clear violation of the
1793 law. Although Gorham's lawyers denied his role in the rescue, Justice

McLean said that if any man "by words or actions . . . encouraged others to make the rescue, he is responsible." Despite those direct instructions, the jury deliberated through the night and returned to McLean announcing that they were unable to agree on a verdict. It took a retrial in November 1848 and a second jury to declare Gorham and his colleagues liable. McLean ordered the abolitionists to pay $6,000 in damages.[64]

In what was surely the most stunning moment of these proceedings, Adam Crosswhite entered the courtroom to testify for the defense. Crosswhite had returned to Michigan at risk of being seized and shipped into bondage, but he was convinced he could offer useful testimony on Gorham's behalf. Those in the crowd, many of whom were black activists, looked on anxiously as Crosswhite took the stand to testify, in effect, against his owner. Given the public knowledge of the case, he could do little but tell the truth: he was "born in Kentucky, the slave of his own father" and, in his significantly vague phrasing, "came to this State in 1843." Acknowledging his fugitive status in the presence of his owner and the men who had been hired to recapture him placed Crosswhite in imminent danger, but he seemed unbothered, confident in the tools of black vigilance. Black Michiganders sprang into action as soon as his testimony concluded. When the fugitive stepped down, "a rush was made to the door with Mr. Crosswhite, by the colored citizens, who soon conveyed him across the Detroit River into Canada."[65] One year after abolitionists whisked Crosswhite away from his rural home in Marshall, black activists liberated him again, this time from inside a U.S. district courthouse in Detroit.

It seems likely that Gorham's lawyers had asked Crosswhite to come back to Michigan, hoping the fugitive would deny that the white townsmen had been the driving force behind the family's rescue. For all its nobility, his decision is stunning; a person who successfully fled slavery and reached Canada returned to a courtroom in the United States. His choice underlines the strength of Michigan's activist community and, perhaps, Crosswhite's dedication to contesting slaveowners' legal claims.

The day after that second rescue, activists gathered at the Detroit City Hall, where they issued resolutions explaining why they had broken the law in terms that conveyed striking arguments about citizen status. They declared in writing the ideas about slavery, freedom, and the law embodied in each of the Crosswhite rescues. They agreed to a series of resolutions, which they later had printed in antislavery newspapers, including one denouncing the decision in favor of Giltner as a restriction of "the rights and liberties of the citizens of the free state of Michigan." While their protest tactics defied legal structures, the activists argued that the law should have a decisive influence in American life. They sought a citizenship that would protect black people from slavery and allow activists, white and black, to challenge limits on that protection. By acknowledging Giltner's claims, McLean and the court had "deprived us of all protection and security in our lives." "Many of us have worn the galling chains of slavery," they confessed. Legally, some of them might still have belonged to other people.[66] Their appeal for legal protection demanded a reorganization of the law in the slaveholding republic. It is not clear whether some or all of those meeting in Detroit had aided the Cross-whites, but they understood that they faced the same threats from slavecatchers and northern lawmakers, and they declared themselves willing to do the same work as the rescuers, refusing to "submit tamely to be converted into goods and chattels."[67]

On that Michigan night in December 1848, African Americans who might legally have belonged in slavery called on the government to create their freedom and in so doing to change its central function. "Live or die, sink or swim, we will never be taken back into slavery," they resolved. The gathered activists wished "to be a peaceable and sober portion of the community," and said they were willing to "abide by the constitution and laws of this and all other states," provided those laws "recognize no slavery within their borders." Their ideas were central to the rescues of the Crosswhite family and more broadly to the intellectual work of vigilance. Black people, from courtrooms, from newspaper offices, and from the plaza of New York's city hall, argued for a citizen status that defended the freedom of individual black women and men. Those words from Detroit expressed the lawmaking potential of organized acts of lawbreaking.[68]

*   *   *

Black activists made arguments about the terms of citizenship by breaking the laws that upheld human bondage. The Detroit meeting illuminates the interconnected legal and extralegal work of black citizenship politics and frames lawbreaking as a targeted claim for legal change. Delegates pledged their lives to fight enslavement, yet also resolved to petition Congress to repeal the Fugitive Slave Act of 1793. If successful, such a petition would cut out the heart of American slavecatching law.[69] For black activists in the North, breaking the law was a way to defend themselves from enslavement and to make freedom more secure and attainable for others. Lawbreaking was a multifaceted project of shifting the legal terrain of black and American life in the nineteenth century. Ultimately, because proslavery interests controlled the federal government in the antebellum period, this form of protest led slaveowners to craft more robust slavecatching legislation. Lawbreaking is destabilizing. To lawmakers and slaveowners interested in controlling black bodies for profit and power, it was egregious and dangerous. The Crosswhite controversy was a key part of the popular political context in which congressmen developed and passed the 1850 Fugitive Slave Act.[70]

Northerners' antislavery law and politics and southerners' proslavery anxieties came to a head in 1850, producing a congressional crisis regarding California statehood, the future expansion of slavery, and the property protections to which slaveowners were entitled. Surveying the political landscape, John Calhoun announced that "it can no longer be disguised or denied that the Union is in danger."[71] Legal questions about slavery were poised to break the nation. Frederick Douglass's *North Star* ensured African Americans kept abreast of congressional efforts at compromise, focusing in particular on new proposals for fugitive slave legislation. In January 1850, James Murray Mason of Virginia introduced a proposal to broaden slavecatching authority, and Douglass detailed the arguments of that "high-minded Virginian." In March, he began printing a "Weekly Review of the Congressional Proceedings." In one such column, Douglass bitterly noted Massachusetts senator Daniel Webster's apparent proslavery turn when he endorsed a law to protect slaveowners' property. For his work on behalf of slaveowners, Douglass said the North's Judas would not "be denied 'the thirty pieces of silver.'" Douglass, in turn, praised William Seward, who had refused to agree to protections for slavery and memorably declared "there is a higher law than the Constitution," calling on Congress to uphold divine principles of human freedom.[72] His radical antislavery sentiments pleased black activists who searched for a champion in Congress, just as it outraged southerners, who read it as an attack on their institutions and their character. In April, Douglass listed dozens of petitions northerners had sent to Congress opposing new slavecatching laws and measures to allow slavery to spread west.[73]

Congress passed a new Fugitive Slave Act in September 1850, part of a series of laws intended to resolve sectional tensions. The law created a massive slavecatching infrastructure for all of the United States. It called for a new and growing set of federally appointed commissioners empowered to hear fugitive cases and sanction the removal of the accused to slaveholding states.

Commissioners had the power to appoint police to arrest fugitives and to call on the people to do so. The measure not only empowered but also technically obligated all people in the United States to uphold rights to human property. "All good citizens," the law proclaimed, "are hereby commanded to aid in the prompt and efficient execution of this law." Slavecatchers had the power to arrest people themselves and bring them to court. Any testimony from an alleged fugitive would not be admitted as evidence. Most notoriously, in a stunningly corrupt provision, if a judge ruled that a person was a slave, he was paid $10 for the case; he received only $5 if he ruled a person was free.[74] The legal expansion of slavecatching was such an important part of the compromise effort because of long histories of antislavery vigilance and violence. Black activists, fleeing slavery and assisting runaways, helped to ensure white southerners that they needed a new law. While the measure was discouraging for those who had called for federal changes like the abolition of the 1793 Fugitive Slave Act, it was likely not a shocking development to people who understood the influence of slaveowners in the federal government. In the 1850s, activists approached arrests and trials of alleged fugitives much as they had before the passage of the strict, new law.[75] For black and white activists, imbued with an ideology built around pursuing both freedom and justice, the Fugitive Slave Act further illuminated the necessity of lawbreaking. At Shiloh Church in New York City in October 1850, a black man stood before the crowd and pledged to protect his family, to "send [a slavecatcher] to hell before he shall accomplish his mission." His pledge met boisterous cheers from the crowd.[76]

Black and white, pro- and antislavery people across the free states were more anxious and angry over the Fugitive Slave Act than perhaps any other piece of antebellum legislation. The law seemed a decisive step toward defining the nation as a republic for slavery rather than freedom. In a practical sense, the Fugitive Slave Act pulled white northerners into the peculiar institution. The act required them to maintain slavery, pushed them to take a position on human bondage, and, because the process of rendition would send an alleged fugitive south before a hearing, compelled northerners to decide who belonged in their legal communities. People's anxieties over the proposed law were on display in New York City on May 8, 1850. That evening, the New York Committee of Vigilance celebrated its anniversary at Shiloh Presbyterian Church on Prince Street in Lower Manhattan, about a mile north of the site of William Dixon's brief liberation from city hall. Samuel Cornish had founded Shiloh Church in the 1820s, and since then, it had served as an important site for antislavery vigilance work, including as a shelter for fugitive slaves as early as the 1830s.[77] Activists celebrated decades of vigilance work in a center of the Underground Railroad, embracing the continuities in antebellum black protest, concrete political strategies, and organizations that endured through the passage of the Fugitive Slave Act.

As though it were a rescue the committee organized, their anniversary celebration became the site of a tense confrontation over the forms and objectives of black citizenship politics. A number of reform societies and antislavery groups had planned to celebrate their anniversaries that May in New York, and some white news editors encouraged city residents to disrupt the proceedings. Editors were especially angry about the forthcoming American Anti-Slavery Society meeting, a gathering of "abolitionists, Socialists, Sabbath-breakers and anarchists." They feared these radicals would misrepresent the North and intensify sectional strife. Refusing to allow "half a dozen madmen [to] manufacture opinion for the whole community," they wanted the events to become forums to debate slavery and urged nonabolitionists to claim a voice in the celebrations. While some of these editors maintained a veneer of nonviolence, others claimed mobbing was their right. Together, white newspaper editors inflamed existing racial and political tensions in the city and pushed protest and counterprotest perilously close to chaos.[78]

The anniversary celebration at Shiloh Presbyterian was a prime target for white northerners who wanted to suppress radical antislavery work. As members and supporters of the New York Committee of Vigilance filed into the church on May 8, they noticed "a set of disgraceful rowdies" joining them, a few occupying the pews on the ground level and many more filling the upper galleries. Activists opened the meeting with prayer and read from Matthew 25, which prophesied Jesus' resurrection and his separation of the sheep from the goats—the righteous from the damned. Charles B. Ray, secretary of the committee, stepped to the stage to present the year's accomplishments. They had liberated 151 fugitives, he said—"for that, you know, is our business"— and members were at work on cases to free forty more from bondage. Ray's brazenness surely angered the antiabolitionists in the crowd; perhaps he relished the chance to tout his success in flouting the laws of the slaveholding republic. Ray, in turn, might have been shocked or startled when the city's police chief walked through the church doors "accompanied by a strong force." His men took up positions around the sanctuary, causing a woman in the audience to faint, overwhelmed by the palpable tension in the church. Ray tried to maintain control of the room, continuing his prepared remarks by reading a letter from Gerritt Smith, who demanded black people have legal access to militias and public schools. The rowdies interrupted Ray with loud hisses and groans. The police presence, however disruptive their entrance, might have been all that prevented a riot in response to this black political event.[79]

The imposing Samuel Ringgold Ward followed Ray at the podium. Tall, broad-shouldered, and proud of his dark skin, Ward was renowned for his booming voice and oratorical skill. As a child, he had escaped slavery with his family, and he reveled in his successful fugitivity. That night, he announced that he and other abolitionists would continue to defend fugitives "in spite of any laws that may be passed." Ward informed the raucous audience that his political work was inspired by his father's service in the American Revolution. He called himself "a black citizen of New York—a black American," amid a rising cacophony of applause, hisses, and mocking laughter from the crowd. As Ward spoke, shouts of "Fire!" spread through the crowd. Flames raged from a nearby building, and a number of volunteer firefighters rushed out of the church, followed closely by panicked or gawking audience members. As he fought to the conclusion of his remarks, shouting over the boisterous crowd, Ward argued that he and his colleagues acted "with perfect legality" when they assisted fugitives. As a citizen, he felt an obligation to violate statutes that denied a human right to freedom. Ward and others pushed their extralegal politics into the realm of lawmaking. When the abolitionist William Burleigh tried to follow Ward's speech, he was shouted down by one Mr. Hill, who bellowed from the audience a resolution that northerners would "never surrender the compromises made . . . to perpetuate the Union." The remaining rowdies cheered Hill's sentiments. Hill and his friends called for other abolitionists to take the stage so the crowd could abuse them directly; they continued until the meeting broke down amid persistent taunts and shouts.[80]

The vigilance committee's anniversary was far more public than most other meetings black activists organized in the antebellum period. They wanted to broadcast their ideas widely in hopes of changing people's minds about the terms of citizenship. Proposals for a new fugitive slave law enthralled white Americans and so offered a valuable spark for black politics. The anniversary meeting points to the potency of black citizenship politics because of the extent and passion of white opposition it inspired. Many white northerners were outraged by black women and men rescuing alleged fugitives on city streets and challenging the legal order of their communities.

FIGURE 6. Portrait of Samuel Ringgold Ward from his *Autobiography of a Fugitive Negro* (1855). With his booming voice and striking physical presence, Ward cut an imposing figure during a raucous May 1850 gathering to denounce the proposed Fugitive Slave Act.

Some of those white northerners believed it was politically important for them to challenge the vigilance committee; Ward, Ray, and others had voices that white people felt the need to silence. Through their radical claims about citizenship, black activists helped to create the context in which the crowd abused them, intensifying legal controversies and nearly causing a riot in their pursuit of change.[81]

The Fugitive Slave Act increased black northerners' anxieties about being kidnapped or arrested, but for many, it also sharpened their twin projects of resisting and reshaping legal structures. In October 1850, black people crowded into the Zion Chapel in Manhattan, a building that could hold up to 1,500 people, to express their thoughts on the recently enacted law. Activists advertised the meeting with a handbill calling on New Yorkers to consider their "DUTY in the CRISIS." William P. Powell, who had been chosen to preside over the meeting, opened by quoting William Lloyd Garrison's radical conviction that the Constitution was a "covenant with death, and agreement with hell." Powell had worked with Garrison since the founding of the American Anti-Slavery Society in 1833, and he roused the crowd by denouncing the nation's laws.[82] Of the Fugitive Slave Act, he declared, to resounding applause, that it "must be trampled under foot, disobeyed, and violated at all hazards." But Powell did believe in the potential for legal change. A few weeks before that meeting at Zion Chapel, Powell and his colleague Lewis Putnam wrote to New York's mayor Caleb Smith Woodhull to express concerns about their freedom. Federal legislation left Powell, Putnam, and other black New Yorkers in "the peculiar position" of relying on "the people of New York, to defend her citizens against the operation of unjust law." They requested details from Mayor Woodhull about the protections the state might offer them and their families. Unsurprisingly, the mayor chose not to reply.[83]

What sort of response might Powell and Putnam have expected? Existing legal structures valued white property rights over black freedom. In response, African Americans insisted that personal security was essential to citizenship. They asked Mayor Woodhull to challenge federal authority, to establish questionably legal protections for black New Yorkers, and to provide public details about those protections. Federal law required "all good citizens" to enforce the Fugitive Slave Act, but activists wanted citizen status to protect them from that federal law. Putnam and Powell wrote of their "earnest desire, to be good law-abiding citizens," and they outlined the terms they felt that legal relationship should entail. They called on "all American citizens . . . to join in the cry of repeal." The form of the U.S. government made it possible for a groundswell of opposition to change an unjust law. But in the final resolution at their October 1850 meeting, they again turned away from the law, soliciting volunteers "to act on the secret committee" and asking fugitives to register themselves so black vigilantes could offer sufficient protection.[84] They made the complex claims that citizen status entitled them to protection both by and from the government and that they would pursue protection through both legal and extralegal work.

During the meeting at Zion Chapel and in printed advertisements for it, activists suggested that personal security was a distinctly masculine responsibility. A handbill advertisement shouted at black New Yorkers that "your Fire-side is in danger of being invaded!" The duty to act was a male responsibility to protect their households. It is somewhat surprising, then, that two-thirds of the people who crowded into the church were black women. Rather than further encouraging those women's evident activist spirit, male speakers subordinated women to men, framing resistance as a quality of black manliness rather than a gender-neutral manifestation of black political power. Black men would be "worthy neither of our homes nor the confidence of our wives and children" if they did not willingly offer their lives in fights with slave catchers. One speaker, who pledged to "send [a slave catcher] to hell," personalized that vision of black resistance. "I am a father," he announced, "and bound by every tie to protect my wife and children."[85] Their language stands in odd contrast with the substantial presence of women at the gathering. The women who are reported to have applauded those sentiments cheered an idealized vision of manly resistance to kidnapping, one that obscured the reality in which they defended themselves and others. Women's presence thus endorsed the speakers' masculinist claims, helping black men present themselves as they wanted to be seen. And the orators seem to have found it especially important to reassert masculine power in that setting.

Claiming a manly duty to resist slave catchers fit with a broader strategy of legitimizing opposition to the law. Lawbreaking was politics, and in the antebellum United States, politics was men's business. Black activists sought a new legal relationship through citizenship, but it was a relationship that remained defined by some of the traditional gender barriers of early republic politics.

*   *   *

The Fugitive Slave Act of 1850 was a response to acts like the rescues of William Dixon and Adam Crosswhite. Crosswhite's liberation was a rich echo of Dixon's rescue from the steps of city hall a decade earlier. Perhaps the most remarkable tie between their stories is that both men ended up free, far from a given as slaveowners and lawmakers worked together to stabilize the system of human property. Black Americans broke the law because they understood how difficult it was to secure their freedom within existing legal structures. The difference between Dixon and Crosswhite is that the former won his freedom through the court. After he was recaptured in a Duane Street coal cellar, Dixon benefited tremendously from the work of his NYCV legal team. The lawyers called several witnesses to testify to his freedom. A white ship captain said that he had occasionally employed Dixon, who he knew as free, since 1831. A black barber came north from Philadelphia to testify that he had known Dixon as a free man for fifteen years. Dr. Allender, the alleged slaveowner, had to prove a far more difficult case. Because the slave he called Jake had run away in 1832, none of Allender's witnesses could say that they had seen the man for at least five years. They then had to prove they could identify one of Baltimore's 20,000 free and enslaved African Americans. Dixon waited in Bridewell Prison for months before learning of Judge Riker's decision to grant him bail.[86]

After his release, Dixon's uncertainty about whether he might be called back to court or possibly arrested or kidnapped added tension to his daily encounters in New York City. Perhaps no single encounter was more frightening than a chance meeting with a runaway slave from Maryland. In his second autobiography, *My Bondage and My Freedom*, published in 1855, Frederick Douglass described the morning he arrived in New York, disembarking from a train just after he escaped slavery in Baltimore in 1839. Lost and lonely as he wandered the streets in his newfound freedom, Douglass felt overjoyed to encounter a black man he remembered from Baltimore, a man he identified as Allender's Jake. "I knew Jake well," Douglass wrote. He had heard that Walter Allender had hired slavecatchers but was glad to see Jake apparently thriving in freedom. Jake was less than pleased to encounter his former friend. He silenced Douglass, declared, "I am 'William Dixon,' in New York!" and left the recent runaway alone in the street.[87]

Perhaps Douglass, writing in the 1850s with antislavery ends in mind, fabricated this story to dramatize the terrifying experience of fleeing slavery. It can be difficult to imagine that on his first morning in a city with more than 16,000 black residents, Douglass stumbled upon a man he knew, a fellow fugitive with his own compelling story of escape.

But histories of slavery and freedom turn on precisely these kinds of chances: the sale of a boy to an owner who decides to teach the child to read;

the young man's opportunity to work in a city where he finds companionship and love with a free woman; the good fortune of a white acquaintance failing to notice a runaway slave riding a train bound north to freedom.[88] And perhaps the chance encounter was not as rare as population numbers suggest. Frederick Douglass had been told to find David Ruggles when he arrived in New York, and Ruggles would eventually help the fugitive reunite with his soon-to-be wife Anna Murray and begin a new life in New Bedford, Massachusetts. Perhaps Dixon lived near Ruggles or had been on a visit to his old ally. Perhaps Ruggles drew around him a community of people who could offer and might need to receive help in encounters with slavecatchers. Most importantly, Douglass's story seems plausible because hundreds of people fled slavery each year, because so many sought community and opportunity in northeastern cities, and because the New York Committee of Vigilance pursued both legal and extralegal tactics to create and secure black freedom. As Douglass did, it makes sense that the man who called himself William Dixon would have begun his work to build a free life in New York City.

Douglass's account suggests that the legal case of the fugitive named Jake might itself have been series of acts of lawbreaking. For Jake, this could have been a simple result of his desire for freedom. Again and again he declared himself "a freeman." He performed freedom in the courtroom and on the streets, using his voice in an effort to change the fact that he was legally enslaved. With his words, the Baltimore runaway redefined his legal status in a way that denied the possibility of human bondage. He was free because no person should be enslaved. A fugitive called Jake appears to have known that the legal landscape of New York could be favorable to those efforts, that he could lie in court, transforming himself into a free man named William Dixon.

Who knew the truth of "Allender's Jake"? The mob that rescued Dixon understood how difficult it was to secure black freedom through established legal proceedings. Regardless of whether they knew Dixon was Jake, they knew there were limits to the justice available to him and their rescue protested that legal reality. When they broke the law, the rioters declared that they would not acquiesce to their marginal legal status, that they would resist anything that stood in the way of a relationship with a government that would safeguard their freedom.

Perhaps more surprisingly, William Dixon and his defense team broke the law repeatedly, brazenly, in a courtroom inside New York City Hall. Their lawbreaking helped move toward a legal precedent of protection for black freedom. It is possible that activists created the character of William Dixon and worked to get a judge like Richard Riker to grant a writ of *homine replegiando*. William Dixon might have been at the center of a test case. If Judge Riker granted the writ, it would have established a precedent securing for alleged fugitives one avenue to a jury trial. This would have been a high-stakes test, but perhaps Jake and his counsel agreed that breaking the law, becoming William Dixon, was his best opportunity to find freedom. Further, one man's risk of bondage could open avenues to freedom for many others. The NYCV and Jake's lawyers built a case, gathered witnesses, and presented the story of William Dixon, a freeman, seeking a writ of *homine replegiando* for a hearing before a jury. For all his condemnation of the collective rescue, it seems likely that Samuel Cornish, a leader in the NYCV, also knew the truth about Dixon. In fact, he might have opposed the city hall mob because of what he knew, anxious that the case be decided in court because he had helped design a character who had so much legal potential. Cornish could have seen the lawbreaking in court as more transformative than that which took place in City Hall Park.

There are many ways to see the logic of making a fugitive into a free man, especially in pursuit of legal protections. But whether or not the case was designed as such, Dixon's perjury was part of the negotiations over how black people would be treated in courts when they were claimed as fugitive slaves. It was part of the contest over African Americans' relationship to American governments, and vocal activists ensured that lawmakers saw this as a struggle over the content of citizenship. In newspapers, in courtrooms, and in the city streets, black New Yorkers broke the law, combining extralegal violence with formal legal processes in a way that could fundamentally trans-form black life across the free states. Black people's legal status was in flux, a truth that was no more vivid than in discussions about how courts would relate to African Americans arrested as fugitive slaves. Activists insisted on legal change and used citizenship to outline a legal relationship predicated on black people's freedom. The fugitive slave issue presented a crisis to white southerners who wanted to protect their system of human property and who believed that controlling black people's movement generally was a corner-stone of the institution of slavery. The ways black people used citizenship in arguments about fugitive slaves spurred intense response from lawmakers interested in upholding white supremacy.

CHAPTER 5

Contesting the "Foul and Infamous Lie" of *Dred Scott*

In the antebellum decades, African Americans worked through the vagueness of citizenship to claim legal protections and make arguments about the relationships between individuals and governments. Their work helped push northern lawmakers to pass personal liberty laws. Even in areas where they did not make tangible gains, activists forced lawmakers to think about the content of citizenship and black people's legal status. Federal lawmakers tried to curtail certain forms of black politics with the Fugitive Slave Act of 1850, but citizenship remained undefined and continued to be useful for black activists. In 1857, Supreme Court Chief Justice Roger Taney looked to foreclose the opportunity of citizenship when he dismissed Dred Scott's freedom suit on the grounds that no black person had been or could be a citizen of the United States. The *Dred Scott* decision threatened black people's work to use citizenship in pursuit of rights. In response, activists adopted new tactics designed to ensure the status remained unsettled and useful for their politics.

The chief questions in Dred Scott's suit concerned slavery in the territories and the processes of emancipation, but much of Taney's decision focused on explaining why black people could not be citizens in order to exclude them from American political, legal, or social communities.[1] The chief justice worried that freedom suits in federal court might destabilize slavery, but he was also concerned about the implications of black citizenship politics. Taney's decision reflected his awareness of black protest strategies and his desire to prevent activists from using citizenship to seek legal protections.

After *Dred Scott*, activists continued to pursue specific legal protections, but Taney's decision permeated black political life. On September 14, 1858, for example, thirty-seven black men gathered for a state convention in Troy, New York, to demand the repeal of the state's property qualification for black voters, which had stood since 1821.[2] In addition to seeking changes in state laws, they spoke out against Chief Justice Taney's opinion. Taney handed down his ruling eighteen months before the Troy convention, but activists refused to leave it in the past. And so William J. Watkins stood before his colleagues at the concert hall in Troy and denied that Roger Taney had the authority to interpret the U.S. Constitution. Watkins was the son of a Maryland activist also named William Watkins. He worked as a teacher in Rochester while also traveling to give abolitionist lectures and collaborating with Frederick Douglass on his publishing work.[3] The younger Watkins did not mince words when he spoke about Taney's ruling. "The *Dred Scott* decision is a foul and infamous lie," he declared, "which neither black men nor white men are bound to respect." The ruling perverted fundamental constitutional principles; it was simply untrue that black people were not citizens. Rather than a statement of legal fact, Watkins called the decision "an utterance of individual political opinions" and urged people to reject the ruling in order to defend the republic.[4]

The chief justice failed to suppress black citizenship politics even as he attempted to foreclose the very possibility of black citizenship. The meeting in Troy in 1858 was typical of gatherings held in the late 1850s to strategize and respond to *Dred Scott*. Free black Americans were anxious and angry in the aftermath of that case; they made radical statements denouncing the nation's laws, they considered violent revolution as a political tool, they questioned whether they should remain in the United States, and some decamped for foreign soil. But many black activists remained in the United States and continued using citizenship in their politics after the nation's highest legal authority declared they could never be citizens. They put forth their own version of American history to challenge Taney's central arguments about black people's legal status in the past and future.[5]

In the late 1850s, black northerners chose to stay in the United States because they saw ways to continue working to secure legal protections through citizen status despite Taney's decision. Longstanding forms of black citizenship politics persisted after *Dred Scott*, helped black people offer potent challenges to Taney's arguments, and convinced many that they had a legal future in the nation. Taney's ruling encouraged activists to continue the work they had done for decades, and it sparked new ideas and arguments. By contesting the chief justice's claims, black people continued to push their way into lawmaking conversations. Watkins's response to the decision—calling it "a foul and infamous lie"—was key to black northerners' political strategy of the late 1850s. By calling the chief justice a liar, rejecting his narrative of the nation's history, and challenging his interpretation of the Constitution, African Americans held onto a space in which they could make public arguments about citizenship. They presented Roger Taney as a radical outlier, working to delegitimize him and push his proslavery, white supremacist ideas out of discussions about the nation's legal future. Taney used *Dred Scott* to define the nation as a slaveholding republic in its past, present, and future. By challenging his opinion, black people made transformative claims about American history, law, and society. Black activists were convinced Roger Taney's opinion would not be the last word on their legal status. The terms of citizenship remained vague after *Dred Scott,* and so African Americans remained in their country, confident that citizenship was a viable tool to shape their legal position in the United States. In the spring of 1857, activists took up their work with the direct, transformative claim "we *are* citizens."[6]

*   *   *

Roger Taney's ruling in *Dred Scott v. Sandford* concluded a decade of tortuous legal proceedings involving several black and white people across multiple state and federal jurisdictions.[7] Dred Scott, born a slave in Virginia around 1800, was transported to St. Louis, where U.S. Army surgeon John Emerson bought him in 1833. Emerson's career required significant travel, and he brought Dred Scott to Illinois and the Wisconsin Territory in the mid-1830s. In Wisconsin, Scott met and married an enslaved woman named Harriet, whose owner then gifted the woman to Emerson.[8] Emerson subsequently moved to New Orleans, where he met and married Irene Sanford, who took the doctor's surname. The Emersons brought the Scotts south to New Orleans, then back north to Illinois. On the return trip, Harriet gave birth to a daughter on a boat in the Mississippi River between Illinois and the Wisconsin Territory. John Emerson died in 1843, and title to the Scott family passed to his wife. After Irene Emerson refused to allow Dred Scott to purchase himself in 1846, Scott and his wife sued for their freedom on the grounds that they had resided in Illinois, territory deemed free under the

Northwest Ordinance of 1787. The Scotts lost their first suit on a technicality, won a retrial in 1850, and then saw the judgment reversed by the Missouri Supreme Court in 1852. In the meantime, Emerson had transferred owner- ship of the Scott family to her brother John Sanford (rendered as Sandford in subsequent records), who lived in New York. This transfer of ownership allowed Dred Scott's lawyers to sue in the circuit court in 1854, presenting their case as a dispute between citizens of separate states. The federal judge instructed the jury to follow Missouri precedent, which led them to uphold Sanford's title. Scott and his attorneys filed a writ of error, requesting a new trial before the U.S. Supreme Court, and the justices agreed to offer Scott his final legal option with a hearing in Washington, D.C.

Sectional politics and questions about slavery's future in the expanding United States shaped the decisions in the suits Dred and Harriet Scott filed. The judge for the Missouri Supreme Court was reluctant to declare Scott free because he wanted to keep himself and his state out of the fight over slavery's expansion. The "inevitable consequences" of antislavery lawmaking "must be the overthrow and destruction of our government," and he wanted no part in encouraging that process.[9] In federal courts, judges recognized that a decision to free the family could empower the national government to restrict slavery in new territories, allow northern states to emancipate the human property of traveling slaveowners, or encourage enslaved people to use the courts to escape their owner's grasp. When Scott appealed to the U.S. Supreme Court, Taney recognized the transformative potential of the suit. The chief justice seized the opportunity to present his vision of a potentially limitless slaveholding republic, a nation with powerful state governments and without black legal personhood.[10]

Roger Taney responded to Dred Scott as both an enslaved person seeking freedom in court and a black person making an argument about the content of citizenship. The complex forms and possibilities of African Americans' politics permeated the chief justice's ruling, which he delivered on March 6, 1857. Taney declared Congress had no authority to govern U.S. territories added after the ratification of the Constitution. This invalidated the North- west Ordinance of 1787, which had barred slavery from Illinois and Wiscon- sin, and prevented the federal government from restricting slavery's future expansion. He also declared unconstitutional both the Missouri Compromise and popular sovereignty, both of which made possible state legal restrictions of slavery.[11] He added that the Fifth Amendment protected an individual's right to bring property, including slaves, anywhere in the country. In theory, his decision opened the entire United States to slavery, answering complex questions about the nation's political geography and curtailing the arguments enslaved people might use in freedom suits.

Taney's vision of slavery expansion called for fundamental changes in the nation's legal structures, but for many observers, his denial of black citizenship was equally stunning and outrageous. Dred Scott's counsel had filed suit in federal court on the grounds that he was a citizen of Missouri and also of the United States. Taney asked whether Scott or any person "whose ancestors were imported into this country, and sold as slaves" could subsequently "become entitled to all the rights and privileges and immunities guaranteed to the citizen?"[12] He responded with a resounding no. In a wide-ranging reinterpretation of the Constitution and the country's history, the chief justice ruled black people could never be considered rights-bearing members of the nation. Each state had the power to decide who was a citizen of that state, he argued. Although a state might confer rights and privileges on an individual, neither the federal government nor any other state had to provide the same protections. Taney imagined his way into the racial attitudes of the founding generation and said black exclusion was logical because when the Constitution was written, black men had "no rights which the white man was bound to respect." And Taney elided disagreement on the court, ruling with a confidence that suggested he wielded all the authority of the federal government and encouraging the impassioned response to his opinion.[13]

"If anything related to the construction of the Constitution can be regarded as settled," Taney wrote, "it is that which we now give to the word 'citizen.'"[14] Despite his confidence, Taney made a series of inconsistent arguments that reflected the vagueness of citizenship in the United States. The content of his opinion indicated the persistent uncertainty in the relationship between rights and citizen status. He concluded that a descendant of slaves could not become a "member of the political community . . . and as such" secure legal protections, including the right to sue in federal court. This argument suggested legal belonging preceded and produced rights. But he also said free black people could never be citizens because states denied them certain legal protections, suggesting that a person's rights determined his or her legal status. He wrote with an air of certainty, but Taney could not describe definitively the relationship between citizen status and a person's rights.

Black activists insisted that Taney's ruling was based on a fundamentally inaccurate reading of the Constitution. At the Troy convention, in addition to calling the chief justice a liar, they said he had falsely claimed the authority to annihilate decades of legal precedent that limited the spread of slavery. His constitutional arguments and his history of the framers were flawed, designed only "to satiate the wolfish appetite of the oligarchy." Taney's argument that citizens of a state did not necessarily possess legal protections in other states contradicted the Comity Clause of the U.S. Constitution and reflected persistent uncertainties about how the federal system should operate. He argued that there were multiple citizenships; a state could declare a person a citizen within its borders, but only state citizens who were also already citizens of the United States could be secured in their legal protections when they entered other states. Rather than clarifying the foundations or content of citizen status, Taney's ruling highlighted its uncertain terms.[15]

Like African American activists, Taney invoked the past to make arguments aimed at crafting the terms of citizenship. His most infamous statement—that black people "had no rights which the white man was bound to respect"—was an assessment of popular opinion on racial categories in the eighteenth century. The key to black people's legal position in the Constitution could be located in the founders' racial ideas, he reasoned. He abandoned recent federal precedent on slavery expansion but looked to the early eighteenth century for colonial laws to support his claims about black rights. Lawmakers in Massachusetts in 1705 and Maryland in 1717 erected barriers to interracial marriage, which Taney said indicated their desire for "a perpetual and impassable barrier" between the races. Taney then looked to the early republic, citing New Hampshire's 1815 law excluding black men from militias and Connecticut's 1833 act to outlaw black schools.[16] Taney used that evidence to claim that an ideology of racial exclusion motivated the nation's founding lawmakers and should continue to determine black Americans' legal status.

Chief Justice Taney understood black activists as a threat to the nation's racial order and crafted his decision to suppress African American politics. Taney acknowledged that black protest and abolitionism had begun to reshape the nation. He recognized some "change in public opinion or feeling, in relation to this unfortunate race" in the United States. Black activists sought to transform the ways lawmakers and other white Americans thought about African Americans, and Taney noted their halting success. In addition, many northern states did confer some rights on black people, such as legal protections for alleged fugitives.[17] But Taney refused to allow antebellum realities to shape his interpretation of the nation's laws. He insisted that he

could not "give to the words of the Constitution a more liberal construction
. . . than they were intended to bear."[18] He ruled that a history of slavery and
exclusion defined the present and future of African Americans' legal status,
regardless of their political aspirations and achievements. Taney's chief aim
was to protect the institution of slavery and justify its expansion. But Taney
revealed his anxiety about black northerners when he denied the significance
of changed public opinion across the country. He wrote so forcefully and at
such length on the question of black citizenship in order to curtail the legal
possibilities the status held out for African Americans. The decision constituted an effort to restrict black voices to the margins in discussions of individuals' rights.[19]

As enslaved black people used the law to seek freedom, they destabilized
slavery and convinced the chief justice of the transformative potential of their
politics. Dred and Harriet Scott were part of a history of enslaved people
who sought and attained access to formal legal proceedings in pursuit of
freedom. They were two of nearly 300 enslaved people who sued for freedom
in Missouri before the Civil War. Each of those suits argued that black people
should have a formal relationship with American lawmaking authorities and,
in the approximately one-third that resulted in freedom, suggested that such
a relationship could threaten slave ownership.[20]

Freedom suits reflected the concerns of enslaved black people beyond
the South and carried meanings for legal developments across the country.
Scott's freedom suit was a claim for formal legal protections through citizen
status. It stood alongside northern black politics and sought the same broad
outcome—a legal connection between black people and governments in the
United States. Scott and his lawyers claimed a black person could be a citizen,
and they used the Constitution to say the status must entail the right to file
suit in federal court. Roger Taney recognized the political threads connecting
Scott to other black southerners in courtrooms and to black northerners in
protest meetings, and he looked to suppress their possibilities through his
ruling on Scott's case. Throughout the decision, Taney indiscriminately cited
legal restrictions on enslaved and free people, North and South. He argued
free black northerners were legally no different from Dred Scott, and he
believed denying Scott's freedom was also a threat to the politics of those
who were already free. One of Taney's chief aims was to ensure that no
African American could make legitimate claims on federal legal entities.

Taney focused nearly half of his opinion on denying black citizenship
because the status was such a potent political tool. To bolster his sweeping

argument, the chief justice cited an 1857 State Department pronouncement denying African Americans passports on the grounds that they were not citizens. Like Taney, those officials declared black people could not be citizens because various states restricted their rights. The State Department's decision was a direct response to a group of free black people who sought a specific legal privilege as citizens.[21] Taney's ruling gave that policy the legal sanction of the Supreme Court. African American activists transformed ideas and debates on citizen status and black people's rights. Roger Taney aimed to end those debates and secure slavery and racial exclusion for the United States.[22]

* * *

There was a compelling logic to the historical arguments at the center of Chief Justice Taney's ruling. He was right to dig for the roots of American racism in the soil of European colonialism and slavery. When the United States broke from England in 1776, and when its leaders crafted a constitution in 1789, few abandoned their convictions that black people were "ordinary articles of merchandise." Most of the nation's founders did see black people as different and inferior, and few denounced prevailing prejudices. As Roger Taney noted, white supremacy had profoundly shaped the nation's legal development.

But Taney's history of the United States was incomplete. The legal precedents he cited, such as the Constitution's fugitive slave clause and state laws against interracial marriage, did not explicitly exclude black people from all rights or deny the possibility that they could be citizens. He willfully ignored a history of black people engaging with legal processes and securing legal protections. In the late 1850s, black activists saw the opportunity to challenge white supremacy by complicating the chief justice's portrait of the past. They revised Taney's history, arguing that state and federal law offered explicit and implicit openings for them to secure legal protections. Taney's bad history provided a clear path for black activists to challenge *Dred Scott*.

William J. Watkins took a lead role in correcting Taney's history during the New York state convention of 1858. Watkins reported resolutions from the business committee to the convention as a whole for debate, and his list began with a direct statement about African Americans' legal position in the country. Black New Yorkers were gathered "for the security of the rights guaranteed to them, as part of '*the people*,' in the Constitution of the United States." They declared themselves "citizens of the State of New York, and, consequently, of the United States," in a direct rebuttal of Taney's central argument. The activists demanded "influence, as a political power," in the country's formal lawmaking structures. Like the chief justice, they looked to the past, citing the nation's legal foundation to prove their case. But rather than citing specific laws that secured their legal position, they spoke more broadly of "the theory of human rights set forth in the Declaration of American Independence" in support of their claims.[23]

These black New Yorkers, like the chief justice, were convinced that their arguments about the nation's history were urgent and legally significant beyond their own concerns. They had "a great work to perform in the conflict being waged between liberty and despotism." Resisting the chief justice upheld the ideal of equality on which the nation had been founded. Black New Yorkers called on others "to trample, in self-defence, the dicta of Judge Taney, beneath their feet." Preserving American freedom required people to oppose the decision, a judicial embodiment of the corrupt and dangerous influence of slavery. From their opening statement that black Americans were part of "the People," these black New Yorkers declared Taney's ruling inaccurate and illegitimate. Their approach suggested they knew the law better and were more suited to defend it than the chief justice. These were powerful claims to make in the midst of the sectional crisis of the 1850s as American people argued over and worried a great deal about how the federal government might influence their lives and shape the nation's future. In that context, black activists presented themselves as legitimate lawmakers by disparaging the chief justice. They worked to marginalize Taney and developed arguments that would encourage the continued fight for legal change. Their work at the Troy convention represented key elements of African Americans' responses to *Dred Scott.*

Black and white activists from across the North joined those New Yorkers in attacking Taney's legitimacy. In November 1858, delegates to an Ohio state convention echoed their colleagues to the east, urging people to "trample the Fugitive Slave Law and the dicta of the *Dred Scott* decision beneath our feet, as huge outrages."[24] Editors of a Boston religious newspaper joined the parade of disrespect, declaring "judges are not infallible." They continued, "We do not believe that this decision of the Supreme Court will command either respect or obedience." Judges should not attempt to "transcend their power to secure partisan ends," and it was particularly outrageous for a Supreme Court justice to do so. "The decision is an attempt to sanctify falsehood and injustice, and it cannot stand."[25]

White lawmakers joined the questioning of Taney's authority, including his colleague Justice Benjamin Curtis. After Taney delivered his opinion on May 6, Curtis read a dissent denying that Taney had the authority to supplant the limits Congress had imposed on slavery.[26] In the summer of 1857, a group of state senators in Maine asked their state supreme court to decide whether free black people could legally vote. According to Maine's constitution, all men could vote who were citizens of the United States and at least twenty-one years of age. But *Dred Scott* seemed to require Maine to disfranchise black men. The state supreme court ruled that no racial qualification existed for Maine's citizen status. Their ruling contradicted the claims of "high judicial authority," but nowhere in Maine's history could the justices find evidence of a racial suffrage restriction, and so, they said, black men were "citizens of the United States" based on state law and practice. Through the history of rights in their state, the justices made arguments about citizen status and explicitly challenged the U.S. Supreme Court.[27] And also like Taney, the Maine court used specific legal protections as evidence of a broad legal status.

The persistent uncertainty in the terms of citizenship made possible legal challenges to Taney's ruling. After *Dred Scott*, people in positions of power, like Maine's lawmakers, continued working to understand citizenship and to secure legal protections for black Americans. Taney was only one among many legal theorists opining on the terms of citizenship. But these challenges also helped instill further uncertainty about the nation's legal structures. The forceful, logical arguments lawmakers made to dispute the chief justice seemed to prove that the ruling was not definitive and urged others to question Taney's ideas about slavery and citizenship. The Maine decision could encourage black protest. Lawmakers' opposition to Taney helped preserve the uncertain legal space black activists had used to claimed citizenship and pursue rights through the status.[28]

At a black state convention held at the New Bedford City Hall in Massachusetts in the summer of 1858, activists took a number of steps to show their disregard for Taney's decision. Charles Remond informed his fellow delegates he was tired of political displays without substance, and he wanted "to see a position taken." He urged his colleagues to take "a defiant position . . . towards legislatures, and congresses, and supreme courts—never forgetting Judge Taney." Activists often declined to use Taney's proper title, choosing instead the diminutive "judge." They refused to acknowledge him as "chief" of anything, particularly justice. Remond was so angry "that he was prepared to spit upon the decision of Judge Taney." "Judge Taney was an old story," he admitted, but Remond felt "he could never say all he wanted upon the subject."[29]

Before the meeting began in city hall, black people claimed public space in ways that denied the authority of state legislators and federal judges who tried to formalize black exclusion. Delegates stood on Elm Street, in the heart of the city, and watched a parade of two black militias. Around ten o'clock on the morning of the convention, the New Bedford Blues greeted the Liberty Guard of Boston for events to commemorate West Indian Emancipation Day. Forty-five armed men marched through the city, accompanied by two brass bands from the nearby towns of North Bridgewater and Malden. These military companies organized, gathered, and marched in flagrant denial of a state law barring black people from joining or creating militias.[30] After a long day winding through "the principal streets" of New Bedford, the men continued on to Pope's Island, just off the coastline, "where a grand chowder was served up." Perhaps the summer weather was pleasant; convention visitors could also have watched a parade of black sailors that ended with a clambake in a park. These groups of black people luxuriated in the public space of New Bedford. On a day when activists gathered to protest the *Dred Scott* decision, black people declared through their public actions that formal legal statements would not confine them to the margins of society. The day's events amounted to a public show of disdain for legislated racial exclusion. Roger Taney had denied black citizenship but could not decisively exclude African Americans from the nation. Even black youths joined the work. The men of the Liberty Guard marched alongside "a company of colored boys, numbering some twenty or more, who were very neatly dressed."[31]

When black activists disregarded the decision or, like William Watkins, called Taney's decision "a foul and infamous lie," they put forth their own interpretations of the nation's history. Attacks on Taney's character did political work, pushing the chief justice to the margins of constitutional interpretation in order to make space for their claims about American law. To call the chief justice a liar was a vicious insult, perhaps even more outrageous than Remond's eagerness to spit on the decision. Much of early American political culture was built around personal reputation and honor, both of which grew out of an individual's trustworthiness.[32] Saying Taney had lied about the law encouraged people to continue seeking answers to questions about black people's legal status. And because the chief justice's ruling was rooted in his reading of American history, calling him a liar argued for an alternative past.

Taney said the country had been created as a white man's republic and that it must remain so, but African Americans insisted that the nation's laws had historically left room for black people to belong. Activists continued to make public statements about the terms of citizenship, building their political claims around alternative historical arguments. Attacking Taney's legitimacy made room for black citizenship politics.

A Fourth of July celebration in 1859 offered a tremendous opportunity for black activists to present their history of the United States. Members of the Banneker Institute gathered in Philadelphia that year to celebrate the eighty-third anniversary of the nation's independence and to denounce the chief justice. Founded in the early 1850s, the institute was a center for black literary and cultural development, sponsoring lectures, debates, and other intellectual events for black urbanites.[33] Jacob White, a Philadelphia teacher, opened the day's events with a speech in which he wondered whether black people had any reason to celebrate American freedom. How should they feel given the "supreme judicial decision" that at the nation's founding, black Americans "had no rights that others were bound to respect"? White informed listeners that the chief justice's position did not demand blind obedience to his claims. The decision demanded critical questioning because it purported to redefine the nation. "An opinion like this, emanating from a body of such learned men as compose our supreme court, should be examined with the greatest scrutiny." The Banneker Institute's decision to celebrate the founding denied Taney's claims that black people had never belonged in the United States. Further, Benjamin Banneker, the namesake of their institute who had helped design the nation's capital, revealed a history in which black Americans had been critical to national development and had earned positions of respect in the country. Jacob White's thesis was simple: "Ladies and Gentlemen, we have rights."[34]

White crafted his own history of the United States, citing alternative foundations to support his sweeping argument. The history of black military service was key to his claims. He celebrated the ideals of the Declaration of Independence, which he described as a document "for whose principles Attucks died." Although White's chronology was imperfect, he invoked Crispus Attucks, a black man killed in the Boston Massacre, to highlight black people's sacrifice and to show that African Americans joined the Revolutionary War because they believed the framers were sincere in the egalitarian words of the Declaration. One could read the nation's true principles in the blood of black men who fought to create it. White reminded his audience that black men had joined the founders in the fight for liberty and, in so doing, had forged an emotional connection linking black people with the United States through a shared history of struggle. And he encouraged his audience to enjoy a spirited celebration of their American history. Their revelry would "broadcast the doctrine of our American citizenship."[35]

William H. Johnson, the main speaker for the day, also crafted an argument through a history of the United States. He was skeptical of Taney's claim that the founders wrote powerful statements about equality while also intending to exclude black people. "Are you willing to believe that they were base enough to have invoked God's presence whilst they committed perjury?" he asked the delegates. Black and white people together had formed the nation and sanctioned its government. A history of cooperation belied "the new dogma which has just been put forth by the head of the Supreme Court."[36] The nation's history proved black people's Americanness and drove their legal challenge to *Dred Scott*. For Jacob White, the depth of his emotional connection to the United States, rooted in African American history, rendered the legal order Taney had proposed impossible. When black Americans slept, he said, they dreamt "of [their] rights as citizens," and they knew lawmakers excluded them only through "a strange perversion of the correct principles of legislation."[37]

Jacob White and William Johnson adapted Roger Taney's argumentative approach, using the nation's history to support their political argument about black people and American citizenship. Their approach had the power to change ideas about black people's legal status because it challenged Taney's narrative of absolute black exclusion across the nation's past. Activists did not intend to prove black people had never been marginalized. Instead, they looked to overcome their exclusion by showing that the nation's history made possible black legal inclusion. By using Taney's tactics and offering their historical narrative, White and Johnson presented the chief justice as a historian who had simply misread the nation's past.

Challenging Taney's history with their own facts and interpretations was key to black politics of the period. Delegates to the 1858 Massachusetts convention spoke about Crispus Attucks as well as Peter Salem, a former slave who joined the army and killed a British officer at the Battle of Bunker Hill. They noted that black soldiers had distinguished themselves in the years since the Revolutionary War, fighting at the Battle of New Orleans and on the Great Lakes during the War of 1812. The United States had declared war on Britain in 1812 in part as a response to the impressment of three sailors, "two

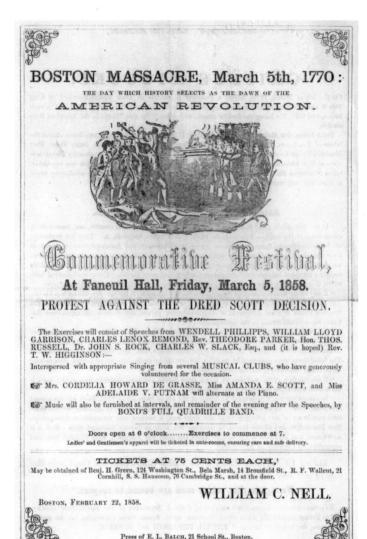

BOSTON MASSACRE, March 5th, 1770:

THE DAY WHICH HISTORY SELECTS AS THE DAWN OF THE

AMERICAN REVOLUTION.

𝕮𝖔𝖒𝖒𝖊𝖒𝖔𝖗𝖆𝖙𝖎𝖛𝖊 𝕱𝖊𝖘𝖙𝖎𝖛𝖆𝖑,

At Faneuil Hall, Friday, March 5, 1858.

PROTEST AGAINST THE DRED SCOTT DECISION.

The Exercises will consist of Speeches from WENDELL PHILLIPPS, WILLIAM LLOYD GARRISON, CHARLES LENOX REMOND, Rev. THEODORE PARKER, Hon. THOS. RUSSELL, Dr. JOHN S. ROCK, CHARLES W. SLACK, Esq., and (it is hoped) Rev. T. W. HIGGINSON:—

Interspersed with appropriate Singing from several MUSICAL CLUBS, who have generously volunteered for the occasion.

☞ Mrs. CORDELIA HOWARD DE GRASSE, Miss AMANDA E. SCOTT, and Miss ADELAIDE V. PUTNAM will alternate at the Piano.

☞ Music will also be furnished at intervals, and remainder of the evening after the Speeches, by BOND'S FULL QUADRILLE BAND.

Doors open at 6 o'clock........Exercises to commence at 7.
Ladies' and Gentlemen's apparel will be ticketed in ante-rooms, ensuring care and safe delivery.

TICKETS AT 75 CENTS EACH,

May be obtained of Benj. H. Green, 124 Washington St., Bela Marsh, 14 Bromfield St., R. F. Wallcut, 21 Cornhill, S. S. Hanscom, 76 Cambridge St., and at the door.

WILLIAM C. NELL.

BOSTON, FEBRUARY 22, 1858.

Press of E. L. BALCH, 21 School St., Boston.

FIGURE 7. "Boston Massacre, March 5th, 1770," Boston (1858). For several years during the 1850s, black Bostonians celebrated Crispus Attucks Day, a festival built around the Boston Massacre and the black man who died in the incident. To many black activists, Attucks, depicted at the center of the engraving, cemented African Americans' place in the nation at the moment of its origins. Combining this celebration with protest against *Dred Scott* offered a forceful rebuke to Taney's claims about black people's position in the nation.

of whom were colored—satisfactory proof, at least, that they were American citizens."[38] Black military history stood at the center of activists' challenges to *Dred Scott*. In Massachusetts, African Americans celebrated Crispus Attucks Day annually in the late 1850s. They observed Crispus Attucks Day on March 5, 1858, at Faneuil Hall, which had been a center of political activity during the revolutionary period and the origin point of Attucks's funeral procession after the Boston Massacre. Inside the hall, visitors found a display of artifacts from Attucks's life as well as gifts black revolutionary soldiers had received for their service.[39] In a series of speeches, activists praised Attucks for his courage in having made "the first move in the cold streets of a revolutionary epoch." William Cooper Nell, an early historian of black American soldiers, described Attucks as "the first to attack, and himself the first martyr" of the Revolution.[40] Crispus Attucks was central to the challenges that activists issued to Roger Taney. Black Bostonians planned the celebration "to commemorate the names and services of Colored Americans in the wars of their country, and to Protest against the Dred Scott Decision which denies them Citizenship." The blood of Attucks and other black forefathers entitled African Americans to legal protections.[41] William Watkins, speaking in Albany in February 1859, summarized this thread of black protest: "Whatever may be said of Justice Taney's law, he was certainly very wide of the mark in his facts of history."[42] African Americans saw how important the past was to Taney's decision. Revising Taney's own revisionist history refuted his argument that black Americans could not be citizens.

*   *   *

While many black northerners refused to accept Taney's portrait of the United States, others saw in *Dred Scott* a confirmation of their longstanding doubts about black life in the country. On learning of the opinion, some stood firm in their convictions that the nation's laws were designed to uphold slavery, and it pushed them to abandon efforts to establish a legal relationship with American governments. A number of prominent black activists considered and encouraged emigration from the country. Most black people chose to remain in the United States, but they took part in complex conversations about legal change in the country. African Americans' ideas about the purpose of the Constitution and the potential of the nation's laws shaped their responses to *Dred Scott*.

In May 1857, Robert Purvis delivered a speech explaining that Taney's ruling fit squarely within an established pattern of American law and government. Purvis spoke at the annual meeting of the American Anti-Slavery Society, the organization he had helped William Lloyd Garrison establish and which had for decades brought together abolitionists who rejected formal politics. In the immediate aftermath of Taney's ruling, Purvis felt assured of his ideas about American laws. "The doctrine of the anti-slavery character of the American Constitution," he said, "seems to me one of the most absurd and preposterous that ever was broached." Both "history and common sense" disproved that doctrine. Purvis said the chief justice had simply told the truth about the nation's racism, and he was disgusted with black activists who thought otherwise. He could not fathom a man who agreed to be "trampled upon and judicially declared to '*have no rights which white men are bound to respect*,' and then turn round and glorify and magnify the laws under which all this is done." He seemed perversely pleased with Taney's decision. The chief justice had confirmed Purvis's longstanding beliefs; the nation's government was proven to be an "atrocious despotism," both "in its formation and essential structure as well as in its practice." The rot of prejudice came from the nation's legal core. Purvis was glad for the opportunity to use Taney to prove the righteousness of his brand of antislavery. He suggested dramatic change outside the bounds of law might be necessary for black people's political aims, and he hoped his fellow abolitionists were prepared for such a struggle. "There is a prospect of this atrocious government being overthrown, and a better one built up in its place." Purvis was ready to take part "in the revolution" for which radical abolitionists had labored and that *Dred Scott* might spark.[43]

Other black activists agreed that the nation's racism came from its legal foundation, but they did not welcome potential revolution. Although William Still read truths in Taney's decision, he urged African Americans to leave the country rather than revolt against it. Only two weeks after Taney's ruling, Still, who had taken the reins of the Vigilant Committee of Philadelphia, described black Philadelphians' disheartened responses to the case. Before *Dred Scott*, black Americans had been hopeful in spite of themselves; many had refused to acknowledge "the proslavery usages and policy of this Government." But he criticized those activists who seemed optimistic. Some seemed to believe the decision would spark a unified push among white and black northerners toward racial justice, an idea Still found to be absurd. He seemed ready to accept Taney's argument that black people could never experience equality in the United States. "I confess," Still wrote, "I see but a faint prospect of any very great change for the better, at least in the present generation." The black Philadelphian echoed the sentiments John Russwurm had expressed before he left the United States for Liberia in 1829. Still's words were not as decisive as Russwurm's, but he did feel black people should look for a better future beyond the United States. He encouraged readers to go to Canada, where African Americans could be "in possession of all our rights—and citizen of the most powerful nation on earth." There, "all the immunities and privileges are as sacred to the black man as to the white."[44] Believing the legal protections Taney denied him were beyond his grasp at home, he turned his eyes abroad to continue the search.

Still explored his doubts about black life in the United States in a letter to Mary Ann Shadd Cary, a person who had years before left the country under a cloud of similar doubts. Shadd Cary was editor of the *Provincial Freeman*, a newspaper based in southwest Ontario, Canada. She had been born free in Delaware in 1823, then left the United States after the passage of the 1850 Fugitive Slave Act, hoping to aid those who fled to Canada in their search for freedom and community. She began publishing the *Provincial Freeman* in 1853 as a way to enable black Canadians to communicate with one another and to remain attuned to legal developments in the United States. Shadd Cary identified William Still as "Our Philadelphia Correspondent," inducting him into a black expatriate community although he still lived in the United States. Still was useful for Shadd Cary because his antislavery vigilance work concerned and connected black people on both sides of the border. But she did not need a correspondent in the United States to tell her readers what *Dred Scott* meant. As she looked south, she found reasons other than Roger Taney to doubt the government would provide black people with legal protections. Shadd Cary criticized the Republican Party's free labor ideology, which appealed to white northerners' anxieties about competing with enslaved people in the labor market. Antislavery politics in the United States often involved elements of white supremacy. She was especially outraged by a speech William Seward delivered in early 1857. He and other Republicans glorified white labor, always, Shadd Cary said, in contrast with "black African slave labor." Republicans denounced black slavery only in contrast with "free white labor," implying that black Americans could be nothing other than slaves. Seward's speech emphasized "distinctions of color," and it had been delivered before the *Dred Scott* decision. To the emigrant editor, Taney's ruling was simply part of its American context. Even when fighting slavery, white Americans did so in a way that marginalized black people, expressing concern not for those in bondage but for white people threatened by the increasingly sprawling exploitation of African Americans. Seward and the Republicans, together with Taney and the Democrats, represented racism so deeply ingrained in the United States that, to Shadd Cary, it was impossible for black people to seek a meaningful citizenship in the country.[45]

Ultimately, William Still did not follow Mary Ann Shadd Cary to Canada. He remained a key player in black Philadelphia's politics through the Civil War years.[46] Still and many others who thought seriously about leaving the United States after *Dred Scott* continued to seek avenues to secure a legal position in their native country. For instance, in 1858, Henry Highland Garnet organized the African Civilization Society, an organization whose title called to mind the old and persistent American Colonization Society. Garnet planned for his ACS to pursue missionary work in West Africa, and he thought of it as an emotionally fulfilling project for black Americans in the wake of *Dred Scott*. In promotional literature for the society, Garnet declared his love for Africa, "the land of his ancestors," and said individuals who chose to emigrate would help build "a Christian nation" and help improve the continent as a whole. Garnet confessed that he was disheartened by legal circumstances in his native country, and he "hoped to see a national flag yet of which he would be proud." Still, Garnet was careful about the society's aims. He refused to promote forced or mass emigration, and he hoped his ACS would serve as a tool to fight slavery and prejudice in the United States.[47] While he looked to other shores, Garnet remained interested in the possibilities of the United States, even after Justice Taney had denied any such possibilities existed.

Despite the brutal plainness of black legal exclusion and Roger Taney's efforts to make it permanent, most African Americans chose not to leave the United States. Many chose to remain because they continued to believe in the potential of their politics. They called Taney a liar, presented themselves as citizens, and persisted in their efforts to establish a legal relationship with American governments. Taney could not suppress the forms of black citizenship politics, and activists, along with white Republican lawmakers, ensured Taney would not stand alone in presenting arguments about the nation's laws. In a way, *Dred Scott* gave black politics more currency because it brought questions about the meaning of citizenship and black people's legal status to the center of sectional disputes of the 1850s. Even for black people who believed the Constitution was proslavery, *Dred Scott* sparked a renewed commitment to pursuing changes in the law. Among those activists was Charles Remond, a longtime ally of William Lloyd Garrison and an outspoken critic of the U.S. Constitution. But in the same speech in which Remond wished to spit on Taney's ruling, he attacked a fellow delegate who called for black migration to Canada. Remond "wouldn't hear of such a thing as liberty in Canada; he must have liberty in America."[48] William Wells Brown, also a Garrisonian ally, said the purpose of the Massachusetts convention was "to proclaim to the world that we have rights" and to call on the state legislature "to assume a defiant attitude towards the Dred Scott decision."[49] Although these activists believed the Constitution was fundamentally corrupt and proslavery and that Roger Taney had affirmed their reading, they remained committed to changing the nation's legal order. In their resolutions, convention delegates noted that Taney's decision contradicted the Privileges and Immunities Clause, using the terms of the Constitution to dispute Taney's proslavery vision. Remond and Brown felt bound to their native country. Brown declared black people were "Americans in every sense of the world," who would rely on "American climate . . . American government, and American manners to sustain their American bodies and minds."[50]

Black activists insisted on remaining in the United States because they saw that they could continue to challenge Taney's interpretation of the laws. They were encouraged by the possibility of using principles like the Privileges and Immunities Clause to make arguments about the terms of citizenship. Activists did not believe Roger Taney had the last word on the nature of American citizenship, and in the late 1850s, their political statements ensured his decision was not definitive. Calling the chief justice a liar and challenging his authority as a historian and constitutional interpreter were critical ways black people worked to sustain the possibility of legal change in the United States.

Alongside their work as constitutional interpreters, many free black northerners invoked their Protestant faith for encouragement and to help craft their arguments against *Dred Scott*. Protestant faith intertwined with historical and constitutional arguments to challenge Roger Taney. Delegates to the 1858 Massachusetts state convention said they possessed rights "not granted by the American Government, but by the creator." Faith helped sustain black activists in the late 1850s. Frederick Douglass explained the politics of his faith in May 1857, when he announced to an audience, "You will readily ask me how I am affected by this devilish decision—this judicial incarnation of wolfishness. My answer is . . . my hopes were never brighter than now." Douglass looked to other authorities. "The Supreme Court of the United States," he said, "is not the only power in this world. It is very great, but the Supreme Court of the Almighty is greater." His Christianity explained his optimism about black people's American lives.[51] For Douglass, this was not simply an expression of hope for a better life in the hereafter. His faith fostered a political statement in response to Roger Taney's denial of black rights, an argument that bridged his ideas about God and about the nation's laws. Douglass believed "the decision of the Most High" determined what was good and what was evil and that the egalitarian language of American founding documents put in writing the nation's commitment to goodness. Try as he might, Roger Taney could not "decide against God." Douglass's religious faith also manifested as a faith in the righteousness of the nation's legal system. The government was designed to encourage "the development of right ideas of liberty and humanity," empowering people to implement "comprehensive plans for the freedom and elevation of all the people of this country." Black religious faith encouraged a conviction that black people could secure change despite the edict of the chief justice.[52]

Some black ministers interpreted *Dred Scott* through their ideas about the divine and used their pulpits to challenge Roger Taney in the late 1850s. In the spring of 1857, congregants of Philadelphia's First African Presbyterian Church settled into their pews to hear a sermon from their pastor, William T. Catto. Reverend Catto had been born free in Charleston, South Carolina, around 1810. He was educated in an informal school in the South and, by the late 1840s, had become involved with local Presbyterians. Seeking opportunities to minister to black people, he settled in Philadelphia and rose through the ministerial ranks at the First African Presbyterian Church.[53] May 1857 marked that church's fiftieth anniversary, and Catto had prepared a sermon for the celebration. Like other black religious leaders, he linked African Americans with the biblical Israelites as large, faithful populations bound by tyrants and hoping for liberation.[54] Catto's sermon asked the congregation to look to the distant past for lessons to shape the future. In the book of Exodus, Moses convinced the pharaoh to liberate the Israelites. Moses then led them out of captivity in Egypt, where the Israelites set up a temporary camp near the Red Sea. But when the pharaoh changed his mind about freeing them and went in pursuit of his former captives, the Israelites blamed Moses for leading a failed Exodus. Reverend William Catto found in that moment the text of his sermon. According to Exodus chapter fourteen,

Moses prayed, and God responded: "Wherefore criest thou unto me? Speak unto the children of Israel that they go forward." The Israelites, Catto told his audience, "did go forward, their difficulties were removed, for the sea was made to part at the lifting up of Moses' rod over it."[55] From that story, the minister preached about the transformative possibilities of faith and offered a broad vision of the relationship between people and governments.

For Reverend Catto, the Bible offered a guide through contemporary problems. "What [was] to the children of Abraham, under their peculiar situation, may to the people of God, in this day, be as important."[56] His sermon was a message about how people overcame oppression with God's help by remaining faithful and actively pursuing deliverance. He preached his sermon two months after Taney delivered his opinion in the *Dred Scott* case, encouraging his congregants to continue working for legal change in the nation. The closest he came to a direct statement about the chief justice was his argument that citizenship was a set of responsibilities. "Regarding men as citizens, it cannot with any show of truth be said upon him there are no claims."[57] The Exodus story described a fruitful relationship between people and an authority figure. Moses was a divinely appointed instrument for the oppressed. The Israelites' "cries ascended to God, and he determined to deliver them." But the relationship imposed obligations on individuals, requiring them to "go forward" and, for black Philadelphians, requiring a continued push toward realizing the egalitarian potential of their nation's government. Black activists must take on the burden of ensuring that Taney's vision was not realized in the United States. Catto's sermon called for religious faith and for political action, asking the congregation to strive optimistically against Roger Taney's claims. The chief justice issued his decision as though it were definitive, but he could not make law without contest, and religious faith was one spur for black people's persistent opposition to his ruling.

*　*　*

The *Dred Scott* decision did not suppress African Americans' arguments about citizenship, but it did change some of the central priorities of black political work. After Taney's ruling, black people at times neglected their efforts to define the content of citizenship. Frederick Douglass used the nation's founding language and his own Christianity to protest *Dred Scott* in May 1857, but much of his speech was a response to Chief Justice Taney rather than a concrete argument about the terms of citizen status. Douglass described Taney's ruling as another imperfect settlement in the ongoing debates over slavery and black people's legal status in the United States. Taney "may decide and decide; but he cannot reverse the decision of the Most High." To support his claim, Douglass retold the history of the founding. "Your fathers have said that man's right to liberty is self-evident."[58] Douglass's pronoun choice echoed his Fifth of July oration and suggests the feelings of alienation with which he often struggled. But here, he saw the value in forcing white Americans to dwell on their connection to the founders' egalitarian language. The men who wrote and signed the Declaration of Independence were not fringe radicals but part of the American mainstream; they had framed a government in terms they felt represented popular sentiments.

Douglass said Taney was not a thoughtful interpreter of the Constitution but was instead similar to the radical abolitionist William Lloyd Garrison. He asked American people to see the chief justice as a fringe ideologue who had no place in the nation's lawmaking conversations. The Constitution had been designed to secure freedom and legal equality, Douglass argued, but Taney, like Garrison, incorrectly read the frame of government as a proslavery document. Taney and Garrison were among "those who seek slavery in the Union," but they and their supporters were "most woefully mistaken." The comparison aimed to push Taney, author of a "devilish decision," out of discussions about American laws. Douglass claimed the power to interpret the nation's law and history, presenting himself as a champion of the founders' vision against an array of corrupting forces. "Law is in its nature opposed to wrong," he proclaimed. Any exclusionary measure departed from "the general system of the law." Taney needed to find "an intention . . . expressed with irresistible clearness" in order to support his sweeping exclusion of black Americans from the benefits of the Constitution.[59]

Douglass's speech highlights central aspects of black people's responses to *Dred Scott* and points to their vital political potential. Activists worked to shift the ground of discussion about the nation's laws, to claim Taney and other proslavery ideologues should have no part in debating the future of slavery or the terms of citizenship. But in Douglass's multilayered argument for black citizenship, he did not say in specific terms what the status would mean for black people's legal lives. Rather than detailing the terms of citizenship, Douglass focused on explaining the reasons Taney was a liar.

The force of the denial of black citizenship from the Supreme Court compelled black activists to focus on claiming citizen status in whatever form

it might take. "We *are* citizens of the State of New York," convention delegates declared in 1858, "and, consequently, of the United States, and should
enjoy all the rights and immunities of other citizens."[60] But what criteria
made them citizens? And what were those rights and immunities? The *Dred
Scott* decision struck at the heart of antebellum black protest. As they worked
to indict Taney and deny the logic of his decision, the truth is that as a
ruling from the U.S. Supreme Court, it was a powerful legal statement that
compelled black people to do different kinds of political work. Taney's judicial position gave his opinion the weight of authority, and *Dred Scott* posed
a serious challenge to a particular strand of black politics.

Still, as they questioned Taney's personal character, his historical analysis,
and his legal reasoning, black activists emphasized that their voices mattered
in discussions about the nation's laws. Taney's decision responded to the real
potential of black people inserting their voices in lawmaking conversations.
In their responses to the ruling, black activists ensured that their longstanding
political forms could continue. The chief justice remained at the forefront of
black activists' political concerns until the sectional crisis turned to war. The
slaveholders' rebellion, sparked in part by Taney's sweeping proslavery claims,
would offer unprecedented opportunities for black men and women to solidify their positions in American communities, to build relationships with
American governments, and to make powerful claims through citizenship
that would influence the process of rewriting the laws of a broken nation.

CHAPTER 6

Black Politics and the Roots
of Reconstruction

On a gray December afternoon in 1863, William Still stood shivering on the exposed platform of a Philadelphia-bound streetcar. Perhaps he ruefully shook his head when the first snowflakes fell on his shoulders and the ride became "utterly intolerable." As the car rumbled south into the city, Still realized "that nowhere in Christendom could be found better illustration of Judge Taney's decision in the *Dred Scott* case." Standing in that cold satisfaction, he might have reflected on the limits of progress borne from decades of political struggle. He rode on the platform because state law allowed private rail companies to deny African Americans seats inside the streetcars that operated in and around Philadelphia. That afternoon, Still had boarded a nearly empty train with a white man he employed and paid two adult fares, at which point the conductor demanded that Still "step out on the platform." The demand was not a matter of personal choice, the conductor insisted; he was simply following rules requiring black exclusion that had been passed down from "the aristocracy." Still tried to explain why his exclusion was unjust: "I told him that I paid taxes, etc., but of course it was to no avail." And so William Still rode through the cold, into the snow, until he finally decided to step off the frigid platform and walk the remaining distance to his Philadelphia office.[1]

That streetcar ride was especially galling because Still had spent the morning visiting Camp William Penn, one of the earliest sites where black soldiers trained to fight with the Union army during the Civil War. His exclusion seemed to illuminate the depth of American hypocrisy, as a black man was forced into the cold after having spent the morning with a group of

African Americans who had pledged their lives on behalf of the nation. During and after the Civil War, William Still would stand at the forefront of a struggle for equal access to transportation in Philadelphia, a fight for new legislation that relied on examples of black men's valor and that intersected with larger debates about African Americans' changing legal status.[2]

In November 1865, two years after Still's wintry ride and a few months after the Union secured victory over rebellious southerners, black soldiers marched into Harrisburg, Pennsylvania, for a celebration of their service. Thousands of their black supporters from in and around the state capital took part, joined by large crowds of white people—"ladies and gentleman," according to news reports. The returning soldiers paraded on streets hung with evergreen arches and laudatory banners, including one that read, "He who defends freedom is worthy of all its franchises." Through these soldiers, black Pennsylvanians made arguments about their legal position in the nation. Black Union regiments became political tools for activists like William Still, and they helped African Americans capitalize on new opportunities to seek specific legal protections in the Civil War era.[3]

Black citizenship politics shifted, expanded, and changed in the 1860s. As they had in earlier decades, activists spoke out in public, demanding legal protections as citizens. But they practiced this politics in a different legal world. Over the course of the war, the federal government played a more direct role in individual Americans' lives and forged new relationships with black people. The presence of the Union army in the South and the laws Congress enacted helped structure the process of emancipation, presented the federal government as an authority that was concerned with African Americans' lives, and allowed black people to use that authority to their own ends.[4] In the Civil War era, black activists sought specific legal protections through their connection to a national government that was increasingly interested in and capable of changing their legal lives. Black people wanted the expansive, active federal government of the Civil War years to survive Appomattox and implement a robust set of legal protections for citizens.[5]

Black activists in the North had long fought slavery and worked to enrich the legal meaning of freedom, and they interacted in important new ways with some of the four million African Americans who gained freedom during the war. As they forged connections across regional lines, activists spoke to a national government that was grappling with the legal questions they had so long sought to answer. Legislating emancipation generated debates about the specific content of citizenship. Black activists thus encountered profound opportunities for their work to shape that status. By continuing to claim rights as citizens, African Americans shaped a radical transformation of the legal order. The political forms of the antebellum period played a critical role in molding the legal transformations of the Civil War era. In the 1860s, Republican lawmakers defined citizenship in ways that aligned with some of black people's longstanding political goals. But African Americans also recognized and critiqued the limits of legal change and continued to claim specific protections through citizenship. Understanding their efforts in the context of the Civil War era illuminates the lawmaking significance of free black northerners' politics. Further, it points to connections between black northerners and the freedpeople of the South, as together those groups would shape the fraught process of defining citizenship. The protest work of antebellum black activists is part of the broader history of African Americans navigating and influencing the legal terms of emancipation. Free black northerners laid the foundations for and helped craft the legal framework of Reconstruction.

*   *   *

Black people began using the history of black military service to claim rights as citizens long before the first guns fired on Fort Sumter. When black New Yorkers protested their disfranchisement in 1840, they noted that black soldiers had served and died in naval battles on the Great Lakes during the War of 1812. Black men's "bones have enriched the most productive lands of our country," they declared, and the nation's "liberties and privileges were purchased by the exertions and blood of our fathers."[6] The field of African American history has its roots in such politicized memories of black service. The black Bostonian William Cooper Nell spent two decades compiling stories of black military service and in 1855 published *The Colored Patriots of the American Revolution*, one of the earliest known histories of black people in the Americas. Nell opened his book with the hope that it could generate change, that it might "deepen in the heart and conscience of this nation the sense of justice" toward black people.[7]

White Americans valued martial behavior as a display of masculinity, and black people used their knowledge of that tendency in their politics.[8] As they invoked the history of black military service, some black people also created militia companies, in part to serve as tangible evidence of their masculine valor. Among those companies were the Attucks Guards, the Attucks

Blues, the Attee Guard, and the Attic Guards, with names that invoked Crispus Attucks, the black victim of the Boston Massacre, a cornerstone of black American military history. These organizations framed black Americans as descendants of Revolutionary War heroes and claimed for militiamen the mantle of noble fighters against tyranny.[9] In many cases, African Americans formed these military companies despite state laws that declared them illegal. When the U.S. Congress passed the Second Militia Act in May 1792, requiring "every free and able-bodied white male citizen" to be enrolled in the militia, it set a precedent for black exclusion from state militia companies.[10] In 1793, Massachusetts followed federal law by limiting militia enrollment to "able bodied white male citizens."[11] In 1839, when a group of women petitioned that state's legislature to remove "distinctions of color" from the laws, a legislative committee defended the measure, describing it as a blessing because it "releases the colored citizen from the burden of service."[12]

But as they did in other cases, African Americans broke laws when they thought it politically useful to do so. On an autumn afternoon in 1857, a group of black men calling themselves the Liberty Guard met at their armory at the intersection of Boston's Cambridge and Joy streets. They organized into ranks and began a set of maneuvers, preparing for a parade through the city. Their uniforms—black from head to toe—would have made the fifty men of the Liberty Guard a distinctive spectacle. Perhaps their bayonets shined in the sun, presenting a striking contrast to their dark clothing. Lewis Gaul, captain of the militia company, understood that their march would anger the public and perhaps state lawmakers as well. Before the parade, Gaul, who worked in Boston as a coachman, instructed the company to "disregard every insult that might be thrown at them by the jealous and rowdy white folks." Shouldering their weapons, the militiamen marched up Cambridge Street, cheered by a number of "highly elated" black supporters. They proceeded to the Massachusetts State House, where they displayed their polish and skill in maneuvers as well as their lack of concern about breaking the law. But as the parade continued, Captain Gaul's predictions proved true. The Liberty Guard attracted a group of angry white followers who taunted the militiamen and the black people present to witness the march. These white Bostonians insulted the guardsmen and attacked their black supporters. First, the rowdies threw pebbles and stones, then they charged on the Liberty Guard's black followers with clubs. The white crowd overwhelmed the militia's black supporters. But when the rioters ripped bricks from the street and threw them at the guardsmen, the militia broke ranks and chased their attackers off the Boston Common, with a few militiamen "fleshing their bayonets in the posteriors" of the slowest assailants. Lewis Gaul urged the victorious Liberty Guard back into their ranks and led their return to Cambridge Street, completing the day's parade.[13]

The violence did not dampen the day's celebratory spirit. In the evening, the guardsmen hosted a party at Faneuil Hall, where they dined on "coffee, pies, apples, and ice creams" and danced with women who had helped organize the parade and the celebration. For all that revelry, the highlight of the celebration came close to midnight when Sarah Hill, who had been chosen to represent the black women at the party, presented the Liberty Guard with a handmade banner. Addressing the gathering, Hill acknowledged that the militiamen were essentially outlaws, barred from receiving a state charter, but she relished the power of their parade, which "proved that you can exist without" legal sanction. Despite injustice and in the face of attack, Captain Gaul and his men had "behaved like gentlemen; and true, brave soldiers." Hill reminded the black people present that they should not be defined by their legal exclusion. She embraced ideas of respectability and masculinity that were central to politicizing valor. But Hill and the other women present worked alongside the guardsmen to claim legal protections through a black militia. The banner Hill presented to the Liberty Guard embodied the multiple kinds of labor involved in arguing that African Americans were critical to the survival of the republic and in claiming citizen status through military valor. Her gift was a silk banner that black Bostonians had won as a tribute to their service during the Revolutionary War; it featured an eagle and a shield representing the United States. Perhaps Hill or another black woman had carefully preserved that banner, stored apart from everyday linens and awaiting an opportunity to make a political statement. Hill had sewn the name "Liberty Guard" into the silk, using the black militia to insert African Americans into the national fabric. After the banner presentation, the band played "The Girl I Left Behind Me," a traditional American march that offered a gendered salute to Hill and other women supporters.

The day's events also inserted black politics into the process of crafting American laws. Lewis Gaul, Sarah Hill, and the other black men and women who took part in the celebration understood that the militia and its parade were not legal. The guardsmen had to fight off those who would exclude them from the republic, those invested in the racialized power structure that outlawed black militias. Both federal and state militia laws explicitly framed participation as the province of white male citizens. By organizing the Liberty

Guard and marching in public, the activists rejected these exclusions, in effect arguing that they were citizens and, as such, were entitled to public space and to a legal relationship with the state and federal governments. As they had in protecting alleged fugitive slaves, black people broke the law in demanding rights for themselves as American citizens. The men who signed up for the militia and the women who supported them announced that military participation should entitle black people to a place within the legal community. Activists understood and expressed this idea in various ways in the antebellum years, and they had powerful new opportunities to do so as the nation once again went to war.

*   *   *

At the outbreak of the Civil War, a chorus of black activists urged African Americans to take up arms in the fight against rebellious slaveholders. Confederate forces bombarded Fort Sumter beginning in the early morning hours of April 12, 1861. The following week, Alfred M. Green, a black teacher and activist in Philadelphia, published a letter on the political possibilities of black service. Green was no stranger to radical politics, having been arrested in March 1860 during an attempt to rescue fugitive slave Moses Horner from a carriage bound for Baltimore and a return to bondage.[14] Now Green considered the transformative potential of black soldiering in a new American war. In a letter he wrote on April 20, he acknowledged that black men's bravery in the past had "failed to bring us into recognition as citizens." Still, Green urged African Americans to seek the duty of defending the country because doing so held out the possibility that they could secure legal protections. The Civil War was "an auspicious moment" for renewing "claims upon the justice and honor of the Republic," he wrote.[15] Green argued that martial valor could establish a new legal relationship between black Americans and government authority. Joining the war effort would allow black people to make their strongest claims yet to rights as citizens.

Many free black people were eager for a fight against slaveowners and to pursue the political opportunities of service with the U.S. military. In April 1861, black men responded to President Lincoln's call for volunteers by forming militia companies and volunteering at recruitment offices in northern cities. But Lincoln had announced that his chief goal was to preserve the union; he instructed recruiters to reject black volunteers because enlisting African Americans might suggest the war was a fight against slavery. White

COME AND JOIN US BROTHERS.
PUBLISHED BY THE SUPERVISORY COMMITTEE FOR RECRUITING COLORED REGIMENTS
1210 CHESTNUT ST. PHILADELPHIA.

FIGURE 8. "Come and Join Us Brothers," Philadelphia (c. 1863). Likely produced during the push for black enlistment that followed the enactment of the Emancipation Proclamation, this broadside issued a forceful call for black men to join the fight and to embody a nobility and manhood that activists hoped would enhance their claims to legal protections as citizens. Prints and Photographs Division, Library of Congress.

northerners generally opposed a war on behalf of the enslaved or in pursuit of black people's rights. Lincoln also hoped to keep proslavery border states from joining the Confederacy.[16] Still, black men tried to enlist, and Frederick Douglass was among those who continued to encourage them to volunteer. In May 1861, Douglass received a letter from a person who wanted to form a black regiment in New York with funding from abolitionists and the state government. "Before we get through with the war," the correspondent wrote, "every man, black or white, able and willing to carry a musket, will be wanted." Douglass agreed, but he also acknowledged, "Those of our number who have offered our services to the Government, have been coldly turned away." In the first years of the war, Douglass understood, black men must fight against Lincoln's exclusionary policy in order to fight against Jefferson Davis's slave-owning rebels. Still, Douglass encouraged black men "to drink as deeply into the martial spirit of the times as possible." He urged African Americans to continue "casting about for an opportunity to strike for the freedom of the slave."[17]

Over the next two years, black people continued organizing and volunteering, and the U.S. government continued to refuse their offers. In the fall of 1861, with rebel armies frustrating U.S. officials, Douglass wrote that black enlistment would give the war a necessary sense of purpose and "would revive the languishing spirit of the North."[18] Some federal officials seemed to agree, including Secretary of War Simon Cameron, who called for the enlistment of enslaved black men, arguing that slaveowners had forfeited their property rights by rebelling. But Lincoln forced Cameron to edit those ideas out of his annual report on the war.[19] And in 1862, when Union generals formed regiments of black volunteers in the occupied areas of Louisiana and South Carolina, Lincoln declined their service and ordered the units disbanded.[20]

Lincoln harbored doubts about African Americans' future in the United States, and in August 1862, he invited a group of black men to the White House and urged them to support emigration. Lincoln asked the men—largely ministers he felt were ideologically pliable—to convince other African Americans to voluntarily leave the country. "But for your race among us there could not be war," he declared. Removing black people, he suggested, would solve American problems.[21]

Lincoln's racial pessimism influenced wartime policy. In the preliminary Emancipation Proclamation that he issued on September 22, 1862, he called on Congress to continue exploring the potential colonization of black Americans "with their consent." Similarly, in the annual message to Congress he

delivered in December, Lincoln declared plainly, "I strongly favor colonization." Lawmakers at the highest level questioned the possibility of an African
American future, and Lincoln's efforts to encourage Congress and black
Washingtonians to support colonization sanctioned persistent efforts to
exclude black people.[22] This was the ideological and political context in
which African Americans had to operate as they pursued freedom and formal
rights during the Civil War. When activists struggled for the opportunity to
enlist and to be seen as useful contributors to the war effort, they fought
against the persistent belief that black people could not be equal members of
American communities.

In the face of those rejections, a number of activists urged black men not
to volunteer. The history of African Americans fighting in the service of the
United States but remaining excluded convinced many that they should not
risk their lives for the thin hope of securing legal change. In the pages of the
Pine and Palm, the white abolitionist James Redpath printed statements from
black people urging their brethren not to seek military service. He published
those letters because he was promoting black migration to Haiti, but African
Americans wrote to him to express their reluctance to serve regardless of how
they felt about leaving the country. Henry Cropper, captain of a black militia
company known as the Frank Johnson Guards, informed readers of the *Pine
and Palm* that neither he nor his fellow militiamen had joined black Philadelphians who had rushed to volunteer immediately after Fort Sumter. Members
of Cropper's militia had "more knowledge of our duty, and also more dig-
nity" than those who were so eager to serve. State laws and federal practice
only allowed white men to serve in the military, and so it was "absurd"
for black men to volunteer. Legal barriers to black enlistment bolstered the
arguments of people like Cropper who discouraged black volunteers.[23]

Redpath printed similar letters from across the free states. A correspondent in Ohio mocked those who tried to volunteer, saying that they
attempted to join a fight to defend "the laws that bind the slave." From New
Jersey came a letter that described the rush to enlist as "evidence of weakness
and want of foresight." A New Yorker urged black men to go to Haiti rather
than "hanging around [Union] camps in menial positions."[24] In the *Pine and
Palm*, black people argued against fighting a war for the Union because state
and federal governments had for so long denied them rights and protections.
They proclaimed that the Civil War was not a fight for African Americans.
But as they discouraged volunteers, these black people also implicitly
sketched a specific kind of exchange for African American service. People on

both sides of the debate over black voluntarism agreed that black Americans were entitled to rights and that the federal government's obligation was to protect those who would enlist in its defense.[25] Black military service must be linked to legal change, suggested those who wrote to the *Pine and Palm*, and their critiques might therefore change the ways lawmakers thought about their obligations to African Americans. Such arguments against enlistment lay the groundwork for transformations of the legal order that characterized the postwar period.

Black men had good reason to doubt their military service would solve the problems of American racism, but as the federal government conducted the war effort, lawmakers took halting steps toward the kind of legal change for which activists had long called. Over the course of the war, the federal government established new legal relationships with black people. The process of war helped produce freedom and political opportunities for black activists to shape the content of American citizenship. In the war's opening months as African American men were turned away from recruitment offices and the Union lines, enslaved black people acted in ways that forced changes in government policy. In the spring of 1861, a few enslaved people fled plantations and made their way to Union troops at Fortress Monroe, near Hampton, Virginia. There, they encountered General Benjamin Butler, who recognized that runaway slaves could offer a tactical advantage in the war. Butler declared the fugitives "contraband of war," and in August 1861 and July 1862, Congress passed confiscation acts that legislated that doctrine and made the army by law a vehicle for black freedom. These measures encouraged more enslaved people to run to Union lines.[26]

Beyond the occupied South, the confiscation acts encouraged black people who hoped the war might transform their legal status. Enacting the policy of confiscation forged a new kind of bond between enslaved black people and the federal government, an important early step in what would be a rapid, dynamic process of building a robust legal relationship. Black people who fled slavery quickly proved their usefulness to the Union army and encouraged officers like Butler to ensure that runaways were not sent back to slaveowners. Escaped slaves provided information about southern terrain and Confederate troop movements, dug ditches and erected fortifications, cooked meals, washed clothes, and moved and buried bodies—they did all the work necessary to facilitate a massive and growing war effort. Congress passed the confiscation acts in response to black people pursuing their freedom and contributing to the war effort, and they initiated a process through which

FIGURE 9. "[Bermuda Hundred, Va. African-American teamsters near the signal tower]" (1864). These black men, identified as former slaves, did essential work with the Union Army, carting military supplies in central Virginia in the late stages of the war. While some black activists anticipated the potential glory of black men taking up arms for the cause of freedom, others understood that black enlistees might be greeted with this reality of hard labor and expressed doubts as to whether African American men should offer themselves for this type of Civil War service. Civil War Photographs, 1861–1865, Prints and Photographs Division, Library of Congress.

African Americans could seek out federal authorities in pursuit of legal protections.[27]

The actions of fugitive slaves and the policy of confiscation together accelerated the process of building a legal relationship between black Americans and the federal government. Black people's multifaceted political work helped generate a rapid series of transformations in the legal connection between African Americans and the government.[28] And the work black people did with the Union army helped push federal officials to develop the connected policies of black enlistment and emancipation more than two years after southern states began to secede. Faced with enduring rebellion and Confederate military successes, Lincoln came to see, as Douglass and others had said, that dismantling slavery would bolster the Union war effort. He announced his preliminary Emancipation Proclamation in September 1862, and it took effect on January 1, 1863. The proclamation freed enslaved people in all areas of the Confederacy that were still in rebellion and allowed for the enlistment of formerly enslaved and free black men in the army. Small numbers of black men had served in the Union navy as early as August 1861, but the formal opening of the army's ranks to African Americans greatly increased black enlistment. Ultimately, close to 200,000 African Americans served in the Union forces during the war.[29]

Both of these processes, born out of the exigencies of war, expanded the reach of the federal government, connected it to black people, and deployed federal power in ways that could provide them with legal opportunities. For activists like Frederick Douglass, they were steps toward justice that had long been denied. He said these changes made real the truth of the Constitution, which recognized no distinctions among slaveholders and slaves, black and white: "all are citizens who are of American Birth."[30] Douglass understood the broad legal implications of military policies, even when they were not explicitly aimed at making black men citizens. Lincoln affirmed black men's place in the national community by calling on them to fight in its defense. And Congress established ties with black people that were, to Douglass and others, key steps toward their aim of a redefined legal position in the country. Black men, Douglass suggested, were fighting to solidify and define a new, formal bond with the federal government.

* * *

The black men who wore Union blue would be essential to black politics because so many white Americans, North and South, continued to reject the proposition that African Americans were entitled to legal protections. In July 1862, on the same day that Congress passed the second confiscation act, they agreed to a new Militia Act. Together those laws resulted in black soldiers being paid less than white soldiers for their service. The Militia Act authorized black men to serve in the military as both soldiers and laborers, but Lincoln did not formally act to include black soldiers until 1863. When black men joined the military, they were paid the $10 monthly wage set for black laborers under the terms of the second confiscation act. In 1863, when black men began enlisting as soldiers, they were still paid $10 a month while white soldiers earned $13 each month. This disparity initially resulted from a kind of legislative accident, but it suggested the ways inequality might persist in the changing legal relationship between black people and the federal government.

Black activists at home and black soldiers in the field made clear their opposition to unequal pay. The terms of their developing relationship with the government were unjust, and they appealed to their value as soldiers to change their legal position. In Baltimore, a group of black Methodist ministers met with current and former Maryland state lawmakers in March 1864 to push for a broad set of rights. Reverend J. P. Campbell informed the white officials that "the colored man of Maryland wants free soil, free speech, free men, and no slaves, with equal pay, equal bounty, equal pensions, equal rights, equal privileges, and equal suffrage." He integrated the desire for soldiers' equal pay with the pursuit of political access on the home front and after the war's anticipated end.[31]

In 1863 and 1864, members of the Fifty-Fourth and Fifty-Fifth Massachusetts regiments refused to accept their unequal wages. James Henry Gooding, a corporal in the Fifty-Fourth regiment, wrote to President Lincoln to remind him that black soldiers had taken on the same burdens and offered the same sacrifices as their white counterparts. "The patient Trusting Descendants of Africs Clime have dyed the ground with blood, in defense of the Union, and Democracy," he noted. Black men had proven themselves "obedient and patient, and Solid as a wall." Gooding posed a simple question to the commander-in-chief: "We have done a Soldier's Duty. Why can't we have a Soldier's pay?"[32] As the pay inequality remained unresolved, members of the Fifty-Fifth Massachusetts Regiment wrote to Lincoln in July 1864. They explained that they had refused to accept unequal pay on principle but also reminded the president that their chief concern was Union victory: "to us money is no object; we came to fight For Liberty justice & Equality. These are gifts we Prise more highly than Gold." Still, they would not accept unequal wages. Seventy-four men who signed the letter requested back pay and asked for their "immediate Discharge[,] Having Been enlisted under False Pretence."[33]

On the same day that the soldiers of the Fifty-Fifth Regiment demanded equal wages, the *Christian Recorder* printed a letter from James Jones, ward master of a New Orleans hospital for the Eighth U.S. Colored Heavy Infantry, which criticized the limits of justice during the Civil War. "As soldiers," he said, "we have little cause of complaint, if we except the gross injustice being practised upon us by the Government in refusing to pay us more than seven dollars per month." Jones might have been particularly disheartened because unequal pay persisted amid tremendous legal change. From his camp in the South, he had learned of "slaveholders, sitting in the slaveholding city of New Orleans, adopting a clause to their Constitution which at once and forever abolishes slavery." But Jones remained hopeful, writing that he and his comrades had a keen sense of "our duty as colored men and as citizens of the United States." Winning battlefield success, he anticipated, might help secure equal pay and a wider set of legal changes in the nation.[34]

James Jones and the soldiers of the Fifty-Fifth Regiment might not have heard news from Washington, but as they were crafting their protest statements, Congress agreed to equalize black soldiers' pay in a measure they enacted on July 12, 1864. The *Christian Recorder* had reported on rumblings from the nation's capital as Congress moved toward a new militia law. "This is right, and never should have been any other way," the editors noted. The decision to provide equal pay and back pay for withheld wages marked the lawmaking possibilities of black protest in the Civil War era.[35] As black people had in the antebellum North, they made public demands for government action, showing themselves as critical contributors to the nation. In the context of the war, the federal government heard their claims and enacted legal change to redress their grievances. Black protest could work in important ways in the Civil War era because of the new connections that were developing between African Americans and the federal government.

Old prejudices and policies stood poised to limit the legal opportunities of the Civil War era, but the black convention movement endured and expanded as a result of the conflict, offering a vehicle to organize African American protest. The antebellum forms of citizenship politics emerged in powerful ways in the South during and after the war as African Americans endeavored to shape the legal changes of the era. Freed men and women recognized the uncertainties of their status, and some began working to shape lawmaking conversations about their new place in the country. The Civil War era created new opportunities for a range of black politics across the South, as African Americans challenged the authority of slaveowners, sought justice for violence perpetrated against them, claimed control in formal government through connections to the Republican Party, and organized for education and economic self-sufficiency.[36] One strand of black southerners' politics involved organizing conventions that extended the political work black people did in the antebellum North by making public demands for rights and protections as citizens.

During and after the Civil War, activists organized political conventions designed to capitalize on the opportunities of the moment and to connect black northerners and southerners. Free and freed black people together worked toward formal political rights in the aftermath of emancipation. In August 1865, black people held a state convention in the lyceum of Alexandria, Virginia. The lecture hall had opened in 1839, but during the war, the Union army appropriated it and converted it to a hospital before making parts of it available to groups like these black activists, a radical change from its origins. More than fifty delegates, many of whom identified themselves as freedmen, came together for the meeting. The activists must have understood the significance of holding the convention just a few miles from Washington, D.C., where federal lawmakers were debating plans and laws related to emancipation.[37] But as the proceedings began, delegates addressed the distinctive challenges and dangers they faced as a result of gathering in a former Confederate state. In his opening remarks, George Cook from Norfolk, Virginia, reported that some white southerners had tried to pay people they had once owned to stay away from the convention. Others tried to warn away potential delegates, saying "that coming here would hurt us at home." But Cook relished the high stakes of their activism, declaring that he would "exert [him]self to secure the franchise in every way that is honorable and just." "If I die in the attempt," he continued, "my children will reverence me for it the more."[38]

George Cook anticipated that the convention could help secure black voting rights in what had been the largest slaveholding state and one of the most important for the slaveholders' rebellion. Such was the radical potential of organized black politics after the Civil War. In the face of mortal danger, activists in Virginia pushed for sweeping legal change that would give substance to their uncertain new status as freedpeople. "We claim," the delegates announced, "as citizens of the State, the laws of the Commonwealth shall give to all men equal protection." They called for a meaningful relationship with the state government, one that would allow any man to "appeal to the law for his equal rights without regard to the color of his skin." And they argued that the franchise was essential to that status, that it could serve as a tangible marker of the bond between citizen and state. The activists also looked beyond Virginia, calling the right to vote "the privilege of the nation," with roots in the Declaration of Independence. They were "natives of American soil" and "citizens of the country," they contended.[39] Their claims to a connection with the government of Virginia were also claims for a connection to the U.S. government for themselves and for all other black Americans. These activists presented a broad vision of postwar legal change through citizen status. They claimed that status on the basis of nativity, attached to it the specific privilege of voting, but also hoped to maintain its breadth as a means to secure equal protection. They continued the antebellum project of building citizenship through claims to rights, but now they did so in the former slave state of Virginia and with a new optimism born of Union victory in the war. George Cook and others had witnessed and experienced the process of emancipation aided by federal authority; they knew that the federal government could exert its will to transform the nation and that government power could be used to defend black people's interests.

The Virginia activists invited honorary delegates to their meeting, including Henry Highland Garnet, an experienced participant in black conventions and a figure whose presence linked postwar southern conventions with those from the antebellum North. They made clear that the convention reflected black Virginians' concerns and was not the product of their "northern friends."[40] Still, the fact and form of the convention revealed ideological and strategic connections that crossed the Mason-Dixon line.[41] Freedpeople in Virginia called themselves citizens, worked to specify the content of that status, and made their claims in public, hoping to influence ongoing debates over the nation's laws. Black Virginians saw value in linking their politics to that of black northerners and extending the aims of antebellum protest. Garnet's presence thus pointed to both continuities of political forms and the geographical expansion of black citizenship politics. War and emancipation had helped to shape forms of black politics emerging in Virginia in 1865. In the late 1850s, Garnet had organized the African Civilization Society, which focused on missionary work in West Africa. After *Dred Scott*, he had come to harbor serious doubts about the possibilities of black people's lives in the

United States. But at the outbreak of the Civil War, he had abandoned the work of his ACS, seeing that the conflict could be an opportunity to rebuke Chief Justice Roger Taney's vision and transform the United States into a nation that would secure black rights.[42]

And so Garnet went to the Virginia convention in the hope of spurring broad legal change for black Americans. He would have found much of the proceedings familiar, but he might have been surprised when the secretary brought to the convention floor a death threat that had been mailed from Washington. "Beware! Beware! Beware!" the message read. "Fields Cook, you and other negroes will die before the autumn leaves fall. . . . You are never to be on an equality with the whites. . . . many of you will die soon if this Freedmen's Convention &c., &c., continues. . . . The South must and shall be avenged!" The threat denied that legal change was possible and suggested that the federal government could not assert its power decisively over rebellious former slaveowners. Fields Cook was a Baptist minister in Richmond and a former slave who had purchased his freedom in the 1840s. He brushed off the threat, declaring, like his colleague George Cook, that he would gladly offer his life "in the discharge of his duty." Garnet joined these men in dismissing the threat. He denounced its author as "a mean, contemptible coward," one among thousands of white southerners with murderous feelings, none of whom would "dare to accomplish what they threatened." Some of the other delegates were less convinced the threat was empty, and a brief debate ensued about how they should respond or what steps they might take to protect themselves. In the end, though, "the letter was thrown under the table by a unanimous vote," and the activists bolstered that defiance by filling the meeting hall with the sounds of "My Country 'Tis of Thee."[43]

The author of the anonymous threat denied the potential of black people's politics and claimed that they would meet violent resistance if they tried to change their legal lives as Americans. As Garnet noted, the threat may have been toothless, but it presaged critical forms of white supremacist politics that emerged after emancipation. White southerners felt especially threatened by efforts on the part of black people and the federal government to remake the laws of their society, and they would brutally suppress those efforts, determined to re-create the legal and social order that had characterized "the South" before the Civil War. The convention delegates rebuked that threat with a hymn of belonging, an unofficial national anthem with lyrics that celebrated freedom and asserted the singers' title to the joys of the "sweet land of liberty." The author of the threat recognized that Union victory in war had made possible this black political convention in Virginia. Black activists understood that connection as well, and they took the opportunity to try to secure further legal changes that would formalize their feelings of belonging in the nation. The war helped African Americans move longstanding forms of citizenship politics to new places and brought the ideas of that politics to the center of national discussions about postwar change.

As they did in Virginia, black people in Tennessee worked together in pursuit of formal political rights with tactics similar to those black northerners had used but that reflected the distinctive opportunities of the war. By the end of February 1862, Tennessee's rebel government had collapsed and the state was largely under Union control for the remainder of the war, which provided black people extensive opportunities to build relationships with federal officials and prove their value to the war effort.[44] In January 1865, a group of 59 African Americans looked to capitalize on their service, demanding equal suffrage as a pillar of the new Constitution state lawmakers were tasked with developing. The petitioners identified themselves as "American citizens of African descent, natives and residents of Tennessee, and devoted friends of the great National cause." Loyalty was central to their claims, and they repeatedly emphasized that "there have been white traitors in multitudes in Tennessee," while black southerners remained dedicated to the Union cause. They said that black enfranchisement was a necessary part of the defense of the United States. "If we are called on to do military duty against the rebel armies in the field," they asked, "why should we be denied the privilege of voting against rebel citizens at the ballot-box?" The petitioners presented their demands as part of a vision for a transformed legal order, arguing that black suffrage was essential in order to "abolish the last vestige of slavery." And they put forth a thorough definition of the terms of citizenship. Black people had proven themselves "good law-abiding citizens" through their multifaceted service to the nation: "praying for its prosperity, rejoicing in its progress, paying its taxes, fighting its battles, making its farms, mines, workshops and commerce more productive." Having taken on these obligations, they asked a simple question about what they presented as a critical right of citizenship: "why deny them the right to have a voice in the election of its rulers?"[45]

When state lawmakers refused to act on their petition for the vote, black Tennesseans organized a convention to further emphasize their demands. On August 7, 1865, Sergeant H. J. Maxwell of the Second Battery, U.S. Colored Light Infantry spoke in pursuit of "life and liberty," which he declared "meant to share in the Government by which they were protected." Maxwell was among many soldiers who attended that convention and enhanced claims to rights based on military service. "We want two more boxes, beside the cartridge box," Maxwell proclaimed, "the ballot-box and the jury box. We shall gain them."[46]

In the aftermath of the Civil War and emancipation, black people both North and South felt renewed optimism and a sense of their political potential. In numerous protest statements, they outlined what would become central aspects of the postwar legal changes that the federal government enacted. Activists from across the country came together for a meeting of the National Equal Rights League, held in Cleveland in October 1865, which extended the ideas of antebellum conventions and integrated newly free black southerners into the movement. At the meeting, James Henry Harris, who had once been enslaved and was now a teacher in Raleigh, North Carolina, declared that "the elevation of the Negro depends upon his own right arm," the arm that had helped to crush the slaveholders' rebellion. Reflecting on that service, John Richards of Detroit demanded that the federal government extend suffrage to freedmen in the South. "As colored men have fought to defend and perpetuate the unity of this Government," he argued, "every principle of honor demands that they should be placed on a footing with other citizens."[47] Richards and others said that black suffrage would help prevent a return to white supremacist government in the South, but they also argued that legal change must follow from the costly war. Only a legally robust freedom could give meaning to the deaths of the hundreds of thousands of American people who had defended the Union.

Black activists' central goal was to forge a relationship with the federal government that would provide them with rights and equal access to legal authorities. At the National Equal Rights League (NERL) meeting, D. B. F. Price of Cairo, Illinois, called for a legal status that would defend against exclusion or oppression. He and other black people in Illinois had been subject to "continued outrages" at the hands of "rebel sympathisers," he testified. Standing before the crowd, Price lifted his shirt and "exhibited marks from wounds received at their hands." Price thus embodied the immediate physical danger black Americans faced, as well as the broader difficulties of freedom without legal protection. But Price remained optimistic, hoping that the NERL would "secure the rights of colored American citizens," and perhaps was convinced that his wounds would show federal lawmakers how important it was to build a substantive relationship with black people.[48]

Black Americans recognized opportunity in the dynamic legal order of the Civil War era and in the expansive federal government that had defeated southern rebels. They claimed specific protections and presented a broad vision of legal change for the nation, built on their continuing arguments about the terms of citizenship. They demanded that the federal government play an active role in American people's lives. Wartime developments encouraged many of them to believe that the U.S. government could change fundamentally, that it could become a vehicle to protect African Americans' freedom and secure their rights.

In early 1866, black activists in the Pennsylvania State Equal Rights League sent a message to the U.S. Congress in the interest of specifying the terms of their uncertain new status. The Thirteenth Amendment, ratified in December 1865, raised questions about the legal position of four million newly freed African Americans. Black Pennsylvanians sent to Congress a series of demands for legal change that would give texture to black freedom. Three men—William Nesbit, Joseph Bustill, and William Forten—signed the message, but they had been chosen to represent dozens who had gathered to discuss their concerns. The signers claimed a broader mantle, identifying themselves as "the representatives of the disfranchised of this country." Perhaps the shared sacrifices of war convinced these black northerners they could speak to the interests of black people across the country. "We are American Citizens," they said, and were "compelled to support the government with money and life." They sought federal laws to ensure their safe travel by rail and steamboat across the nation. And because they had fulfilled their obligation to support the national government, they declared that "protection and equal right to the ballot and the law, are due to us."[49] "We wish to be politically and legally equal with our white fellow citizens," they proclaimed, outlining their broadest goals.

Throughout their message, the activists argued that citizenship should include an indivisible array of rights. Many lawmakers and theorists in the nineteenth century understood rights to exist in discrete categories—natural, civil, political, social—but black activists argued that citizenship comprised all those rights.[50] To secure black people's civil rights, these activists said, Congress must propose an additional constitutional amendment that outlawed racial discrimination. With that measure in place, all laws barring black suffrage should "be declared *void*" because they would be unconstitutional. Black disfranchisement was "anti-republican," they insisted, and any steps toward civil rights without political rights would therefore represent an incomplete reform of the nation's laws.[51]

This message from Nesbit, Bustill, and Forten reflected their sense of the federal government's capacity to effect change through the law. Enforcing the Thirteenth Amendment required "that every vestige of this foul, barbarous, and unscrupulous enemy of man and his inalienable rights, shall be forever swept from this land."[52] The amendment called on Congress to remove all legal markers of bondage, all vestiges of inferior status based on race. Their claims reflected critical ways that Republican lawmakers would justify the Civil Rights Act and subsequent postwar enactments. Black people believed Congress could produce such extensive change because they had experienced the wartime expansion of the government and had seen the legal destruction of slavery. Black politics of the Civil War era thus made arguments both about the kind of legal changes the federal government should implement and about the kind of government that should produce those changes. Federal lawmakers had proved themselves capable of and willing to address black people's concerns, and they had a responsibility to continue to do so after emancipation.

While they spoke about the broad potential of legal change, the Pennsylvania activists did not neglect the limits of government influence. They did not expect legal changes to alter the prejudices of white Americans, including lawmakers who might enact that legislation. "Hate us as you will, turn from us at your pleasure," they wrote, "we ask you not to allow us to be robbed of the price of our blood, our sufferings, and that which is ours by birth-right and taxation."[53] They did not anticipate that congressmen could eradicate racism, even from their own hearts, but they did believe that the federal government could provide the legal instruments by which black people could defend themselves from manifestations of that racism. Their focus was on changing legal facts across the country. They called for a bond with the federal government that would produce tangible legal change as a step toward justice, which they believed to be more powerful than ephemeral feelings of love or brotherhood.

When black people gathered for conventions in the North and South and capitalized on the legal opportunities the Civil War produced, they performed much the same political work and pursued many of the same ends that black activists had since at least the 1820s.[54] They called themselves citizens and bolstered that claim by citing their contributions to the United States. They demanded a raft of legal protections, chief among them the franchise, "this safeguard, indispensable to the protection, prosperity, and happiness of the citizen." They asked to be "recognized as an integral part of the American people in every State in this Union."[55] Arguments about their contributions were more vivid in the aftermath of the war, but the claims echoed earlier arguments in pursuit of rights. Black activists saw the Civil War as a chance to reiterate and expand on their antebellum work. In particular, the postwar period seemed to be a moment of possibility because the nation's lawmakers seemed especially interested in working to give freedom a robust legal meaning.

The political work African Americans did to imagine a new legal system reached beyond established centers of activism in the free states. Black citizenship politics spread southward as northern black activists traveled to the southern states and as some black southerners themselves seized opportunities of the moment to shape the legal terms of their freedom. In addition to attending the state convention in Alexandria, Henry Highland Garnet joined a group of activists in Norfolk, Virginia, who issued a message to the people and the lawmakers of the United States demanding the right to vote. Like their colleagues in Pennsylvania, they made what they characterized as a simple demand, "that a Christian and enlightened people shall, at once, concede to us the full enjoyment of those privileges of full citizenship." To these black southerners, voting was essential to citizenship and the most powerful safeguard of their newly won freedom. They were not interested in "expensive aid from military forces," a garrison state designed to uphold black rights. Instead, they sought the self-protecting power of the vote. "Give us the suffrage, and you may rely upon us to secure justice for ourselves," they said.[56] Changing the laws with the backing of federal government authority, they maintained, would transform their lived experiences.

*   *   *

Black activists' statements paralleled the policies that federal lawmakers enacted in pursuit of a legal settlement of the war. Both activists and lawmakers wanted solid legal foundations for wartime emancipation. They hoped to ensure that proslavery southerners could not return to dominate national, state, or local governments; reinstate slavery; or produce another rebellion. They wanted to ensure that black people had access to formal legal outlets to defend their freedom. The Civil War raised questions about African Americans' status in the nation, and black people pushed their way into the ensuing debates, helping to define the legal terms of freedom.

Black activists paid careful attention to the legal developments moving through Congress as the war ended, and they worked to influence change by producing public statements at the meetings they held in the aftermath of military conflict. It is difficult to know whether Republican lawmakers read those statements and, if so, exactly how activists influenced the legislative process. But it is important that congressional measures called for the federal government to structure freedom in much the same ways that black activists had envisioned. The legal developments of Reconstruction fulfilled many of the demands of black activists. Congress enacted laws and amended the Constitution in ways that established a legal bond between black people and the federal government. The measures declared citizenship a birthright and made clear that citizenship was a rights-bearing status. And as they crafted these legal changes, congressmen offered some of the same constitutional arguments to justify them that black activists had put forward. Both black activists and lawmakers argued that the federal government had the authority to intervene in laws of the states because of the constitutional provision that required Congress to ensure to each state a republican form of government.[57] And as they considered what the nature of black freedom should be, lawmakers turned to citizenship as a means to provide individuals with rights and protections. Federal lawmakers came to embrace the vision that black activists had long promoted, namely that citizen status should include rights. Activists had worked to make citizenship a legal phenomenon with specific protections, and in the Civil Rights Act of 1866, Congress made that vision the law.

Among the Republicans in Congress who pursued legal change, many did so because they were convinced that the government was responsible for defining and defending black freedom. Many lawmakers saw the Thirteenth Amendment as a first step in that direction, a foundation from which they could enact new laws that would secure the abolition of slavery in law and in fact. Black Americans, especially those in the South, needed to be assured that they would not be reenslaved or subject to oppressions that bore the marks of bondage. The legal regime that emerged under President Andrew Johnson's lenient policies, characterized by Black Codes that restricted labor, movement, and property ownership, showed congressmen that it was vital to offer a formal legal definition of freedom.[58]

Congress designed the Civil Rights Act of 1866 as an outline of the essential elements of black freedom. It declared black Americans citizens by birth and extended to them a set of legal protections through that status. It secured to black people, freeborn and formerly enslaved, the rights to make contracts, to file lawsuits, to testify in court, and to hold and transfer property. And it secured to black people "full and equal benefit of all laws and proceedings for the security of person and property, as is enjoyed by white citizens." Further, the act prohibited any punishment for crime "different than is prescribed for the punishment of white persons," protecting black people from state laws that might deem particular behaviors criminal among them or impose harsher penalties for criminal acts.[59] Essentially, the act provided black people access to courts and equal protection under the law. As a measure that defined black freedom, it built a new relationship between all individuals and the U.S. government. And it included a striking acknowledgment of the power of whiteness in law, using the access and protection afforded to white people as a baseline of rights for American citizens as a whole.

The Civil Rights Act of 1866 transformed the legal order of the United States. It offered a clear answer to the question of who could be a citizen and clarified the significance of that status by attaching to it a specific set of legal rights. It included all native-born black people in the citizenry. And it shifted responsibility for determining individuals' rights away from the states and to the federal government. The fact that the federal government had been the legal force behind emancipation policy positioned Congress to shape the terms of black freedom.[60] The text of the act bound together black freedom and black citizenship, both of which were direct legal products of the Civil War.[61]

Republicans in Congress were concerned that the new legislation might easily be changed, so they solidified it by embedding its ideas in the Constitution.[62] The Fourteenth Amendment echoed key provisions of the Civil Rights Act, declaring citizenship a birthright and connecting it to equal protection of the laws. Like the Thirteenth Amendment, it authorized enforcement by Congress and thereby enriched the relationship between individuals and the federal government. Together, these measures changed the way the federal government related to black people and to all individuals in the nation, and they held the potential for further change by providing a broad outline of citizenship and allowing lawmakers to continue defining its terms.

The laws Congress enacted in the aftermath of the Civil War reflected some of black people's most important concerns. Federal legislators crafted these measures in a context shaped by black politics. Black activists made public statements about the kinds of legal changes Congress should implement just as lawmakers were imagining and debating the terms of a new legal order. Further, the lawmakers who shaped Reconstruction policy were products of an antebellum United States in which black people had long made public arguments about the legal terms of citizenship.[63] Many Republican lawmakers came from states in which black people had for decades sought legal protections through citizen status. In particular, white northerners could have become familiar with black activists' legal arguments as they related to fugitive controversies, which were points of concern for many in northern states who strove to prevent slavery's intrusion into their territory. White northerners who challenged slaveowners' influence in the free states could not have remained oblivious to black people who called themselves citizens in search of protection from slave catchers. By calling themselves citizens and by deploying the forms of popular politics in print and on the streets, African Americans shifted ideas about legal possibilities, helping people to imagine and legislate black citizenship. And by insisting that citizenship should be a foundational legal status, a robust connection between individuals and the nation's government, black people also shaped the language available to lawmakers. In their decades of political work, black activists had helped produce a legal culture in which members of Congress saw citizen status as a viable foundation for the legal protections they thought would secure black freedom. Black citizenship politics, before and after the Civil War, helped to make the legal changes of Reconstruction.

*   *   *

As black activists had hoped, the Civil Rights Act and the Fourteenth Amendment contained transformative possibilities. These measures inserted into the nation's law the principle that African Americans belonged in the country and that they possessed a legal status that entitled them to a set of protections. The laws made the federal government an important presence in black people's lives and empowered Congress to uphold principles of legal equality.

Black people recognized these possibilities immediately. A group of activists gathered in Buffalo in the spring of 1866 to celebrate the creation of a new legal order. According to one observer, the purpose of the event was "to have a general jollification over the passage of the Civil Rights Bill." Those who came together drafted and approved a message to lawmakers in Washington in appreciation of the law.[64] James Jackson, a black minister in Tarboro, North Carolina, perhaps hoped to organize a similar celebration, but first he wanted to be sure that his congregants knew the details of the act. He wrote to the black editors of the *Christian Recorder*, requesting "fifty copies of the issue that contained the Civil Rights Bill."[65] A law that declared black Americans citizens and connected them to the federal government made tangible the networks within which activists had labored. Black people communicated across borders with other activists and with lawmakers in ways that were shaped by legal change. Like their brethren in Buffalo, a group of black Chicagoans met in May 1866 and made plans to send an address to Congress. Their message conveyed "the grateful and patriotic feelings of the colored citizens of Chicago toward the Senate and House of Representatives."[66] African Americans recognized that the legal changes enacted in Congress empowered them, clarified their status, and connected them to the authority of a federal government interested in defining and defending freedom.

Activists worked in that new order to secure practical changes in their own legal lives. After William Still was ejected from a Philadelphia streetcar, he and other African Americans hoped federal legal developments would alter the way they traveled around the city. Still and other activists would test how and to what extent Civil War–era legal change could reshape Philadelphia. While lawmakers declared black people citizens, black Philadelphians struggled to shape the terms of the status. Their project pointed to further possibilities of federal legal change.

Pennsylvania law allowed private streetcar companies to regulate passenger access, and the vast majority of those companies barred black riders. Philadelphia had an extensive history of rioting and violence stemming from racial and ethnic prejudices. Company executives' exclusionary policies might have reflected their personal prejudices or their desire to limit racist violence on the rails.[67] But the policies excluded black people from an affordable method of transportation in Philadelphia and its vicinity. Black Philadelphians had been organizing against the streetcar exclusion long before Still's snowy 1863 trip. They saw that their work was connected to larger legal questions; transit was a proving ground for arguments about black people's status. They framed their struggle for equal access in the terms of *Dred Scott*, hoping that their work could determine "whether the prescribed [*sic*] Americans of Philadelphia have 'rights which white men are bound to respect.' "[68] Access to transit gave people access to a city, and fighting for black access to the streetcars was therefore an important metaphor for the larger project of securing black people's access to the United States. Their work paralleled that of federal lawmakers after the Civil War who wanted to give black freedom legal substance. In the midst of war, seeking to ride in streetcars might have seemed trivial, but both black and white Pennsylvanians believed that transportation had high stakes for questions about race and rights. One activist suggested that the streetcar fight was in miniature "one in which the whole civilized world is engaged, that of liberty and equality arrayed against despotism and slavery."[69]

The geography of the Civil War made Philadelphia transit a vital issue. The Union army used several hospitals on the outskirts of the city that were accessible most conveniently by streetcar. William Still was traveling on a streetcar into Philadelphia from Camp William Penn when he was required to step out onto the frigid platform. The white abolitionist William Kelley condemned the streetcar inequality and the prejudice permeating even the purportedly liberal state of Pennsylvania. White residents of the state, it seemed, would "rather see the yawning pit of hell swarm with new-born demons, than that the sanctity of our street cars should be profaned by . . . a pious wife or mother hurrying to a hospital to sanctify the last moments of her dying husband or son!"[70] Still noted that "the soldiers have been fighting bravely in the Union ranks," a fact that Philadelphians should have known, given that "thousands of wounded colored soldiers" were convalescing in the city at Satterlee General Hospital, the largest Union medical center during the war. In 1864, he wrote to the executives of the streetcar companies, informing them of the scope of black military service, believing his message would "make the managers feel how cruelly unjust to colored citizens they were." But the exclusionary policies remained in place, allowing only those black people who could afford "eight or nine dollars" in carriage fare to visit wounded soldiers.[71]

Black activists thus forced the issue, and a number of white lawmakers pushed back. African Americans filed assault charges against conductors who removed them from the cars, and those legal proceedings kept some measure of attention on their political project. In September 1865, Democratic state lawmakers spoke fearfully about the ways federal legal change might affect Pennsylvania. Republicans, they believed, were promoting not only "negro suffrage" but also "social equality," the terrifying result of equal access to the streetcars. According to these Democrats, black access would bring white men shame, as they would be "pronounced to be *only* the equal of the negro of Dahomey or of Congo." State legislators challenged congressional efforts to include black people through the law, presenting African Americans as essentially foreign and denying that they could belong in the United States.

They made their feelings plain: "We believe in the superiority of our race, and we are unwilling to degrade ourselves either socially or politically."[72] Equal access to streetcars would undermine white supremacy, which was important to many white northerners and increasingly fragile as they fought a war to end slavery.[73]

William Still centered black military service in his campaign against the streetcar exclusion, but he also buttressed his claims by describing the many other ways black Americans supported state and federal governments. "Colored people pay more taxes here than is paid by the same class in any other northern city," he emphasized. Still had made the same argument when he was booted from a streetcar in 1863, informing the conductor "that I paid taxes, etc., but of course it was of no avail." Still was arguing for a legal relationship between black people and governments rooted in mutual concern and contribution, one in which both parties worked on the other's behalf. He noted bitterly that American governments failed to uphold their responsibilities, while black people made essential contributions to their communities. "Nobody," Still wrote, "insults a colored man or woman in the Tax Receiver's office."[74]

The fight for access to streetcars spanned the Civil War, and in 1867, Still published a pamphlet that described the long struggle, hoping to capitalize on the legal changes that Republicans in Congress had implemented. In that pamphlet, Still argued that black people were entitled to equal legal protections because of their upright conduct, financial contributions, and loyal military service. He added specific local texture to citizen status by pursuing the right to travel in Philadelphia, and he sketched both the rights and obligations he believed should link individuals and governments. Still and other black Philadelphians connected their political work to the broader transformation of the nation's laws. They cited the interconnected problems African Americans had faced: "the enslavement of the Black Man at the South, and contempt for him at the North." Because the Thirteenth Amendment had abolished slavery, they suggested, congressional measures like the Civil Rights Act should establish a citizenship that would eliminate laws that reflected contempt for black northerners. Again, Still invoked the power of the armed service of black men. "The slow and heavy car wheels of prejudice," he remarked, "were moved mightily at Fort Wagner, Milliken's Bend, Allusta, &c." by black soldiers. Perhaps his assessment was correct.

Still's efforts finally succeeded in 1867, when Pennsylvania's legislature passed a measure that prohibited racial exclusion on Philadelphia streetcars as well as on any other railway in the state.[75] The arguments Still made in seeking equal black travel underline the steep costs of the legal changes that produced black citizenship. Further, they highlight the ways African Americans understood citizen status. Legal declarations of black equality did not mean black political work would end. Still and other activists saw that the law required them to continue their efforts to build citizenship by giving it the texture of specific legal protections and obligations. In Philadelphia in 1867, they succeeded.

Caroline LeCount, a black teacher and activist who lived in Philadelphia, tested the effects of the new state legislation in the weeks after it passed. Waiting at a streetcar stop, LeCount prepared to board when a conductor breezed past her, choosing that simple means of denying black ridership. But LeCount put the new state law to work and reported the incident to the police, who arrested and fined the offending conductor.

Years of organized protest, black service in a cataclysmic war, and the continuing identification and prosecution of the opponents of black rights combined to produce a victory in the streetcar fights. All of that work was necessary for African Americans to practice a right they had understood as a direct challenge to Roger Taney's denial of black citizenship. Together, that labor comprised the arduous process of building citizenship, brought to fruition through the transformations of war.[76]

The framers of the Civil Rights Act and the Fourteenth Amendment rightly anticipated that white Americans would continue to pursue black exclusion. They designed the law to allow black people to continue to make claims as citizens through the broad idea of equal protection of the laws. But this breadth also demanded constant vigilance and posited a continuous struggle by black people against those who would deny them rights. And while these measures conveyed the transformative vision of the federal government, they did nothing to secure the vote, which many black people believed to be a distinctly powerful and transformative right. After the horrors of war, the limits of legal change were clear and disheartening indeed.[77]

The history of Civil War–era legal changes comprises more than legal texts, their potential, and the ideals of their framers.[78] A key part of that history is the ways black people who had imagined and argued for change experienced new legal developments. Black Chicagoans, writing to the U.S. Congress in 1866, reflected some of the complex feelings black Americans harbored about the nation's developing legal structures. Because of black military service, the activists believed they were owed more than the Civil

Rights Bill. "In these blood stained periods of our country's history," they said, "colored Americans have ever been found faithful to the flag." They had offered their devotion and, in many cases, their lives. "Giving to her the whole heart, we ask from her the *whole hand!* The *suffrage* of the citizen is the strength of the republic."[79] In Chicago and elsewhere, black people reveled in the significance of an act that declared them citizens while condemning the fact that it failed to secure voting rights to black men. Reverend Elisha Weaver, the editor of the *Christian Recorder*, expressed doubt that any white person could genuinely believe that "the black man should not have his natural and civil rights protected, and share equally with others, political privileges." Most who opposed black suffrage said that it would lead to "social equality," which Weaver argued was a baseless superstition used to obscure the reality that there was no danger in black people possessing formal political rights.[80] The insufficiencies of postwar legal change—the fact that black people were declared citizens yet not voters—left room for white supremacists to make these arguments against black suffrage. Reverend Weaver reminded white lawmakers of the danger of those insufficiencies. The decades during which federal authorities allowed states to maintain systems of racial slavery and discrimination had led only to "the most terrible civil war that the sun ever shone upon." Securing black voting rights would realize "the great political principle of the American government."

More broadly, Weaver was concerned about the daily circumstances of black life in the freedom and citizenship that lawmakers had constructed. "Why is it," he asked, "that the Freedmen in most places are not paid their wages and are terribly maltreated?" He doubted that black people could thrive in freedom when "there is scarcely a county in a single State of the South, where the public sentiment of its citizens would tolerate a colored school." Reconstruction required structures of enforcement, including federal military force and measures to secure to black people the independent power of the franchise. Only government authority could suppress the rebellious spirit of defeated southerners. "Coaxing seldom cures the lawless," he wrote. "The lawless must be made to feel that there is in reserve a power to execute law which they cannot resist."[81]

Weaver understood the broad implications of federal legal changes. The government had declared that black people belonged in the country, that they possessed a legal status and were entitled to protections. But like activists from the antebellum period, he wanted to use the law to change black people's lives, and he worried about the limits of measures like the Civil Rights

Act. For Weaver and others, the fact that the law separated voting rights from citizenship was a powerful symbol of its limits as a tool to improve African Americans' daily legal lives.[82] The Civil Rights Act and the Fourteenth Amendment were radical transformations, and they would not be the final legal steps of Reconstruction. But the ways that black activists reacted to these measures highlights the fact that while radical, they were limited in critical ways. Black people felt that the U.S. government was obligated to ensure that they possessed rights and protections in their daily lives and believed that it was capable of doing so. They saw these legal changes as failures because of their limited enforcement capacity and because they implicitly withheld political rights. The Civil Rights Act and Fourteenth Amendment established a relationship between black people and the federal government, the foundation of black politics for decades. But the laws required continuing struggle to specify the terms of that relationship. Elisha Weaver and other black activists recognized that the citizenship the government built was profoundly transformative and profoundly limited. In the aftermath of these changes, they would continue their longstanding political work, molding and challenging the specific language of the law, continuing to shape the terms of citizen status.

The Enduring Search for Home

African Americans worried about the legal settlement of the Civil War, even in the wake of ostensibly sweeping changes like the Civil Rights Act. Black people wanted the federal government to be an active force in their lives, but it was not clear that the legal changes of the mid-1860s would effectively define their connection to that government and secure the protections they desired.

In April 1865, Frederick Douglass outlined his hopes for a radically transformed legal order in a speech he titled "What the Black Man Wants." "I have had but one idea for the last three years," Douglass announced. "I am for the 'immediate, unconditional, and universal' enfranchisement of the black man, in every State in the Union." Any gesture toward legal inclusion would be meaningless without black suffrage; if disfranchised, African Americans would remain "the slave[s] of society." Douglass called on activists to wave the bloody shirt. The scale of black men's deaths during the Civil War offered an unparalleled opportunity to push for black suffrage, he argued. Women were also entitled to the vote, he said, but black men's military service was the center of his argument. Further, he claimed black men should vote in order to continue defending the republic against defeated Confederates after the war. "If he knows enough to shoulder a musket and fight for the flag, fight for the government, he knows enough to vote." Military service across the nation's history had made African Americans citizens. "In 1776 he was a citizen. . . . In 1812 Gen. Jackson addressed us as citizens. . . . And now, when you come to frame a conscription bill, the negro is a citizen again. . . . Shall we be citizens in war, and aliens in peace?"[1] Citizenship without the right to vote was nothing more than alienage, he argued. He called for a citizen status that entailed formal political rights as part of a robust legal relationship between individuals and the government. Suffrage was the critical dimension of a legal order in which black people had formal voices and in which the national government was obligated to hear those voices and address African Americans' concerns. In the aftermath of emancipation, Douglass and other black people insisted that the powerful national government exhibit its capabilities by ensuring rights and protections to African Americans.

The Fourteenth Amendment, which Congress passed and sent to the states for ratification in June 1866, laid the foundation for a transformed relationship between black people and the national government. Broadly, congressmen designed the amendment to secure freedpeople's rights against any limitations southern individuals and governments might impose. Under the amendment, any person born in the United States was a citizen and was connected to both state and federal governments through that status. It barred states from enacting laws that would "abridge the privileges or immunities of citizens of the United States," and it secured to all citizens "equal protection of the laws." The Fourteenth Amendment took effect in July 1868, but it signaled a shift in the nation's core legal structures from the moment it passed through Congress in the summer of 1866. The amendment made citizenship a critical aspect of an individual's legal identity, suggested new connections between the federal government and American people, and secured an array of legal protections based on birth in the nation.[2]

For all its transformative possibilities, black activists and some radical Republicans in Congress criticized the Fourteenth Amendment because it failed to secure black men's voting rights. In fact, Section 2 of the amendment dictated that if a state denied a citizen's right to vote, the state would lose congressional representation in proportion to the number of people disfranchised. Republicans intended this as a repeal of the three-fifths compromise—which had given slaveholding states unequal power in the federal government—and as an implicit endorsement of black suffrage. States would enhance their representation in the federal government if they allowed black men to vote. But Section 2 separated citizen status from formal political rights; under the terms of the amendment, black men who were citizens could legally be denied the vote. The Fourteenth Amendment failed to secure one of the rights that had been at the center of black protest for decades. Congress approved the Fifteenth Amendment in February 1869, which protected voting rights regardless of race. But up to that point, it was unclear whether the changing legal order of the Civil War era would allow any black people to vote.

Many African Americans believed the Fourteenth Amendment author-ized their disfranchisement. Frederick Douglass denounced the measure as fundamentally unjust in the days after it passed through Congress. Black men paid taxes and fought for the nation. They had been "citizens in war," as he had previously said.[3] But on reading the Fourteenth Amendment, Douglass felt that "in all that respects voting and representation, I am but as so much inert matter."[4] He reiterated arguments from the antebellum period. Activists had long said citizenship without suffrage was a status without value; they had used citizenship to secure specific rights, including the electoral franchise. For these black activists, the late 1860s presented a disheartening new kind of crisis. African Americans would be included in the national community, connected to the federal government. But the government seemed uninter-ested in specifying the legal terms of belonging in ways that would empower black people to defend their interests and shape the country. While the Four-teenth Amendment did change the nation's legal foundations, black activists found themselves again required to make claims about the content of citizen-ship in pursuit of the rights they believed were essential.

In October 1868, a group of activists began planning for a national convention to meet the following year in Washington, D.C. They wanted to gather for a discussion of how best to confront "the partial or total exclu-sion of colored citizens from the exercise of the elective franchise and other citizen rights." They recognized the flaws in the developing Constitution. "Surely, the Fourteenth Amendment . . . does not justify such exclusion," they gasped. "Surely," they continued, "citizenship, as declared by that amendment, carries with it the rights of citizens."[5] The amendment must ensure black suffrage in order to align with the principles of the Constitu-tion. The nation's frame of government required "a liberty-loving and loyal Congress . . . to see that a Republican form of government is guaranteed to every State." Section 2 of the amendment, as well as any other measure by which "any state is permitted to withhold . . . the rights of citizens," contra-dicted an essential constitutional principle. Mentioning loyalty raised the stakes of black disfranchisement—they reminded Congress of the recent southern rebellion, which had been predicated on black people's legal exclu-sion. The status of freedmen and freedwomen was "the all-absorbing ques-tion of the present," and they urged black activists to use all the tools at their disposal to push for the franchise "by petition, by personal appeal, by protest, and by what votes we have." In the late 1860s, some black people organized their politics around opposition to the terms of the Fourteenth

Amendment because they believed so strongly in the power of the franchise. Securing the vote, they said, "will necessarily secure to us other rights of which we are now deprived."[6]

Henry Highland Garnet presided over the national convention when it met in January 1869. Nearly 200 official delegates gathered in Union League Hall on Ninth Street NW in downtown Washington. The building stood two blocks from Pennsylvania Avenue, the wide boulevard that links the U.S. Capitol building and the White House.[7] Garnet and his fellow delegates wanted to shape ongoing discussions about the legal future of black Americans and of the United States more broadly. Garnet looked to strike while black military service was fresh in American minds; activists found themselves in "the most auspicious time" for their political work, he argued. It was critical for "the disfranchised and newly emancipated citizens of the United States" to gather and publicize their concerns. For African American activists, securing the franchise was "the one great object to be accomplished." Black northerners had often protested their position by calling themselves disfranchised citizens, and the gap between the adoption of the Fourteenth and Fifteenth Amendments made that position a legal reality.[8] On the first day of the convention, John Mercer Langston of Ohio denounced "the unjust features" of what many Republicans saw as their crowning achievement. The Fourteenth Amendment "virtually endorsed the wickedness of those States which disfranchised a large part of their citizens." It posited a hypothetical disfranchisement of black citizens and laid out a punishment should any state choose that path.

Black people had broader concerns about the uncertain enforcement power for the ideals of the Fourteenth Amendment. "The concession of rights in a legal form," the convention delegates noted, "is comparatively valueless and often a mockery unless supported by the whole judicial and military power of the country."[9] Delegates wanted the government to make clear the means by which they would actualize the citizenship the Fourteenth Amendment constructed. And they offered a helpful suggestion to lawmakers unsure about further expanding the government's reach. Enfranchising black men was the first step toward realizing the ideals of equal privileges and immunities and equal protection of the laws, they argued. As voters, African Americans could influence the lawmaking process to sustain the legal order the amendment's first section had called forth.

The Fourteenth Amendment offered federal government sanction for black activists who claimed rights through citizenship. The nation's law undeniably identified black people as citizens and made the status a conduit to individual rights. But the amendment required continued protest to mold the specific content of citizenship. Black activists recognized that the Fourteenth Amendment fundamentally changed the nation's government and that it had essential, dangerous limitations. Citizenship without suffrage seemed little better than nominal freedom or a tenuous hold on personal security, which had defined the lives of so many black northerners before the Civil War. In early 1869, the delegates who gathered in Washington, D.C. as well as all other African Americans remained disfranchised citizens. After decades of protest, it must have been tremendously disheartening to see the limits of the remade Constitution that a cataclysmic war produced.

In the years between the adoption of the Fourteenth and Fifteenth Amendments, black activists confronted citizenship as a problem. By declaring birthright citizenship, the Fourteenth Amendment fundamentally redefined legal belonging in the United States, and black activists had to convince lawmakers that the transformation was insufficient. Citizenship had been perhaps the easiest achievement of antebellum black politics. The vagueness of citizenship allowed activists to claim the status without a clear legal doctrine to deny their claims. In conventions and public meetings, they rhetorically made themselves citizens, acting always in pursuit of other legal protections. The Fourteenth Amendment repudiated the *Dred Scott* decision and codified African Americans' decades-old legal arguments. But that measure established a nebulous and labor-intensive citizenship. The amendment made citizen status available to all by birth and, simultaneously, explicitly demanded continued political struggle on the part of marginalized people to give texture to the status.[10]

What were black Americans to do in the face of a measure that so fundamentally transformed their legal status yet seemed to do so little for their lived experiences? How could activists articulate the limits of citizenship after the Fourteenth Amendment? The letter of the law in June 1866 said African American men should have all the privileges and immunities of white men. But black activists were intimately familiar with the politics of lawbreaking. For decades they broke the law, denouncing measures they saw as unjust and pushing legal structures to align with their vision of the republic. In the years after the Civil War, African Americans encountered a new wave of resistant lawbreaking. White southerners attacked black people's privileges and immunities by blending extralegal terrorism with structured state and local challenges to a vision of Reconstruction that included black equality. The law would be diminished and in many ways broken by these challenges. In 1873, for instance, white Democrats murdered dozens of black Republicans in Colfax, Louisiana, in an effort to steal the governorship. None of the perpetrators were convicted of any crimes. In 1876, the U.S. Supreme Court ruled that the federal government did not have authority to punish individuals, like white Democrats in Colfax, for crimes against individual black people's civil rights. Deciding that only state governments could be punished for violating the 1866 Civil Rights Act, the Supreme Court gave white Americans tremendous freedom to terrorize and marginalize black people who pursued rights or power. Generally, the broad individual rights the Fourteenth Amendment conferred encouraged government officials to withdraw their authority and limit the ways they worked to create justice in individuals' lives. The Fourteenth Amendment enabled black people to appeal to the federal government for redress of grievances, yet subsequent legal, social, and political developments distanced black Americans from the government and military bodies that might care about and work to confront injustice.[11]

Citizenship was a tremendous, transformative legal reality that obscured the daily experiences that denied African Americans equality. Citizen status offered a new foothold for black people to continue an old struggle in pursuit of legal protections, appealing to a national government that increasingly believed its work on behalf of African Americans was done.

Henry Highland Garnet was pastoring Shiloh Presbyterian Church in New York City as that struggle took shape. The Civil War had changed Garnet's relationship with the United States. He abandoned his work with the African Civilization Society and the project of emigration, and he invested anew in the possibility of an African American future. In September 1861, Garnet traveled to Europe with a passport signed by Republican Secretary of State William Seward. "This fact must fill Judge Taney with horror," one black editor imagined.[12] But in 1863, having returned to Manhattan, Garnet and his family struggled through the New York City draft riots. According to one account, his daughter removed a sign bearing his name from the door of their home, denying Garnet's personal history and his activist identity in order to survive a racist mob.[13] After the riots, Garnet remained hopeful about the prospects of the war and worked to recruit black troops for the Union military. But in early 1869, he was forced to continue protesting the nation that disfranchised him. In the 1870s, he witnessed the judicial attack on the Reconstruction amendments and the grassroots work of white supremacy to deny black people equal protection of the laws. Garnet told a

JAMES U. STEAD,   989 6TH AVE. N.Y.

FIGURE 10. Henry Highland Garnet, albumen silver print by James U. Stead, 1881.
Garnet, photographed here on the eve of his departure for Liberia, had long cultivated
an interest in connecting black Americans with communities in West Africa.
National Portrait Gallery, Smithsonian Institution.

The Magnificent Steamships
EGYPT AND SPAIN.
Of the National Steamship Line, between New York and Liverpool.
OFF SANDY HOOK, ENTERING AND LEAVING THE PORT OF NEW YORK.

FIGURE 11. "The Magnificent Steamships Egypt and Spain." New York (1879). Surely Garnet understood the symbolic significance as he stepped on board the steamship *Egypt* to leave the United States and begin a journey to a new home in Africa. He sailed first to England, then to what he hoped was a more just future in a place he identified as his ancestral home. Popular Graphic Arts Collection, Prints and Photographs Division, Library of Congress.

friend that he longed to "reach the land of my forefathers and with my feet press her soil."[14] After decades of protest and legal change, he was unsure whether the United States could or should be his home.

In 1881, Garnet took a government position as minister to Liberia, sailing from New York City to Liverpool on the steam ship *Egypt*, then on to Monrovia, where he arrived in December of that year. His voyage retraced the path John Russwurm had traveled fifty-four years earlier.[15] Perhaps Garnet felt then what Russwurm had in 1827, that it was "a mere waste of words to talk of ever enjoying citizenship" in the United States. Perhaps he accepted the position in Liberia because he continued to harbor doubts about his native country, because he was unsure whether black Americans could secure the legal protections he and other activists had so long demanded. Henry Highland Garnet, born into slavery in Maryland in 1815, fell ill at his new home in an African American nation across the Atlantic. He died in February 1882, still searching for a place where he might truly enjoy citizenship.

NOTES

INTRODUCTION

1. Winston James, *The Struggles of John Brown Russwurm: The Life and Writings of a Pan-Africanist Pioneer, 1799–1851* (New York: New York University Press, 2010), pp. 5–25.

2. John B. Russwurm, "The Condition and Prospects of Haiti" (1826), accessed March 20, 2017, http://www.blackpast.org/1826-john-b-russwurm-condition-and-prospects-haiti; Winston, *The Struggles of John Brown Russwurm*, pp. 16–25.

3. "To Our Patrons," *Freedom's Journal*, March 16, 1827.

4. When they launched the paper, Cornish agreed to work as a coeditor for only six months. Cornish said that health concerns led him to leave the city and also wrote that he planned to pursue ministry work for the Presbyterian Church "in the country." He declared his full confidence in the enduring "usefulness and necessity" of the paper and in Russwurm's capabilities as editor. He took what may have been a ceremonial position as a general agent for the paper during his travels. "To the Patrons and Friends of *Freedom's Journal*," *Freedom's Journal*, September 14, 1827.

5. "Liberia," *Freedom's Journal*, February 14, 1829.

6. Ibid.

7. "Intelligence. Liberia," *Boston Recorder and Religious Telegraph*, April 28, 1830. Russwurm wrote that he had arrived in Liberia on November 12 "after the uncommonly long passage of 58 days."

8. I use the term "activists" to describe those people who did work to fight slavery and enrich freedom. Most of the black Americans who appear in this book were abolitionists, but I am interested in the work they did beyond the fight against slavery, in pursuit of legal change and a broader sense of freedom and justice.

9. Black newspapers offered political advice and instruction to black readers, printed debates over activists' goals and tactics, conveyed legal arguments designed to sway legislators, and challenged prejudice in the hope of changing white Americans' ideas about black people in the country. Using the forms of print culture helped to legitimize black politics in the minds of white observers and helped connect a community of activists across a broad geography. See Richard Newman, "Protest in Black and White: The Formation and Transformation of an African American Political Community During the Early Republic," in *Beyond the Founders: New Approaches to the Political History of the Early American Republic*, ed. Jeffrey L. Pasley, Andrew W. Robertson, and David Waldstreicher (Chapel Hill: University of North Carolina Press, 2004); Lara Langer Cohen and Jordan Alexander Stein, eds., *Early African American Print Culture* (Philadelphia: University of Pennsylvania Press, 2014).

10. "An Error Corrected," *Rights of All*, June 12, 1829.

11. "Importance to Our City," *Rights of All*, July 17, 1829.

12. "Elective Franchise," *Rights of All*, October 9, 1829.

13. I frame this story as part of the long history of the early republic, spanning the period from the ratification of the Constitution in 1789 to the outbreak of the Civil War in 1861. In these decades, critical questions about the nation's government were unsettled and contested. Although that uncertainty did not end after the Civil War, the legal settlement of the conflict did offer clear answers to major questions, declaring the supremacy of the federal government over the states, asserting who legally belonged in the nation, and outlining a set of individual rights for citizens. I use the terms "early republic" and "early United States" interchangeably to refer to this period. On the legal settlement of the Civil War era, see Laura Edwards, *A Legal History of the Civil War and Reconstruction: A Nation of Rights* (New York: Cambridge University Press, 2015).

14. U.S. Constitution, Article I, Sections 2 and 3; Article II, Section 1; Article III, Section 2; Article IV, Section 2.

15. Douglass Bradburn writes, "Anyone who called for a strong national state or encouraged a national standard for American citizenship dissented from the common view." Douglas Bradburn, *The Citizenship Revolution: Politics and the Creation of the American Union, 1774–1804* (Charlottesville: University of Virginia Press, 2009), p. 2. Because citizenship was ill-defined at the nation's founding, people continued to partially construct and reconstruct the status in a series of struggles over its meaning in the nineteenth century. See Linda Kerber, "The Meanings of Citizenship," *Journal of American History* 84, no. 3 (December 1997): 833–854; James Kettner, *The Development of American Citizenship, 1608–1870* (Chapel Hill: University of North Carolina Press, 1978); William J. Novak, "The Legal Transformation of Citizenship in Nineteenth-Century America," in *The Democratic Experiment: New Directions in American Political History*, ed. Meg Jacobs, William J. Novak, and Julian E. Zelizer (Princeton, NJ: Princeton University Press, 2003); Rogers Smith, *Civic Ideals: Conflicting Visions of Citizenship in U.S. History* (New Haven, CT: Yale University Press, 1997).

16. U.S. Attorney-General, *Opinion of Attorney General Bates on Citizenship* (Washington, D.C.: Government Printing Office, 1863), pp. 3–4, quotation from p. 4. Bates was responding to a question about the status of a black man who was commanding a Union naval vessel. He concluded that birth in the nation marked black people as citizens, although he remained uncertain about the legal implications of that status.

17. On the relationship between ideas about sovereignty and the uncertainties surrounding citizenship, see Bradburn, *The Citizenship Revolution*, esp. pp. 61–100. On the importance of local institutions in determining individuals' rights in the early nineteenth century, see Laura Edwards, *The People and Their Peace: Legal Culture and the Transformation of Inequality in the Post-Revolutionary South* (Chapel Hill: University of North Carolina Press, 2009); Novak, "The Legal Transformation of Citizenship in Nineteenth-Century America."

18. On black northerners' communities, cultures, and institutions, see, for instance, Gary B. Nash, *Forging Freedom: The Formation of Philadelphia's Black Community, 1720–1848* (Cambridge, MA: Harvard University Press, 1988); James O. Horton and Lois E. Horton, *In Hope of Liberty: Culture, Community, and Protest Among Northern Free Blacks, 1700–1860* (New York: Oxford University Press, 1997); Leslie Harris, *In the Shadow of Slavery: African Americans in New York City, 1626–1863* (Chicago: University of Chicago Press, 2002); Patrick Rael, *Black Identity and Black Protest in the Antebellum North* (Chapel Hill: University of North Carolina

Press, 2002); Erica Armstrong Dunbar, *A Fragile Freedom: African American Women and Emancipation in the Antebellum City* (New Haven, CT: Yale University Press, 2008); Richard Newman, *Freedom's Prophet: Bishop Richard Allen, the AME Church, and the Black Founding Fathers* (New York: New York University Press, 2009).

19. Both Stephen Kantrowitz and Andrew Diemer acknowledge the uncertainties of citizen status, but each writes in ways that obscure the work activists did with citizenship. Describing political struggles as the effort "to be included in the nation as full citizens" or naming African Americans as "colored citizens" diminishes the scope of African Americans' work to use language in ways that could secure them specific legal rights. Beyond claiming citizenship or arguing over whether African Americans could be citizens, black and white Americans were debating what citizenship would be, negotiating the terms and content of that status. Black people born in the United States were a problem community for lawmakers interested in upholding white supremacy, and African Americans lived under an ambiguous legal status. But more than that, black activists understood that ongoing negotiations allowed them to make arguments about citizenship that could help them secure rights. Because of the uncertainty surrounding citizenship, black people did a particularly potent kind of political work when they called themselves citizens. The precise ways African Americans used citizenship made their political claims a part of the process of defining the republic. In the ways many historians use citizenship, they have overlooked this aspect of antebellum black politics. See Kantrowitz, *More Than Freedom: Fighting for Black Citizenship in a White Republic* (New York: Penguin Books, 2013); Andrew Diemer, *The Politics of Black Citizenship: Free African Americans in the Mid-Atlantic Borderland, 1817–1863* (Athens: University of Georgia Press, 2016), quotation from p. 22; Nikki M. Taylor, *Frontiers of Freedom: Cincinnati's Black Community, 1802–1868* (Athens: Ohio University Press, 2005), quotation from p. 27. See also Graham Russell Gao Hodges, *David Ruggles: A Radical Black Abolitionist and the Underground Railroad in New York City* (Chapel Hill: University of North Carolina Press, 2010); Leslie Alexander, *African or American? Black Identity and Political Activism in New York City, 1784–1861* (Urbana: University of Illinois Press, 2008); Leslie Harris, *In the Shadow of Slavery: African Americans in New York City, 1626–1863* (Chicago: University of Chicago Press, 2002).

20. I look to build on Martha Jones's scholarship on black legal culture and activism in Baltimore and its environs in the mid-nineteenth century. Jones highlights the ways the instabilities and uncertainties of citizenship and rights provided opportunities for African Americans to enrich their legal lives, noting that black people "drove lawmakers to refine their thinking about citizenship." Jones explores the breadth of people who engaged in this politics, especially through her focus on black people's legal maneuverings in local courtrooms. I am interested in the ways African Americans confronted these same legal uncertainties, although I look to tell a story of a different thread in their protest work. I focus here on the ways black activists structured their politics to craft the terms of citizen status and use it in pursuit of legal change. And I am especially interested in the ways black people built an interstate political community, connecting across borders to broadcast their claims and to expand the reach of the work individuals did in conventions, in print, in courtrooms, and in public. Martha S. Jones, *Birthright Citizens: A History of Race and Rights in Antebellum America* (New York: Cambridge University Press, 2018), quotation from p. 9.

21. In a study of black people working and traveling in the Midwest and Upper South, Anne Twitty has shown how people formally excluded from legal spaces came to know the workings of the law and deployed them in pursuit of their interests. Black people in the North, subject to various restrictions and exclusions by state and federal law, also came to be familiar

with the workings of those exclusionary structures. See Anne Twitty, *Before Dred Scott: Slavery and Legal Culture in the American Confluence, 1787–1857* (New York: Cambridge University Press, 2016).

22. Here I follow Elizabeth Pryor, who highlights the ways black people "redefined segregation as a crime," calling for a different kind of legal order than that which excluded them from public conveyances in the North. I look to expand on this discussion by considering the broad array of rights black people claimed through citizenship and the sweeping changes they demanded and helped usher into the nation's legal structures. Elizabeth Pryor, *Colored Travelers: Mobility and the Fight for Citizenship Before the Civil War* (Chapel Hill: University of North Carolina Press, 2016). For more on black people molding legal development in the nation, see Kate Masur, *An Example for All the Land: Emancipation and the Struggle for Equality in Washington, D.C.* (Chapel Hill: University of North Carolina Press, 2010); Sarah Cornell, "Citizens of Nowhere: Fugitive Slaves and Free African Americans in Mexico, 1833–1857," *Journal of American History* 100, no. 2 (September 2013): 351–374; Kimberly Welch, "Black Litigiousness and White Accountability: Free Blacks and the Rhetoric of Reputation in the Antebellum Natchez District," *Journal of the Civil War Era* 5, no. 3 (September 2015): 372–398; Jessica Marie Johnson, "Death Rites as Birthrights in Atlantic New Orleans: Kinship and Race in the Case of María Teresa v. Perine Dauphine," *Slavery and Abolition* 36, no. 2 (July 2015): 233–256. My thinking here also reflects presentations and discussions from the conference "Emancipations, Reconstructions, and Revolutions: African American Politics and U.S. History in the Long Nineteenth Century," held at the McNeil Center for Early American Studies, Philadelphia, PA, February 2017.

23. Both Erica Armstrong Dunbar and Susan Zaeske emphasize the creative ways that black and white women made spaces for their political work despite gendered constraints. See Dunbar, *A Fragile Freedom*, esp. pp. 70–119; Susan Zaeske, *The Signatures of Citizenship: Petitioning, Antislavery, and Women's Political Identity* (Chapel Hill: University of North Carolina Press, 2003). On women's work to make possible black conventions, see Psyche Williams-Forson, "What Did They Eat? Where Did They Stay? Black Boardinghouses and the Colored Convention Movement," Colored Conventions Project, accessed April 6, 2018, http://colored conventions.org/exhibits/show/williams-forson-exhibit. David Blight's work shows that Anna Douglass and Ottilie Assing were central to maintaining Frederick Douglass's fragile financial and emotional stability. David Blight, *Frederick Douglass: Prophet of Freedom* (New York: Simon and Schuster, 2018).

24. Joanna Brooks has suggested that racial and class barriers restricted African Americans from accessing the traditional public sphere, but black people relied extensively on traditional political tools and helped expand the public sphere. African Americans were convinced that they needed a black press. "We struggle against opinions," a group of activists announced in 1847. "Our Warfare lies in the field of thought." Because of their political techniques and the legal issues in which they engaged, black Americans helped to create and engaged in a broad public sphere for the early United States. See Joanna Brooks, "The Early American Public Sphere and the Emergence of a Black Print Counterpublic," *William and Mary Quarterly* 62, no. 1 (January 2005): 67–92; "Proceedings of the National Convention of Colored People, and Their Friends, Held in Troy, N.Y. on the 6th, 7th, 8th, and 9th October, 1847," in *Minutes of the Proceedings of the National Negro Conventions*, ed. Howard Holman Bell (New York: Arno Press, 1969), p. 18; Geoff Eley, "Politics, Culture, and the Public Sphere," *Positions* 10, no. 1 (Spring 2002): 219–236. On early American street politics more generally, see Simon P. Newman, *Parades and the Politics of the Street: Festive Culture in the Early American Republic* (Philadelphia: University of Pennsylvania Press, 1999); David Waldstreicher, *In the Midst of Perpetual*

Fetes: The Making of American Nationalism, 1776–1820 (Chapel Hill: University of North Carolina Press, 1997, published for the Omohundro Institute of Early American History and Culture, Williamsburg, VA).

25. The *Colored American* listed several people across the North who could take subscriptions for the paper, including Charles Remond in Providence, Rhode Island; Amos Beman in Hartford, Connecticut; Samuel Ringgold Ward in Newark, New Jersey; Abraham Shad in Chester, Pennsylvania; and William Whipper in Columbia, Pennsylvania. These people helped make possible the *Colored American* as a kind of black regional newspaper, and many likely read closely and corresponded with the paper. See "Agents for the American," *Colored American*, April 8, 1837.

26. Scholars of wartime emancipation have challenged the idea that the Civil War should stand as a fundamental break in U.S. history, in particular Hannah Rosen, *Terror in the Heart of Freedom: Citizenship, Sexual Violence, and the Meaning of Race in the Postemancipation South* (Chapel Hill: University of North Carolina Press, 2009); Tera Hunter, *To 'Joy My Freedom: Southern Black Women's Lives and Labors After the Civil War* (Cambridge, MA: Harvard University Press, 1997). One of my goals is to include free African Americans living in the North in the story of postemancipation legal changes.

27. Studying black politics and the development of American citizenship connects the long history of emancipation with that of the process of creating the nation's legal structures. As lawmakers ended slavery and restricted black freedom, they encouraged a black political response that helped to remake the nation's laws. That politics raised questions about the legal terms of belonging in the United States. As African Americans pushed for a more robust set of rights, they demanded answers to the critical question of how people related to one another and to governments in the nation. On the process of ending slavery, see Ira Berlin, *The Long Emancipation: The Demise of Slavery in the United States* (Cambridge, MA: Harvard University Press, 2015); Patrick Rael, *Eighty-Eight Years: The Long Death of Slavery in the United States, 1777–1865* (Athens: University of Georgia Press, 2015).

CHAPTER 1

1. The contested terms of citizenship are an essential and understudied aspect of black protest against colonization. Scholars have tended to suggest that black people, dissatisfied with their freedom, sought to secure full citizenship or that they worked to attain the rights of American citizens, writing in a way that obscures the uncertainties surrounding that status and those rights. The vagueness of citizenship allowed black people to protest organizations like the American Colonization Society by arguing that they were entitled to access and protections as citizens. See Diemer, *The Politics of Black Citizenship*; Horton and Horton, *In Hope of Liberty*; Alexander, *African or American?*

2. On Cornish, see Jane H. Pease and William H. Pease, *Bound with Them in Chains: A Biographical History of the Antislavery Movement* (Westport, CT: Greenwood, 1972), chap. 7; C. Peter Ripley et al., eds., *The Black Abolitionist Papers, Volume 3: The United States, 1830–1846* (Chapel Hill: University of North Carolina Press, 1991), p. 95. On the connected lives and experiences of free and enslaved black people, see Newman, *Freedom's Prophet*, esp. pp. 27–77; Ira Berlin, *Slaves Without Masters: The Free Negro in the Antebellum South* (New York: Pantheon, 1974).

3. 14 Prov., KJV. As a whole, Proverbs 14 exalts wisdom and truth and derides foolishness, dishonesty, and hubris. Among the other especially intriguing verses: "There is a way which seemeth right unto a man, but the end thereof are the ways of death" (v. 12); "A wise man feareth, and departeth from evil: but the fool rageth, and is confident" (v. 16); and "The simple inherit folly: but the prudent are crowned with knowledge" (v. 18). Cornish's readers likely would have understood the context of that quotation immediately, particularly as it came from such a popular, quotable book of the Bible. Mark Noll notes that knowledge of scripture, particularly the Old Testament, was a central facet of the Evangelical Protestantism that drove much of American theological development in the antebellum period. The Bible emerged in the nineteenth century as an essential element of people's public and private lives to the extent that "broad familiarity with its contents characterized both ordinary people and elites." See Mark Noll, *America's God: From Jonathan Edwards to Abraham Lincoln* (New York: Oxford University Press, 2002), esp. pp. 365–372, quotation from p. 372.

4. "To Our Patrons, and the Publick Generally," *Rights of All*, May 29, 1829.

5. Ibid.

6. "An Error Corrected," *Rights of All*, June 12, 1829. Russwurm had been appointed superintendent of schools for Liberia, a fact that went largely unmentioned in criticisms of his decision but may have sparked rumors that he had been bribed away from the United States, persuaded by, as Cornish suggested, "lower or baser motives." See also *Connecticut Courant*, August 11, 1829, and *Rhode-Island Republican*, September 17, 1829.

7. "An Error Corrected."

8. "Mr. Russwurm," *Liberator*, April 30, 1831.

9. See, for instance, a series of articles titled "The Colonization System" that ran in the *Observer* from January through March 1833. Editors appear to have taken notice of Russwurm's change of opinion, noting in 1829 that Russwurm had "renounced his opposition to the colonization society and will hereafter advocate its views." Quoted in *Portsmouth Journal and Rockingham Gazette*, March 7, 1829.

10. Several papers filed brief notices that they reprinted from one another, announcing that Cornish, "a man of colour," was editor of the New York City–based paper. See *American Traveller*, June 19, 1829; *Baltimore Gazette and Daily Advertiser*, June 23, 1829; *Norwich Republican*, June 24, 1829; and *Baltimore Patriot and Mercantile Advertiser*, June 24, 1829. Later, another paper included the *Rights of All* among a list of new publications, noting that Cornish was "an opponent to the plan of colonizing his brethren at Monrovia." *Boston Recorder*, August 13, 1829.

11. Regardless of the extent of literacy among free black people, in the early United States, "newspapers were kept on hand in many public gathering places, especially taverns, coffeehouses, and hotels, where they were often read aloud or in groups. . . . Information and ideas contained in newspapers moved by word of mouth, and passed hand to hand in clippings and letters." Jeffrey L. Pasley, *The Tyranny of Printers: Newspaper Politics in the Early American Republic* (Charlottesville: University of Virginia Press, 2002), p. 7.

12. White newspapers published many of the same sorts of items, although in the early nineteenth century, they were dominated by party politics. Black newspapers focused on broader racial concerns. African American newspapers also had an inherent political significance as markers of black people seizing public voices and taking a place within the increasingly important world of print culture. On the partisan political emphasis of newspapers in the early United States, see Pasley, *The Tyranny of Printers*. Also see Christopher Daly, *Covering America: A Narrative History of a Nation's Journalism* (Amherst: University of Massachusetts Press, 2012), pp. 31–85.

13. On antebellum black newspapers and their power in providing public voice, see Horton and Horton, *In Hope of Liberty*, pp. 206–209. Emphasizing pamphleteering but with an eye toward black print culture as a whole, Richard Newman shows that "the public sphere of print—decentralized, virtually impossible to shut down, and long enshrined in American culture as an open forum—offered room for black views." While it is difficult to say for certain, the circulation of language and ideas through print culture suggests that men like Cornish must have reached a far broader audience than a list of subscribers or correspondents would indicate. See Richard Newman, "Protest in Black and White: The Formation and Transformation of an African American Political Community During the Early Republic," in *Beyond the Founders: New Approaches to the Political History of the Early Republic*, ed. Jeffrey L. Pasley et al. (Chapel Hill: University of North Carolina Press, 2004), pp. 180–204.

14. "Civil Rights of the Jews," *Rights of All*, June 12, 1829.

15. "Barbarism in America," *Rights of All*, August 7, 1829.

16. While many people criticized John Russwurm's support of emigration, those black activists who remained in the United States at times expressed serious uncertainty as to whether they could be secure in their lives in the United States. At an 1832 black national convention, delegates appointed a committee to consider migration to Canada, examining the question of whether "we, as a people, will be compelled to leave this our native land, for a home in a distant region?" The committee members said they were "unable to answer; it belongs to the fruitful events of time to determine." It seems that delegates considered migrating to Canada in part as a way to head off a potential forced "repatriation" to West Africa or the Caribbean. "Minutes and Proceedings of the Second Annual Convention, for the Improvement of the Free People of Color . . . 1832," in *Minutes of the Proceedings of the National Negro Conventions*, ed. Howard Holman Bell (New York: Arno Press, 1969), p. 19.

17. James Forten, *To the Honourable the Senate and House of Representatives of the Commonwealth of Pennsylvania: The Memorial of the People of Colour of the City of Philadelphia and Its Vicinity, Respectfully Sheweth . . .* ([Philadelphia], 1832), p. 1, New-York Historical Society.

18. On petitioning as a political form, see Susan Zaeske, *The Signatures of Citizenship: Petitioning, Antislavery, and Women's Political Identity* (Chapel Hill: University of North Carolina Press, 2003).

19. Forten, *To the Honourable the Senate*, pp. 1–2. This latter claim that all people should have a "remedy by due course of law" was not a direct quotation from the Constitution, but it distills the sentiment conveyed in a number of provisions on the importance of access to courts, jury trials, and the opportunity to protect property by seeking redress before legal authorities. See Pennsylvania Constitution, Articles VIII–XI, accessed July 23, 2018, http://avalon.law .yale.edu/18th_century/pa08.asp#1.

20. Forten, *To the Honourable the Senate*, p. 3. On anxieties surrounding free African Americans in the North and their connections to legal developments, see Leon Litwack, *North of Slavery: The Negro in the Free States* (Chicago: University of Chicago Press, 1961); Horton and Horton, *In Hope of Liberty*; Rael, *Black Identity and Black Protest in the Antebellum North*; Newman, *Freedom's Prophet*.

21. Forten, *To the Honourable the Senate*, p. 3.

22. Forten had also led the opposition to an earlier proposal. See James Forten, *Letters from a Man of Colour, on a Late Bill Before the Senate of Pennsylvania* (Pennsylvania, 1813).

23. Forten, *To the Honourable the Senate*, pp. 6–8.

24. Sean Wilentz, *Chants Democratic: New York City and the Rise of the American Working Class, 1788–1850* (Oxford: Oxford University Press, 1984), pp. 172–218.

25. "Importance to Our City," *Rights of All*, July 17, 1829. This approach to labor and rights persisted well into the antebellum period. Martin Delany, a leading advocate of self-help as a path to racial equality, repeatedly called upon African Americans to become valuable participants in the economic sphere. In a unique series of editorials, Delany argued that black people had become too reliant on religion and that in seeking to use "heavenly means for the attainment of earthly ends," they had neglected the necessity of economic development. "Let us then at once, get to business," he wrote, offering vague instruction to enter "into the various enterprizes." If black Americans became sellers as well as buyers, then they might also become subjects in, rather than simply objects of, American law and society. Delany described the United States as a corporation in which all citizens should share an enterprising spirit. But by his accounting, black Americans had invested no capital in the business of nation making and left the burden upon their white countrymen. Delany adopted a more critical approach than Cornish, but the men shared a belief in the importance of black people working as well as the problem of barriers to that labor. That this rhetoric remained so important throughout the antebellum years underlines the influence of early leaders like Cornish in forging later protest ideology. "Domestic Economy," *North Star*, April 20, 1849. See also two articles under the same title in *North Star*, March 23, 1849, and April 13, 1849, and "Political Economy," *North Star*, March 16, 1849.

26. Graham Russell Hodges, "The Legal Bonds of Attachment: The Freemanship Law of New York City, 1648–1801," in *Slavery, Freedom and Culture among Early American Workers*, ed. Graham Russell Hodges (New York: Routledge, 1998).

27. Richard Newman highlights the links between abolition and uplift, as well as an interracial "moral-uplift discourse" in the early nineteenth century. See Newman, *Freedom's Prophet*, pp. 57–58, 153–155. For another important examination of uplift ideology in antebellum politics, see Rael, *Black Identity and Black Protest in the Antebellum North*. Rael introduces the concept of racial synecdoche, in which the behavior of black individuals was taken to represent the nature and capabilities of the race as a whole. Prominent black activists advocated moral uplift in part because they wanted to limit opportunities to denounce the race as degraded, intemperate, slothful, or extravagant, all traits that white observers attributed to the free black masses. Activist elites often assumed especially proper demeanors and habits in the hope that they could use synecdoche to their advantage, presenting themselves as representatives for the race.

28. On the dimensions of uplift politics in the nineteenth and twentieth centuries, see Kevin K. Gaines, *Uplifting the Race: Black Leadership, Politics, and Culture in the Twentieth Century* (Chapel Hill: University of North Carolina Press, 1996); Rael, *Black Identity and Black Protest in the Antebellum North*; Newman, *Freedom's Prophet*. In exploring the ways activists politicized moral reform programs, these authors have not fully considered the ways those programs intersected with black advocacy for legal change through the concept of citizenship. Uplift was critical to the ways black people articulated their ideas about and claims to legal rights as citizens.

29. "Agriculture," *Rights of All*, May 29, 1829; "Agriculture," *Rights of All*, June 12, 1829. Twenty shillings, or £1, in 1829 would have the purchasing power of £83 in 2017, or roughly $100. A group would need to attain the equivalent of nearly $10,000 to purchase a plot of the land Cornish advertised. While it is difficult to ascertain individual or average wages for black people in the free states, Leonard Curry demonstrates the extent to which laws and social

strictures limited economic opportunity for black urbanites. In 1850, more than 70 percent of black men in New York worked in unskilled, semiskilled, and personal service jobs. See "Purchasing Power of British Pounds from 1270 to the Present," accessed July 25, 2018, https://www.measuringworth.com/calculators/ppoweruk/; Leonard Curry, *The Free Black in Urban America, 1800–1850: The Shadow of the Dream* (Chicago: University of Chicago Press, 1981), chap. 2 and Appendix B.

30. Cornish and his colleagues reflected a common trope of the period in praising the virtue of the small farmer. In his December 1832 State of the Union address, Andrew Jackson announced that "the wealth and strength of a country are its population, and the best part of the population are cultivators of the soil. Independent farmers are everywhere the basis of society, and the true friends of liberty." Walter Johnson notes that Jackson's message became "a staple of nineteenth century agricultural journals." See Walter Johnson, *River of Dark Dreams: Slavery and Empire in the Cotton Kingdom* (Cambridge, MA: Harvard University Press, 2013), p. 34.

31. "Constitution of the African Female Benevolent Society of Troy," in *Address Delivered Before the African Female Benevolent Society of Troy, on Wednesday, February 12, 1834. By Elizabeth Wicks. To Which Is Annexed an Eulogy on the Death of Mrs. Jane Lansing, with an Address by Eliza A. T. Dungy* (Troy, NY: Printed by R. Buckley, 1834), p. 13. Library Company of Philadelphia.

32. Ibid., pp. 3, 4.

33. Ibid., pp. 4–6.

34. For more on the AMRS, see Howard H. Bell, "The American Moral Reform Society, 1836–1841," *Journal of Negro Education* 27, no. 1 (Winter 1958): 34–40.

35. William Watkins, *An Address Delivered Before the Moral Reform Society, in Philadelphia, August 8, 1836* (Philadelphia: Merrihew and Gunn, 1836). Historical Society of Pennsylvania. Any education that did not address morality was "radically deficient."

36. C. Peter Ripley, ed., *The Black Abolitionist Papers, Vol. 3: The United States, 1830–1846* (Chapel Hill: University of North Carolina Press, 1991), pp. 96–97.

37. Watkins, *An Address Delivered Before the Moral Reform Society*, p. 6.

38. Ibid., pp. 11–12.

39. Ibid., pp. 13–14.

40. Ibid., p. 9.

41. For background on and excerpts from that convention, see William Yates, *Rights of Colored Men to Suffrage, Citizenship, and Trial by Jury: Being a Book of Facts, Arguments and Authorities, Historical Notices and Sketches of Debates—with Notes* (Philadelphia: Merrihew and Gunn, 1838). John Z. Ross's reasoning for the proposed restriction is quoted in Yates, *Rights of Colored Men*, p. 10.

42. Their proposal exempted from taxation those who were denied the vote, a purported benefit of the legal change. Yates, *Rights of Colored Men*, pp. 23–24. William Yates wrote to Samuel Cornish with details of those convention proceedings. See "Albany September 9th, 1837," *Colored American*, September 30, 1837.

43. Yates, *Rights of Colored Men*, pp. 26–27, 29.

44. "Proposals for Publishing *Freedom's Journal*," *Freedom's Journal*, March 23, 1827. After Cornish's departure, Russwurm reprinted that prospectus in the issue of April 25, 1828, adding a note that after "over one year with encouraging success," he felt it necessary to reiterate his request for financial support in order to sustain the paper.

45. While many did, not all of the laws explicitly demanded that voters be citizens. Russwurm suggested that citizenship denoted residency in a place, and states that did not explicitly connect citizenship to suffrage did require voters to have resided in the state for at least six months to a year. "Votes in the Several States," *Freedom's Journal*, August 22, 1828.

46. "Elective Franchise," *Rights of All*, October 9, 1829.

47. "The Second Constitution of the State of New York, 1821," Article II, Section 1, accessed July 24, 2018, https://www.nycourts.gov/history/legal-history-new-york/documents/Publications_1821-NY-Constitution.pdf.

48. "The British Settlement of Honduras," *Rights of All*, June 12, 1829.

49. Leonard Curry has shown that the black population of Cincinnati grew gradually from approximately 400 in 1820 to slightly more than 1,000 people in 1830 and that the proportion of black people in that city did not increase over that period. While this was only one city, the statistics might lend credence to observers who felt prejudice spurred the move to enforce the state's black laws. Curry, *The Free Black in Urban America*, pp. 250–251.

50. "For the Rights of All. 'It Is Not a Little Singular . . . ,' " *Rights of All*, September 18, 1829. For more on those legal developments, see Stephen Middleton, *The Black Laws: Race and Legal Progress in Early Ohio* (Athens, OH: Ohio University Press, 2005). On the politics of black travel and movement in the antebellum period, see Pryor, *Colored Travelers*.

51. "A Voice from the West," *Liberator*, September 17, 1831.

52. Voting in the nineteenth century helped create American communities, as it gave a segment of the population a specific physical experience of membership. Disfranchisement barred people from the community of concerned participants made manifest each Election Day. See Alan Taylor, *William Cooper's Town: Power and Persuasion on the Frontier of the Early American Republic* (New York: Vintage, 1995); Kate Masur, *An Example for All the Land: Emancipation and the Struggle for Equality in Washington, D.C.* (Chapel Hill: University of North Carolina Press, 2010).

53. *Opinion of the Hon. John Fox, President Judge of the Judicial District Composed of the Counties of Bucks and Montgomery, Against the Exercise of Negro Suffrage in Pennsylvania. Also: The Vote of the Members of the Pennsylvania Convention on the Motion of Mr. Martin, to Insert the Word "White," as One of the Proposed Amendments to the Constitution* (Harrisburg, PA: Packer, Barrett and Parke, 1838). Historical Society of Pennsylvania. Quotations from pp. 3, 5. Fox ruled that black people were not intended to be included because they did not descend from the framers of the state constitution.

54. For details on the convention, see Roy H. Akagi, "The Pennsylvania Constitution of 1838," *Pennsylvania Magazine of History and Biography* 48, no. 4 (1924): 301–333. Akagi notes that the amended constitution passed by quite a narrow margin, with 113,971 favoring it and 112,759 opposed.

55. Ripley, *The Black Abolitionist Papers*, pp. 81–82.

56. *Appeal of Forty Thousand Citizens, Threatened with Disfranchisement, to the People of Pennsylvania* (Philadelphia: Merrihew and Gunn, 1838), quotations from pp. 4, 15.

57. Ibid., pp. 2–3; "A Very Numerous and Respectable Meeting . . . ," *Pennsylvania Freeman*, March 22, 1838. Black Philadelphians famously gathered in Bethel AME Church in 1817 to denounce emigration and the ACS. See Horton and Horton, *In Hope of Liberty*, p. 150; Newman, *Freedom's Prophet*, pp. 202–207.

58. *Appeal of Forty Thousand Citizens*, pp. 5, 6.

59. Kate Masur and Laura Edwards both show that as federal lawmakers discussed the legal terms of freedom during the Civil War, black people pushed their voices into those

conversations in ways that had the potential to influence the legal lives of all individual Americans. See Masur, *An Example for All the Land*. Laura Edwards has also, along with William Novak, highlighted the limited significance of federal legal power and constitutional ideas like citizenship in shaping the terms of individuals' legal lives in the early nineteenth century. At the same time, it was important that the Constitution connected rights to citizen status and that that frame of government presented the status as an important position for people in relation to state and federal governments. Edwards, *A Legal History of the Civil War and Reconstruction*; William Novak, "The Legal Transformation of Citizenship in Nineteenth-Century America," in *The Democratic Experiment: New Directions in American Political History*, ed. Meg Jacobs, William Novak, and Julian E. Zelizer (Princeton, NJ: Princeton University Press, 2003).

60. *Appeal of Forty Thousand Citizens*, pp. 3, 9–10, 12, 16. For more on the uses of reform work and military participation as bases for citizen status, see Chapters 3 and 6, respectively.

61. *Appeal of Forty Thousand Citizens*, p. 3; Eric Ledell Smith, "The End of Black Voting Rights in Pennsylvania: African Americans and the Pennsylvania Constitutional Convention of 1837–1838," *Pennsylvania History: A Journal of Mid-Atlantic Studies* 65, no. 3 (Summer 1998): 279–299; Christopher Malone, "Rethinking the End of Black Voting Rights in Antebellum Pennsylvania: Racial Ascriptivism, Partisanship and Political Development in the Keystone State," *Pennsylvania History: A Journal of Mid-Atlantic Studies* 72, no. 4 (October 2005): 466–504.

62. "After We Had Put to Press . . . ," *Rights of All*, August 7, 1829.

63. Ibid.

64. "Our People and Our Paper, NEW ARRANGEMENTS," *Weekly Advocate*, February 25, 1837. See also "Title of This Journal," *Colored American*, March 4, 1837, in which Cornish offers a similar explanation for the chosen name, concluding that it is "one which is above reproach."

65. Christopher Malone, *Between Freedom and Bondage: Race, Party, and Voting Rights in the Antebellum North* (New York: Routledge, 2008); Sean Wilentz, *The Rise of American Democracy: Jefferson to Lincoln* (New York: Norton, 2005).

66. *Colored American*, March 4, 1837. For more on the uses of Jackson's message in antebellum protest, see Chapter 4.

67. "To Our Patrons, and the Publick Generally," *Rights of All*, May 29, 1829.

68. "The Importance of Agricultural Pursuits," *Colored American*, April 15, 1837. Cornish promoted an agrarianism that had roots in the ideas of Thomas Jefferson, who had envisioned the nation as an "empire for liberty" composed of prosperous, white, small-scale farmers. That vision profited from, encouraged, and obscured histories of Native American removal and the expansion of slave ownership in the southern states. See Adam Rothman, *Slave Country American Expansion and the Origins of the Deep South* (Cambridge, MA: Harvard University Press, 2007); Steven Hahn, *A Nation Without Borders: The United States and Its World in an Age of Civil Wars, 1830–1910* (New York: Penguin, 2017); Johnson, *River of Dark Dreams*.

69. It is not entirely clear when or why, but Cornish left the *Colored American*. Beginning with the June 1, 1839, issue, Samuel Cornish and James McCune Smith, who had previously been listed as editors, were no longer named as such in the masthead, although the paper noted that letters should be sent to the editors "as above," suggesting that the men may have remained with the publication in that capacity. The July 13 issue bore the heading "Charles B. Ray & Co.—Proprietors." In March 1840, the masthead named Ray as editor, proprietor, and publisher. For more on Charles Ray, another black minister based in New York, see Chapter 2.

70. "The Following Is an Editorial Article . . . ," *Colored American*, June 30, 1838; "Agriculture," *Rights of All*, May 29, 1829.

71. "The Farmer," *Colored American*, December 1, 1838.

72. "For the Colored American. ENCOURAGE THE COLORED PEOPLE TO BECOME FARMERS," *Colored American*, August 3, 1839.

73. "The Petition of Our People," *Colored American*, January 12, 1839.

74. Rothman, *Slave Country*; Hahn, *A Nation Without Borders*; Amy Greenberg, *Manifest Manhood and the Antebellum American Empire* (New York: Cambridge University Press, 2005).

75. John F. Denny, Esq., *An Essay on the Political Grade of the Free Coloured Population Under the Constitution of the United States, and the Constitution of Pennsylvania; in Three Parts* (Chambersburg, PA: Hickock & Blood, 1836), pp. 4, 9–10, 17, 59. John Marshall read and commented on a draft of Denny's manuscript in 1834. Denny practiced law in Franklin County, Pennsylvania. See Alfred Nevin, *Men of Mark of Cumberland Valley, PA 1776–1876* (Philadelphia: Fulton, 1876), 425.

76. *Appeal of Forty Thousand Citizens*, p. 10.

77. Ibid., p. 14.

78. Theodore S. Wright, Charles B. Ray, and James McCune Smith, *An Address to the Three Thousand Colored Citizens of New-York Who Are the Owners of One Hundred and Twenty Thousand Acres of Land, in the State of New-York, Given to Them by Gerrit Smith, Esq. of Peterboro, September 1, 1846* (New York: Library Company of Philadelphia, 1846), pp. 3–5.

79. Ibid., pp. 8–9.

80. Ibid., pp. 9–10.

81. They reinforced this masculine ideal with a verse that exalted agricultural work over that of the military: "Cheerly on the axe of labor, / let the sunbeam dance / Better than the flash of sabre / or the gleam of lance!" Ibid., p. 12.

82. Ibid., pp. 13, 17. Capitalization in original.

83. Willard B. Gatewood Jr., ed., *Free Man of Color: The Autobiography of Willis Augustus Hodges* (Knoxville: University of Tennessee Press, 1982), pp. 20, 22.

84. Ibid., pp. 39, 44–45. In the introduction to this autobiography, historian Willard Gatewood notes that "by living frugally," Hodges saved enough money to open a grocery store. Ibid., p. xxx.

85. Ibid., p. 46.

86. Ibid., p. 53.

87. Ibid., pp. 75–77. On the referendum and its defeat, see Phyllis F. Field, *The Politics of Race in New York: The Struggle for Black Suffrage in the Civil War Era* (Ithaca, NY: Cornell University Press, 1982), esp. pp. 43–79.

88. "The Smith Land Again," *Ram's Horn*, November 5, 1847. This is the only extant issue, although the paper survived for nearly a year, including for some time after Hodges departed to the Smith Lands.

89. Gatewood, *Free Man of Color*, pp. 50, 80.

90. Peter J. Gaile, *The New York State Constitution: A Reference Guide* (Westport, CT: Greenwood, 1991), pp. 10–11; Phyllis F. Field, *The Politics of Race in New York: The Struggle for Black Suffrage in the Civil War Era* (Ithaca, NY: Cornell University Press, 1982), pp. 52–53. Hodges, having returned south after the Civil War to take part in the Virginia Constitutional Convention of 1868, announced during the gathering that he had served as collector in Franklin County and had refused to resign when asked by other country residents. He did not specify

the year of his election. His testimonial is recorded (in dialect) in *Southern Opinion*, March 14, 1868.

91. Jelani Cobb, "Contingent Citizenship: Race and Democracy in the Age of Ferguson and Baltimore," International Festival of Arts and Ideas, New Haven, CT, June 14, 2015, accessed September 14, 2015, http://artidea.org/video-podcast/2085.

CHAPTER 2

1. John F. Watson, *Annals of Philadelphia and Pennsylvania in the Olden Time: Being a Collection of Memoirs, Anecdotes, and Incidents of the City and Its Inhabitants, and of the Earliest Settlements of the Inland Part of Pennsylvania*, vol. 3 (Philadelphia: E. S. Stuart, 1899), pp. 376–377. In 1840, 47,854 free black people lived in Pennsylvania, about 3,000 fewer than the free black population of New York State. *Negro Population in the United States, 1790–1915* (Washington, D.C.: Government Printing Office, 1918; reprint, New York: Arno Press, 1968), p. 57. In 1843, a Philadelphia writer estimated the black population at 30,000, likely accounting for the entire metropolitan area. "Politics in Philadelphia County—a Split—Protection-Tylerism—The Riots, &c.," *New-York Daily Tribune*, August 6, 1842.

2. "Address to the Free Colored People of These United States of America" (Philadelphia, August 1845), p. 1, Historical Society of Pennsylvania.

3. Ibid., p. 6.

4. Beverly Tomek, *Colonization and Its Discontents: Emancipation, Emigration, and Antislavery in Antebellum Pennsylvania* (New York: New York University Press, 2011), esp. pp. 86, 167, 202.

5. "Address to the Free Colored People of These United States of America," p. 2.

6. Laura Edwards shows that local legal authorities were important in individuals' lives in the early nineteenth-century South and that government officials had to work in the antebellum period to make state statute authoritative against a longstanding legal culture based on the preservation of a community concept of order. Many people in the first half of the nineteenth century tended not to seek justice through formal legal structures, especially not those of the federal government. At the same time, as lawmakers formalized state law, black people increasingly turned to the law, using its persistent uncertainties to pursue power and freedom for themselves. Black Americans and others seeking to secure or stabilize their power, including slaveowners, turned to formal legal authorities, increasingly after 1830, to support their claims. See Edwards, *The People and Their Peace;* Twitty, *Before Dred Scott*; Novak, "The Legal Transformation of Citizenship in Nineteenth-Century America."

7. Andrew Diemer offers a history of the meanings of the ACS and its argument that black people were not Americans. But his exploration of the politics of black citizenship—debates over whether black people could be citizens or whether they found the status desirable—obscures the reality that citizenship was not a clear status to be won or lost and thus largely overlooks the necessary work black people were doing to build citizen status, to make it a concept that would secure them a physical space in the nation. Diemer, *The Politics of Black Citizenship*. On the limits of federal government involvement in individuals' lives in the early nineteenth century and the uncertain relationships between state and national citizenships, see Douglas Bradburn, *The Citizenship Revolution: Politics and the Creation of the American Union, 1774–1804* (Charlottesville: University of Virginia Press, 2009), esp. pp. 61–100; Kettner, *The Development of American Citizenship, 1608–1870*.

8. On the vagueness and fragmentation of citizenship, see Bradburn, *The Citizenship Revolution*. The Civil War was the most tragic consequence of the ambiguity of sovereignty and allegiance in the early republic. The essential radicalism of the Fourteenth Amendment was that it defined the citizen in relation to the nation and empowered the federal government to protect his rights. James Kettner suggests that there was a general settlement regarding the meaning of citizenship by the 1790s, but this obscures some of the enduring tensions that emerge in lawmakers' statements on citizenship well into the antebellum period. See Kettner, *The Development of American Citizenship*, p. 17. Black activists were calling for a reordering of federalism that would be central to the legal order in the Fourteenth Amendment, particularly by connecting individuals to the federal government under national citizen status. See Kermit Hall, *The Magic Mirror: Law in American History* (Oxford: Oxford University Press, 1989), p. 145.

9. Michael P. Johnson, "Denmark Vesey and His Co-Conspirators," *William and Mary Quarterly* 57, no. 4 (October 2001): 915–976.

10. W. Jeffrey Bolster, *Black Jacks: African American Seamen in the Age of Sail* (Cambridge, MA: Harvard University Press, 1997), pp. 1–2, 190–191; Thomas D. Morris, *Free Men All: The Personal Liberty Laws of the North, 1780–1861* (Baltimore: Johns Hopkins University Press, 1974), pp. 59–61; Michael Schoeppner, "Peculiar Quarantines: The Seamen Acts and Regulatory Authority in the Antebellum South," *Law and History Review* 31, no. 3 (August 2013): 559–586, esp. p. 559.

11. Schoeppner, "Peculiar Quarantines," p. 577. Daley's story highlights the challenges of enforcing any racially exclusive law, as his counsel argued that he was Native American and should be exempt from the law that applied specifically to descendants of "negroes [or] mulattoes." His opponents offered typical appeals to Daley's hair texture and the degree of his skin's darkness to make Daley black through the law. Schoeppner, "Peculiar Quarantines," p. 559. Charleston was the most important slave port of the British North American colonies and the point of disembarkation for a significant proportion of Africans brought into the United States through the banning of the slave trade in 1808. Ira Berlin, *Many Thousands Gone: The First Two Centuries of Slavery in North America* (Cambridge, MA: Belknap Press of Harvard University Press, 1998), p. 22; Estimates Database, *Voyages: The Trans-Atlantic Slave Trade Database* (2010), accessed January 26, 2018, http://slavevoyages.org/assessment/estimates.

12. *A Memorial of George Bradburn, by His Wife* (Boston: Cupples, Upham and Company, 1883). Bradburn later traveled and worked extensively with Frederick Douglass in an effort to arrange 100 antislavery conventions. See *The Life and Times of Frederick Douglass: From 1817–1882, Written by Himself; with an Introduction by the Right Hon. John Bright*, ed. John Lobb (London: Christian Age Office, 1882), part 2, chap. 5.

13. *Report on the Deliverance of Citizens, Liable to Be Sold as Slaves* (Commonwealth of Massachusetts: House of Representatives, March 6, 1839), pp. 3–7. New-York Historical Society. Bradburn denied that his opinion had any "connexion whatever, with the 'existing topic,' so called, of abolition," p. 9.

14. Ibid., p. 35.

15. See especially Novak, "The Legal Transformation of Citizenship in Nineteenth-Century America," as well as Bradburn, *The Citizenship Revolution*, and Kettner, *The Development of American Citizenship*.

16. House of Representatives, Commonwealth of Massachusetts, *Report on Sundry Petitions Respecting Distinctions of Color*, (Boston: Committee on the Judiciary, February 25, 1839), pp. 5, 12–14. Main Collection, New-York Historical Society. On women's petitioning in the

antebellum period, see Susan Zaeske, *The Signatures of Citizenship: Petitioning, Antislavery, and Women's Political Identity* (Chapel Hill: University of North Carolina Press, 2003).

17. Scott noted that people called "freeman" had traditionally voted in Pennsylvania. For context on the status of freeman, see Hodges, "Legal Bonds of Attachment."

18. *Hobbs and others v. Fogg*, 6 Watts 553, 1837 Pa. LEXIS 136 (Supreme Court of Pennsylvania, Western District, Sunbury 1837), pp. 1–2. Hobbs was the plaintiff on appeal. On Judge Scott, see George B. Kulp, *Families of the Wyoming Valley: Biographical, Genealogical, and Historical Sketches of the Bench and Bar of Luzerne County, Pennsylvania*, vol. I (Wilkes Barre, PA, 1885), pp. 392–402.

19. *Hobbs and others v. Fogg*, pp. 3–7. Gibson's argument appears as a precursor to Roger Taney's logic in *Dred Scott v. Sandford*, 60 U.S. 393 (1857), in which he cited a variety of specific state exclusions to show that it was impossible to see black people as possessing a legal status that would entitle them to rights.

20. *Opinion of the Hon. John Fox*, p. 3. Historical Society of Pennsylvania. Reportedly, the margins of victory for those two elections were twenty-five and two votes, respectively. There is no clear basis for their assumption, but the plaintiffs argued that black people had voted for the victorious candidates and that a ruling against black suffrage amounted to a reversal of the election results. See Eric Ledell Smith, "The End of Black Voting Rights in Pennsylvania," *Pennsylvania History* 65, no. 3 (Summer 1998): 279–299, esp. p. 289.

21. *Opinion of the Hon. John Fox*, pp. 4–5, 8–13. Fox thus fit into a common antebellum pattern in which lawmakers defined a citizen as one who possessed a particular set of rights, a definition that often excluded free African Americans due to wide-ranging state legal restrictions imposed upon them. Fox was able to use that twisted legal reasoning precisely because citizenship was a nebulous concept. He denied black people citizen status based upon their exclusion from certain rights in particular states. He then used that denial to support his ruling that black Pennsylvanians could not legally vote. See Kettner, *The Development of American Citizenship, 1608–1870*, p. 321.

22. David Thomas Konig, "The Long Road to Dred Scott: Personhood and the Rule of Law in the Trial Court Records of St. Louis Slave Freedom Suits," *University of Missouri-Kansas City Law Review* 75, no. 4 (Fall 2006): 53–80; Twitty, *Before Dred Scott*.

23. On Augustine/Woodson, see Floyd J. Miller, "The Father of Black Nationalism: Another Contender," *Civil War History* 17, no. 4 (December 1971): 310–319; "Lewis Woodson to Samuel E. Cornish, 7 February 1838," *Black Abolitionist Papers* Archive, accessed January 8, 2018, http://bap.chadwyck.com.proxy-um.researchport.umd.edu/searchBap/displayBapFulltextFromId.do?QueryName=bap&fromPage=browse&ItemNumber=1&ItemID=11451&SearchEngine=FastESPSearchEngine&ItemID=11451.

24. "For the Colored American. Mr. Editor. . . ," *Colored American*, July 28, 1838.

25. *Speech of John Quincy Adams, of Massachusetts, upon the Right of the People, Men and Women, to Petition on the Freedom of Speech and of Debate in the House of Representatives of the United States; on the Resolutions of Seven State Legislatures, and the Petitions of More Than One Hundred Thousand Petitioners, Relating to the Annexation of Texas to This Union. Delivered in the House of Representatives of the United States, in Fragments of the Morning Hour, from the 16th of June to the 7th of July, 1838, Inclusive* (Washington, DC: Gales and Seaton, 1838).

26. Edward Rugemer, "Robert Monroe Harrison, British Abolition, Southern Anglophobia and Texas Annexation," *Slavery and Abolition* 28, no. 2 (August 2007): 169–191, esp. pp. 177–180.

27. *Proceedings of a Convention of Delegates, Chosen by the People of Massachusetts, Without Distinction of Party, and Assembled at Faneuil Hall, in the City of Boston, on Wednesday, the 29th of January, A.D. 1845, to Take into Consideration the Proposed Annexation of Texas to the United States* (Boston: Eastburn's Press, 1845), pp. 4, 16.

28. Rugemer, "Robert Monroe Harrison, British Abolition, Southern Anglophobia, and Texas Annexation"; Bruce Levine, *Half Slave and Half Free: The Roots of Civil War* (New York: Hill and Wang, 1992), pp. 160–176.

29. "To the People of Colour Throughout the United States," *Rights of All*, August 7, 1829. Nineteenth-century newspapers were often vehicles of political parties, designed to promote a particular group's vision for the country, which further emphasizes the importance of a black newspaper, a tool of communication that could be deployed by people who were excluded from traditional political realms. On the expansion and increased influence of newspapers in the antebellum period, see Levine, *Half Slave and Half Free*; Daniel Walker Howe, *What Hath God Wrought: The Transformation of America, 1815–1848* (New York: Oxford University Press, 2007).

30. "Constitution of the American Society of Free Persons of Colour . . . Also the Proceedings of the Convention . . . ," in *Minutes of the Proceedings of the National Negro Conventions, 1830–1864*, ed. H. H. Bell (New York: Arno Press, 1969). See also "Barbarism in America," *Rights of All*, August 7, 1829, for Samuel Cornish's expression of concern with the Ohio bond law.

31. "American Colonization Society. Mr. Garrison's Second Lecture," *Patriot*, July 10, 1833; *Liberator*, October 19, 1833.

32. "National Reform Convention of the Colored Inhabitants of the United States of America," *Colored American*, July 25, 1840.

33. "A Convention," *Colored American*, May 2, 1840; "National Convention," and "For the Colored American. A Convention," *Colored American*, June 13, 1840; "For the Colored American. Esteemed Friend," *Colored American*, June 20, 1840.

34. Beyond the cost and time, Elizabeth Pryor's work highlights the array of physical and verbal assaults to which black travelers were exposed in the antebellum period. Pryor, *Colored Travelers*.

35. "For the Colored American, National Convention," *Colored American*, July 4, 1840; "For the Colored American, Great Conventional Meeting at Pittsburgh," *Colored American*, July 18, 1840.

36. "For the Colored American. A Voice from New Haven," *Colored American*, August 1, 1840.

37. "Another Voice from New Haven," *Colored American*, September 5, 1840.

38. "National Reform Convention," *Colored American*, September 19, 1840.

39. On September 7, David Ruggles, Joseph Williams (of Connecticut), and David Winn met at Charles Birch's house after being barred from local churches. They read the convention call, the "Maryland Black Law," and parts of Exodus 19, in which God speaks to Moses from Mount Sinai and identifies the Israelites as his chosen people, "a peculiar treasure unto me above all people." They then adjourned to meet the following day, when they were joined by John T. Hilton and S. R. Alexander, the latter of whom blamed poor attendance on misinformation and poor publicity. In early October, the *Colored American* printed a letter with some corrections, noting that the men were forced to gather in a church in a section of New Haven "generally known as 'poverty square'" and highlighting the vocal opposition to the convention

as evidence that people knew about and consciously rejected it. See "National Reform Convention," *National Anti-Slavery Standard*, September 24, 1840; "For the Colored American. Correc-
tion," *Colored American*, October 10, 1840.

40. Paul Gilje has argued that New York experienced increasing racist mob action in the
1830s. Paul Gilje, *The Road to Mobocracy* (Chapel Hill: University of North Carolina Press,
1987), esp. pp. 143–170.

41. "Politics in Philadelphia County."

42. H. C. Wright, "The Philadelphia Mob of Aug. 1st, 1842," *Liberator*, August 19, 1842.

43. "The Philadelphia Mob," *National Anti-Slavery Standard*, August 11, 1842. The paper
estimates the parade at 1,200 people, although it is not clear whether the marchers were all
black or an interracial body. It notes that a local temperance society "invited friends to join"
the parade, which suggests that the event was not racially exclusive.

44. Reporting in the *New-York Daily Tribune* challenged claims that the banner read
"Liberty or Death." "Politics in Philadelphia County."

45. Ibid. On urban space and politics in the early republic, see Newman, *Parades and the
Politics of the Street*; Waldstreicher, *In the Midst of Perpetual Fetes*.

46. "Had the Firemen of Philadelphia . . . attempted to save the African Hall and the
Church from the devouring flames, the passions of a brutal and excited mob would have been
at once turned upon them, as was distinctly threatened." "The Philadelphia Riots," *New-York
Daily Tribune*, August 5, 1842.

47. "The Philadelphia Mob," *National Anti-Slavery Standard*, August 11, 1842. The
National Anti-Slavery Standard also noted that many African Americans sought protection by
sheltering in city police stations. Nearly 70 black Philadelphians were provided refuge in the
mayor's office by August 3. See "The Letter of Our Philadelphia Correspondent . . . ," *New-
York Daily Tribune*, August 4, 1842.

48. "Politics in Philadelphia County." The *National Anti-Slavery Standard* made notice
of this account and decried its unjust portrait of black politics.

49. On the complexities of black people's identities in the antebellum period, see Rael,
Black Identity and Black Protest in the Antebellum North. Andrew Diemer's *The Politics of Black
Citizenship* emphasizes the extent to which black people made political arguments based on
their native birth in the country.

50. *Minutes of the National Convention of Colored Citizens: Held at Buffalo on the 15th,
16th, 17th, 18th, and 19th of August 1843. For the Purpose of Considering their Moral and Political
Condition as American Citizens* (New York: Piercy and Reed, 1843), p. 3.

51. William J. Richardson, "The Life and Times of Samuel H. Davis: An Anti Slavery
Activist," *Afro-Americans in New York Life and History* 33, no. 1 (January 2009): 47–89.

52. *Minutes of the National Convention of Colored Citizens*, pp. 4–7.

53. Ibid., pp. 27–30. Like most antebellum black newspapers, the *Colored American*
appears to have struggled with financial difficulties. On Christmas Day, 1841, Ray printed a
notice that a special supplement through which the paper had covered Congress in 1840 would
not be repeated due to insufficient funds. As for the paper as a whole, he wrote, "We publish
this number without sufficient means at hand to meet the expense; and when we shall have
paid for this number, then we shall issue another . . . *we can promise nothing more.*" See "Our
Winter Paper," *Colored American*, December 25, 1841.

54. *Minutes of the National Convention of Colored Citizens*, pp. 30–36.

55. On black identity in relation to anticolonization, see Tomek, *Colonization and Its
Discontents*; Diemer, *The Politics of Black Citizenship*.

56. *Minutes of the National Convention of Colored Citizens*, p. 3.

57. Munroe's name is also rendered "Munro" or "Monroe" in the record and at times with multiple spellings within a single document. I have chosen Munroe because it seems to have been the most common spelling, and it also helps to distinguish him from another man named William C. Munro, also a black minister, who lived in Providence, Maine.

58. On Munroe's presidency of that society, see "For the Colored American. Tribute of Respect," *Colored American*, September 19, 1840. On travel across Lake Erie during the 1840s, see "The City of Buffalo, 1840–1850," accessed February 3, 2018, http://history.buffalonet.org/1840–50.html.

59. "Annual Report of the Colored Vigilant Committee of Detroit . . . ," *Signal of Liberty*, January 23, 1843.

60. "Right of Suffrage in Michigan.—Action of the Colored People," *Colored American*, March 20, 1841. In the 1850s, Munroe became a vocal supporter of emigration, participating in an 1854 convention on the subject and eventually moving to Canada himself. North of the border, he hosted two meetings in Chatham in 1858 at which John Brown tried to recruit black people for his planned raid on the arsenal at Harper's Ferry. "Proclamation," *Provincial Freeman*, May 10, 1856; Fred Landon, "Canadian Negroes and the John Brown Raid," *Journal of Negro History* 6, no. 2 (April 1921): 174.

61. See, for instance, "Convention of Coloured Citizens," *Non-Slaveholder*, January 1849; "Colored Citizen's Convention," *Weekly Anglo-African*, September 17, 1859.

62. E. A. Marsh, "The Colored Convention," *Liberator*, September 8, 1843.

63. Ibid.; *Minutes of the National Convention of Colored Citizens*, p. 16.

64. Berlin, *The Long Emancipation*, esp. pp. 106–157; Horton and Horton, *In Hope of Liberty*, esp. pp. 155–268; Middleton, *The Black Laws*.

65. Leon Litwack notes congressional measures that prohibited people of African descent from being naturalized, enrolling in militias, and carrying the mail but also shows that these restrictions were complicated by black participation in U.S. military ventures. Leon Litwack, *North of Slavery: The Negro in the Free States* (Chicago: University of Chicago Press, 1961), pp. 64–112. Historians of emancipation have examined the work of building citizenship as a reciprocal relationship between individuals and the government, especially through black women's political work during the U.S. Civil War. See Sharon Romeo, *Gender and the Jubilee* (Athens: University of Georgia Press, 2016); Rebecca Scott, *Degrees of Freedom: Louisiana and Cuba After Slavery* (Cambridge, MA: Harvard University Press, 2008); Rosen, *Terror in the Heart of Freedom*; Chandra Manning, *Troubled Refuge: Struggling for Freedom in the Civil War* (New York: Vintage Books, 2016).

66. W. P. Neuman, "REPORT," *Cincinnati Weekly Herald and Philanthropist*, October 18, 1843.

67. "Address to the Free Colored People of These United States of America," pp. 1–3.

68. *Negro Population in the United States, 1790–1915*, p. 57.

69. Henry Highland Garnet, "An Address to the Slaves of the United States of America," Buffalo, New York, 1843, published in Henry Highland Garnet, *Walker's Appeal, with a Brief Sketch of His Life. And Also Garnet's Address to the Slaves of the United States of America* (New York: J. H. Tobitt, 1848), pp. 90, 92–94.

70. The Colored Conventions project notes that Garnet's 1843 speech was delivered orally and not entered into the convention record, and so the printed version of the speech was not publicly available until 1848. The project's contributors note that Garnet's message broadcast radical protest statements on behalf of free people in New York, bound together free and

enslaved as American citizens, and claimed legal protections for enslaved men and women. "Henry Highland Garnet's 'Address to the Slaves,'" *Colored Conventions: Bringing Nineteenth Century Black Organizing to Digital Life* (2016), accessed February 4, 2018, http://colored conventions.org/exhibits/show/henry-highland-garnet-address.

71. Garnet, "An Address to the Slaves of the United States of America," p. 94.

72. *Minutes of the National Convention of Colored Citizens*, pp. 12–13.

73. Ibid., p. 13. On Garrisonian antislavery, see Caleb McDaniel, *The Problem of Democracy in the Age of Slavery: Garrisonian Abolitionists and Transatlantic Reform* (Baton Rouge: Louisiana State University Press, 2013), esp. pp. 89–112.

74. *Minutes of the National Convention of Colored Citizens*, pp. 13–19, 23–24. Only thirty-seven out of a total of fifty-eight delegates voted on the question of Garnet's speech, which might indicate something of how activists approached conventions. It is possible that they would have planned short trips around such meetings, arriving for a day or two before moving on to other business or returning home. It is also possible that delegates were simply truant, attending occasional sessions but not fully dedicating their time to meetings that sometimes devolved into debates on tedious points of order and repetitive, long-winded arguments among a few activists.

75. Garnet and Douglass embodied a growing schism in American abolitionism between Garrisonians and those who had turned to new antislavery tactics. In 1839, abolitionists in western New York had formed the Liberty Party, a group that looked to end slavery by working within traditional political structures. Black and white activists who had tired of slavery's intransigence after a decade of moral suasion rallied to support the new party. Soon after the 1843 convention closed, the Liberty Party held its own such meeting in Buffalo to nominate candidates for national office. Garnet attended and offered another fiery address in support of their cause. "NATIONAL ANTI-SLAVERY CONVENTION," *Niles' National Register*, September 16, 1843. That unsympathetic paper quoted an account of Garnet's speech from the Buffalo *Advertiser*, which called it "infinitely the best both in manner and matter" delivered at the convention. They continued, "His remarks were clothed in beautiful language, relieved by genuine sparkling wit, or burning with fiery indignant eloquence." On the Liberty Party generally, see Reinhard O. Johnson, *The Liberty Party, 1840–1848: Antislavery Third-Party Politics in the United States* (Baton Rouge: Louisiana State University Press, 2009). Garnet delivered a long speech in support of the Liberty Party in Massachusetts in early 1842. See *Emancipator*, March 4, 1842.

76. *Minutes of the National Convention of Colored Citizens*, pp. 15–16, 21–22. For the roll of delegates, see p. 10. The resolution on the Liberty Party "was adopted with but 7 dissenting votes."

77. Middleton, *The Black Laws*.

CHAPTER 3

1. Tom Chaffin, *Giant's Causeway: Frederick Douglass's Irish Odyssey and the Making of an American Visionary* (Charlottesville: University of Virginia Press, 2014), pp. 1–6; Pryor, *Colored Travelers*, p. 126; David Blight, ed., *Narrative of the Life of Frederick Douglass, an American Slave, Written by Himself, with Related Documents*, 2nd ed. (Boston: Bedford/St. Martin's, 2003), pp. 17–18.

2. "Frederick Douglass to Garrison, Dated Belfast January 1, 1846," in Carter G. Wood-son, *The Mind of the Negro as Reflected in Letters Written During the Crisis, 1800–1860* (New York: Russell and Russell, 1969), p. 391.

3. Blight, *Narrative of the Life of Frederick Douglass*, p. 175.

4. Richard Blackett's work is a foundational study of the political meanings of black abolitionists traveling in Europe. Blackett notes that African Americans successfully cultivated European opposition to American slavery and racism, practicing a politics of shame in their efforts to change the United States. Europe's revolutions made that politics of shame a tool accessible to a broader community of black activists because circumstances on the continent were so well known and often discussed. Blackett also shows that activists made statements of biting scorn about the United States but that they "generally stopped short of total condemna-tion" of their native country. The political uses of citizenship help to explain why activists moderated their rhetorical attacks on the United States. They were invested in the possibility of a changed legal relationship in their native country because it was a republic, because the concept of citizenship was undefined, and because they had been working to build it in a way that would change their legal relationship with the government. See Richard Blackett, *Building an Antislavery Wall: Black Americans in the Atlantic Abolitionist Movement, 1830–1860* (Baton Rouge: Louisiana State University Press, 1983). On Anglo-Atlantic antislavery networks in an earlier period, see Christopher Leslie Brown, *Moral Capital: Foundations of British Abolitionism* (Chapel Hill: University of North Carolina Press, 2006, published for the Omohundro Insti-tute of Early American History and Culture, Williamsburg, VA). Elizabeth Pryor has added critical texture to Blackett's account, focusing on the U.S. side of black travel abroad, especially the struggle to secure passports and the tensions activists like Douglass encountered during their overseas voyages. Pryor, *Colored Travelers*, pp. 103–148.

5. "First of August Celebration; Frederick Douglass' Address," *North Star*, August 4, 1848. Frederick Douglass and his *North Star* in particular examined African Americans' international consciousness. Published from late 1847 through early 1851 (at which point the work was trans-ferred to *Frederick Douglass' Paper*), this newspaper reveals the ideas driving a segment of influ-ential African Americans and antislavery activists during the course of revolutions in Europe. At the time, African American activists generally accepted this Rochester publication as a sort of national voice, and while they likely disagreed with some of its sentiments, it is clear that a great deal of free black northerners were quite aware of the subjects the paper addressed. Dele-gates to the Colored National Convention of 1848, held in Cleveland, resolved to publish their proceedings in the *Cleveland Herald* and the *North Star*, acknowledging the latter as a paper of importance to free black people across the United States and one that would provide them with a broad audience for the issues addressed at their meeting. See "Report of the Proceedings of the Colored National Convention, Held at Cleveland, Ohio, Wednesday September 6, 1848," in *Minutes of the Proceedings of the National Negro Conventions, 1830–1864*, ed. Howard Holman Bell (New York: Arno Press, 1969), p. 9. Douglass himself had toured throughout Europe in the mid-1840s, instilling in him a reverence for the continent (as I will deal with at length later in this chapter) and inspiring the concern that would shape the way he edited and editorialized for the *North Star*. William Wells Brown is also of remarkable importance for similar reasons, as he traveled throughout Europe in various capacities in the late 1840s.

6. Europe had a complex presence in black American politics in the nineteenth century. Extending Richard Blackett's work, Elizabeth Pryor has examined free black people's struggle for passports, a contentious issue because African Americans wanted the legal protection that they symbolized and federal officials often were reluctant to offer that symbol of status. Pryor

has also investigated black people's ocean travels to Europe as spaces of negotiation over equal access to transit. My exploration of the place of Europe in black politics builds on Blackett and Pryor, considering how the combined experiences of being in Europe and reading and writing about the 1848 revolutions were useful to black activists in the United States looking to build citizenship and make concrete changes to their legal position in the nation. Pryor, *Colored Travelers*, esp. pp. 103–148. Elisa Tamarkin suggests that when black activists expressed emotional affinity for England in particular, they were drawing on a larger cultural language of American admiration for an idealized image of the British Empire. That admiration was an important part of U.S. nationalism, and so it would be a fruitful ground for black activists looking to shame the United States in contrast to the United Kingdom. Elisa Tamarkin, *Anglophilia: Deference, Devotion, and Antebellum America* (Chicago: University of Chicago Press, 2008). Black abolitionists joined their white counterparts in connecting with activists overseas. William Lloyd Garrison in particular believed fervently that his antislavery struggle was linked to a larger fight against tyranny that spanned the Atlantic Ocean. Caleb McDaniel shows how connections with Europe shaped both the ideas and the actions of Garrison and his colleagues and that the revolutions of 1848 led some Garrisonians to reconsider their doubts about the possibilities that politicians might produce radical change. Black activists agreed with Garrison on the political possibilities of international connections, but they were concerned with not only an end of American slavery but also a redefinition of the laws that curtailed American freedom. Black activists' interests in legal change and in the search for a community in which they might belong, both rooted in their blackness, led them to respond to the 1848 revolutions with more optimism than the Garrisonians and by considering how they might deploy that set of events to shape their lives in the United States. McDaniel, *The Problem of Democracy in the Age of Slavery*, esp. pp. 66–86.

7. Among the few things that the Constitution made clear in regard to citizen status is that the framers understood it as a connection between an individual and a physical space. The president was required to be "a natural born Citizen," and each state was required to preserve "all privileges and immunities of citizens in the several states." Citizenship was framed as a product of birth or residency, but in each case, it was defined by a person's relationship to U.S. territory. Amid Europe's revolutions, black people would consider a citizenry that was not territorially defined. On citizenship in relation to the territory of the United States, see Linda Kerber, "The Meanings of Citizenship," *Journal of American History* 84, no. 3 (December 1997): 833–854; Pauline Maier, "Nationhood and Citizenship," in *Diversity and Citizenship: Rediscovering American Nationhood*, ed. Susan Dunn and Gary Jacobsohn (Lanham, MD: Rowan and Littlefield, 1996).

8. For general treatments of these revolutions, see Jonathan Sperber, *The European Revolutions, 1848–1851* (New York: Cambridge University Press, 2005); Peter Stearns, *1848: The Revolutionary Tide in Europe* (New York: Norton, 1974).

9. Sperber, *The European Revolutions*, p. 116.

10. On the extent of newspaper publication in the early United States, especially its centrality to partisan political work, see Jeffrey L. Pasley, *The Tyranny of Printers: Newspaper Politics in the Early American Republic* (Charlottesville: University of Virginia Press, 2013), esp. pp. 1–23; Alexis de Tocqueville, *Democracy in America, Abridged with an Introduction by Michael Kammen* (Boston: Bedford/St. Martin's, 2009), chap. 19. Similarly, although with an emphasis on the interactions between a local press and the nineteenth-century struggles for national unification, see Trish Loughran, *The Republic in Print: Print Culture in the Age of U.S. Nation Building, 1770–1870* (New York: Columbia University Press, 2013).

11. Jeffrey Kerr-Ritchie, *Rites of August First: Emancipation Day in the Black Atlantic World* (Baton Rouge: Louisiana State University Press, 2007); Edward Bartlett Rugemer, *The Problem of Emancipation: The Caribbean Roots of the American Civil War* (Baton Rouge: Louisiana State University Press, 2008), esp. pp. 222–257.

12. "First of August Celebration; Frederick Douglass' Address," *North Star*, August 4, 1848.

13. Ibid. Douglass revisited this point in his famous Fifth of July oration from 1852: "Oceans no longer divide, but link nations together. From Boston to London is now a holiday excursion. Space is comparatively annihilated. Thoughts expressed on one side of the Atlantic are distinctly heard on the other." See Blight, *Narrative of the Life of Frederick Douglass*, p. 170.

14. "Foreign News," *North Star*, March 24, 1848. In 1845, the *Cambria* crossed the Atlantic from Liverpool to Halifax in the remarkable time of nine days, twenty hours, thirty minutes at an average speed of 10.71 knots. See "The Blue Riband of the North Atlantic, Westbound," at http://www.greatships.net/riband.html, accessed May 19, 2019. Readers of the *North Star* were made well aware of events outside of their immediate vicinity; "Foreign News" was a regular column, and the paper also included frequent contributions from a correspondent in London. See, for instance, "From the London Weekly Dispatch," *North Star*, January 7, 1848.

15. "Fifteen Days Later from Europe," *New-York Daily Tribune*, March 20, 1848. For another celebration of the revolutions, see "Mass Meeting of the Friends of Republican of Al Countries," *New-York Daily Tribune*, March 22, 1848.

16. Timothy Mason Roberts, *Distant Revolutions: 1848 and the Challenge of American Exceptionalism* (Charlottesville: University of Virginia Press, 2009), esp. pp. 11–15. Roberts notes that the 1848 revolutions occasioned both self-celebration and critical reflection in the United States on the goals and process of the American Revolution, while at the same time producing questions that would persist about foreign policy and the nation's responsibilities to aid free-dom fighters in other parts of the world. American people were more aware of the revolutions than earlier international events because of the proliferation of newspapers and because a num-ber of major U.S. papers sent correspondents to cover events in Europe. Black activists invoked the revolutions of 1848 as part of a larger interest in events from the early nineteenth century in which people pursued work to broaden freedom and self-determination in various parts of the world. Mitch Kachun, "'Our Platform Is as Broad as Humanity': Transatlantic Freedom Movements and the Idea of Progress in Nineteenth-Century African American Thought and Activism," *Slavery and Abolition* 24, no. 3 (December 2003): 1–23, esp. 7.

17. "Minutes of the State Convention of the Coloured Citizens of Pennsylvania, Con-vened at Harrisburg, December 13th and 14th, 1848," in *Proceedings of the Black State Conven-tions, 1840–1865*, vol. 1, ed. Philip S. Foner and George E. Walker (Philadelphia: Temple University Press, 1979), pp. 119–138.

18. Ibid., pp. 123–124.

19. Ibid., pp. 123–124.

20. Presumably, he referred to U.S. Constitution, Article I, Section 8, Clause 15. Douglass rightfully read slavery into the text of that measure, which also justified calling a militia "to execute the laws of the union."

21. "Selections. Speeches," *North Star*, June 15, 1849.

22. Ibid.

23. Black activists engaged with and expanded on the arguments that David Walker made in his *Appeal*, first published in 1829. Walker invoked a community he addressed as "coloured citizens of the world" and which crossed established political borders. He sought a broad,

international political coalition rooted in racial identity. And he also spoke briefly to the array of legal restrictions under which black Americans lived, North and South. Black activists in the later antebellum period built on Walker's work by connecting their gestures toward people around the Atlantic directly to their arguments about the legal protections they believed should be part of citizenship. They reflected, at times explicitly, on the forceful critiques of racism and calls for unity that defined Walker's project, but in the work of later black activists, the concept of the citizen meant something more specific and held a different kind of legal significance than it had in Walker's *Appeal*. Walker, *Walker's Appeal, in Four Articles, Together with a Preamble, to the Coloured Citizens of the World, but in Particular, and Very Expressly, to Those of the United States of America* (Boston: Revised and published by David Walker, 1830); Peter P. Hinks, *To Awaken My Afflicted Brethren: David Walker and the Problem of Antebellum Slave Resistance* (Philadelphia: University of Pennsylvania Press, 1997).

24. Legal authorities in the United States did not formally make birth a basis for citizen status until the Fourteenth Amendment. Still, lawmakers had long acknowledged nativity as an important foundation for people's claims to rights and legal status in the United States. See Kettner, *The Development of American Citizenship, 1608–1870*, esp. p. 342.

25. In addition, Irish people planned to hold a "general meeting" in every parish in the country on St. Patrick's Day for further revelry, although some anticipated that British officials would step in to limit the celebrations. "Foreign News. The News from Europe by the Caledonia," *North Star*, March 31, 1848.

26. Ibid. Alongside these anecdotes of cultural connections, the *North Star* cited market circumstances that conveyed the inextricable links of communities across the continent. In the wake of the revolution, the Paris stock exchange closed for several days, hindering European and Atlantic commerce, especially in England, where people were uncertain "as to the permanency of the present order of things." The New York *Emancipator* also noted that "the news of the Revolution in France produced the deepest alarm in Madrid. . . . The whole of the Court balls were stopped, and Queen Christiana [*sic*] had taken to her bed." *Emancipator*, April 5, 1848.

27. "Frederick Douglass' Address," *North Star*, August 4, 1848.

28. The revolutionary movements across the continent were connected in part by the fact that early political uprisings in France inspired rebels and frightened established leaders further east in Europe. Jonathan Sperber's account of the revolutions, though, emphasizes the extent of nationalism as a motivator in the various places that uprisings occurred and also highlights the variety of ideas that produced rebellious action among people within particular nations. There were national and local contexts important to the development of uprisings across Europe. Sperber, *The European Revolutions*.

29. "Foreign News. The News from Europe by the Caledonia," *North Star*, March 31, 1848.

30. "From Zion's Watchman. European Opinions of Southern Institutions," *Colored American*, September 29, 1838; Blackett, *Building an Antislavery Wall*; Manisha Sinha, *The Slave's Cause: A History of Abolition* (New Haven, CT: Yale University Press, 2014), esp. pp. 339–380.

31. "Presentation and Farewell Meeting," *Liberator*, July 27, 1849. On the place of international events in American discussions on slavery, see Edward Bartlett Rugemer, *The Problem of Emancipation: The Caribbean Roots of the American Civil War* (Baton Rouge: Louisiana State University Press, 2008).

32. "Presentation and Farewell Meeting," *Liberator*, July 27, 1849. Traveling abroad provided black activists with a complicated kind of power. British abolitionists welcomed African Americans and were delighted with the crowds that black speakers drew. And their overseas experiences were important for black activists' political development. But ideological tensions within the antislavery movement led British abolitionists to pull their black colleagues in multiple directions and at times to try to dictate the language and ideas black activists conveyed in their speeches. White Britons, like white Americans, helped secure black activists with critical opportunities to speak but shared controlling impulses rooted in ideas of black inferiority. Blackett, *Building an Antislavery Wall*, pp. 140–141. Slave narratives written and promoted by black and white abolitionists offer a useful window into the fraught power relations between the two. Douglass's 1845 *Narrative*, for instance, carries two prefatory statements, one from William Lloyd Garrison and the other from Wendell Phillips, in which the two white activists vouch for Douglass's story and certify that he was its writer, work that was necessary among readers, both pro- and antislavery, who harbored doubts that black people could be literate, let alone skilled and evocative writers. On the narratives, see William Andrews, *To Tell a Free Story: The First Century of Afro-American Autobiography, 1760–1865* (Urbana: University of Illinois Press, 1986).

33. "Presentation and Farewell Meeting," *Liberator*, July 27, 1849.

34. "Frederick Douglass' Address," *North Star*, August 4, 1848.

35. Douglass's travel in Europe in the mid-1840s gave him a unique perspective, and when other black activists began expressing concern with Europe in 1848, Douglass had already begun to emphasize the importance of Atlantic activism. Writing to William Lloyd Garrison from Scotland in February 1846, Douglass linked his previous experiences in enslavement to the widespread poverty and oppression that he witnessed in Ireland. "He who really and truly feels for the American slave," Douglass wrote, "cannot steel his heart to the woes of others; and he who thinks himself an abolitionist, yet cannot enter into the wrongs of others, has yet to find a true foundation for his anti-slavery faith." He reversed that self-critique when he later criticized American people for ignoring slavery at home while celebrating revolutions against tyranny abroad. As early as 1846, he claimed to "know [that] the cause of humanity is one the world over" and began to encourage others to think and work globally. For Douglass's letter, see "Frederick Douglass to Garrison, Dated Montrose, Scotland, February 26, 1846," in Woodson, *The Mind of the Negro*. Garrison printed the letter in his *Liberator*, March 27, 1846.

36. See articles titled "The Hyperion" in *North Star* August 3, 1849, and August 31, 1849. Douglass opened his paper for voices that represented multiple black political perspectives, but it is difficult to say exactly how he felt about this group of activists who were criticizing his editorial work. On August 3, Douglass seemed quite pleased to announce the "beautifully printed and ably conducted Journal," writing that the newspaper would "be extensively circulated, and exceedingly useful to our oppressed fellow-countrymen." By August 31, his optimism had faded, and he suggested that black activists anoint and support a single paper as their public voice "instead of squandering their money and mis-applying their energy on a multitude of papers which can never be supported." Perhaps Douglass was glad to see the failure of a paper that might be a rival to his own for subscriptions. While his statements from August 31 might have resulted from a self-serving desire to head the single black American paper, it is possible that Douglass would have embraced any number of black newspapers so long as they offered strident, competent critiques of American slavery and racial policy and aimed at securing rights for African Americans.

37. "From the Hyperion. ADDRESS TO THE COLORED PEOPLE OF THE UNITED STATES," *North Star*, August 10, 1849.

38. "Liberia," *Freedom's Journal*, February 14, 1829.

39. "William Wells Brown to His Former Slave Owner," dated London, November 23, 1849, in Woodson, *The Mind of the Negro*, p. 215.

40. On nationalism and identity in the early nineteenth-century United States, see Wald-streicher, *In the Midst of Perpetual Fetes*. Waldstreicher notes that shared rituals, celebrations, and expressed ideals built the United States as a nation, including collective public commemo-rations of the nation's revolution, all of which became critical to how many in the young nation understood themselves as Americans.

41. "Redemption of Cuba," *North Star*, July 20, 1849. Edward Rugemer cites another instance of black people embracing violent revolution against tyrants, noting a toast that black Ohioans offered to slave rebels Nat Turner, Cinque, and Madison Washington during an 1849 first of August celebration. Rugemer, *The Problem of Emancipation*, pp. 222–223.

42. On the struggle for and meaning of passports among black Americans, see Pryor, *Colored Travelers*, pp. 103–125.

43. Clayton's rejection letter is excerpted in *The Annual Report of the American and For-eign Anti-Slavery Society: Presented at New York, May 7, 1850: With the Addresses and Resolutions* (New York: Published by the A. & F. Anti-Slavery Society, 1850), p. 128.

44. "Selections—from the Liberator—Letter from William Wells Brown," *North Star*, December 14, 1849.

45. For more on this, see Blackett, *Building an Antislavery Wall*, pp. 3–46. Blackett argues that black abolitionists used their work in Europe to create a "moral cordon," in which univer-sal condemnation of the United States might lead to abolition in that country.

46. "Extract, from the Address Read to the People's Convention at Worcester," *North Star*, July 14, 1848. For more on the Whig Party, see Daniel Walker Howe, *The Political Culture of the American Whigs* (Chicago: University of Chicago Press, 1979); Michael Holt, *The Rise and Fall of the American Whig Party: Jacksonian Politics and the Onset of the Civil War* (New York: Oxford University Press, 1999).

47. "Anti-Slavery Feeling in Virginia," *North Star*, June 9, 1848.

48. "From the London Times HYPOCRITICAL SYMPATHY—ATROCIOUS PRAC-TICE," *North Star*, December 1, 1848.

49. It was an uphill struggle to convince American people to stand against slavery given the centrality of slave-produced cotton to the U.S. economy and to wider networks of credit and commerce that spanned the Atlantic. Still, the reception of slave narratives, the endurance of antislavery organizations, and the significance of Britain as a cultural touchstone for the United States might have encouraged activists that they could stir public opinion against slav-ery. See Edward Baptist, *The Half Has Never Been Told: Slavery and the Making of American Capitalism* (New York: Basic Books, 2014); Sven Beckert, *Empire of Cotton: A Global History* (New York: Vintage, 2014); Blackett, *Building an Antislavery Wall*; Sinha, *The Slave's Cause*; Tamarkin, *Anglophilia*.

50. "A Column of Atrocities," *North Star*, July 13, 1849. The excerpts reflected what Carol Lasser has described as voyeuristic abolitionism, a political form focusing on depictions of sexual violence and other forms of physical brutality that Saidiya Hartman argues have predom-inated both in abolitionist literature and in more recent discussions and representations of the terrors of slavery. See Carol Lasser, "Voyeuristic Abolitionism: Sex, Gender, and the Transfor-mation of Antislavery Rhetoric," *Journal of the Early Republic* 28, no. 1 (Spring 2008): 83–114;

Saidiya Hartman, *Scenes of Subjection: Terror, Slavery, and Self-Making in Nineteenth-Century America* (Oxford: Oxford University Press, 1997).

51. "American Democracy—What It Is," *North Star*, April 20, 1849.

52. For more on the *Pearl* incident and its meanings, see Richard C. Rohrs, "Antislavery Politics and the Pearl Incident," *Historian* 56, no. 4 (Summer 1994): 711–726. Rohrs indicates that seventy-six enslaved black people escaped on the *Pearl*, while John Dick put the number at seventy-four. Douglass printed an early description of the events under the title "Capture of Runaway Slaves," *North Star*, April 28, 1848.

53. "Drayton and Sayres. Fined for What?" *North Star*, June 1, 1849.

54. "Minutes of the State Convention of the Coloured Citizens of Pennsylvania, Convened at Harrisburg, December 13th and 14th, 1848," in *Proceedings of the Black State Conventions, 1840–1865*, vol. 1, ed. Foner and Walker, p. 125.

55. Ibid., p. 125.

56. This critique might reflect a general gap between vocal activist figures and black northerners more broadly. See, for instance, Rael, *Black Identity and Black Protest in the Antebellum North*, pp. 54–81.

57. "Appeal to the Colored Citizens of Pennsylvania," in *Proceedings of the Black State Conventions, 1840–1865*, vol. 1, ed. Foner and Walker, pp. 126–127. The title of their address seems to have reflected on David Walker's work, and the activists took a similar approach, looking to political actors abroad as inspiration and admonition for more ardent protest among black Americans at home.

58. "Report of the Proceedings of the Colored National Convention, Held at Cleveland, Ohio, on Wednesday, September 6, 1848," in *Minutes of the Proceedings of the National Negro Conventions, 1830–1864*, ed. H. H. Bell (New York: Arno Press, 1969), pp. 7–8, 17–19.

59. "A Call for a State Convention," *Impartial Citizen*, August 8, 1849.

60. As these examples suggest, black activists' references to Europe open a window to consider how vocal leaders related to the wider African American populace. Like Robert Purvis in Pennsylvania or Jermain Loguen in New York, John Roberts, a proponent of Boston's all-black Smith School, tried to use Europe to convince other African Americans to support his cause. Roberts said that the segregated school was an initial "opening" in the move toward a new racial order. In the same way, he said, Europe's revolutions marked the dawn of a new era for progress. "The age is one of improvement and advancement," he declared, "and liberty is on her march of triumph through the world." Boston's school board favored Roberts and voted to preserve the Smith School, but passionate opposition from other black Bostonians indicates that Europe's example did not always garner African American support for a given cause. Roberts undoubtedly lost some standing among black Bostonians because he supported a segregated Smith School. While he and other vocal figures referenced Europe to push people in particular political directions, they remained beholden to the concerns and desires that motivated their constituents. "Meetings of Colored Citizens of Boston, on the Subject of Equal School Rights," *Liberator*, September 7, 1849. For more on the Smith School controversy, see Kantrowitz, *More Than Freedom*, pp. 122–130.

61. "Auburn Celebration," *Impartial Citizen*, August 8, 1849.

62. "Communications. The Morning Dawn!" *North Star*, May 5, 1848.

63. "Government and Its Subjects," *North Star*, November 9, 1849.

64. Ibid.

65. Ibid.

66. On European immigration and some of its implications in the United States, see Kerby Miller, *Emigrants and Exiles: Ireland and the Irish Exodus to North America* (New York: Oxford University Press, 1988); Mischa Honeck, *We Are the Revolutionists: German-Speaking Immigrants and American Abolitionists After 1848* (Athens: University of Georgia Press, 2011); Herbert Gutman, *Work, Culture, and Society in Industrializing America* (New York: Knopf, 1976).

67. "Meetings of Colored Citizens of Boston, on the Subject of Equal School Rights," *Liberator*, September 7, 1849.

68. Exploring the history of American citizenship, Linda Kerber has suggested that non-citizens have been essential for the understanding of citizenship. The nature of citizenship as a desirable yet undefined status has led people to seek it by distinguishing themselves from those they deem outsiders. African Americans knew that they wanted to make citizenship a status available to the native born, and they bolstered that argument by suggesting that those who were foreign born were not citizens and were less entitled to the opportunities the U.S. government might provide. The white immigrant other was a tool for African Americans looking to define and claim citizenship. See Linda Kerber, "The Stateless as Citizen's Other: A View from the United States," *American Historical Review* 112, no. 1 (February 2007): 1–34.

69. "Selections. Speeches," *North Star*, June 15, 1849.

70. For brief background treatments of nativism as a cultural and political force in the North, see Sean Wilentz, *Chants Democratic: New York City & the Rise of the American Working Class, 1788–1850* (New York: Oxford University Press, 1984), pp. 266–269; Bruce Levine, *Half Slave and Half Free: The Roots of Civil War* (New York: Hill and Wang, 1992), pp. 201–203. On stereotypes and cultural conceptions concerning Irish immigrants in particular, see Noel Ignatiev, *How the Irish Became White* (New York: Routledge, 1995).

71. "Irishmen," *North Star*, May 5, 1848.

72. "A Southern Argument," *North Star*, April 20, 1849.

73. "Irishmen." In some of the same issues of his newspaper in which Douglass celebrated the possibilities of Europe's revolutions and praised republican revolutionaries, he perpetuated stereotypes of European immigrants in the United States.

74. Like Linda Kerber, Rogers Smith highlights the extent to which exclusionary arguments have been central to the contested process of building American citizenship. See Rogers Smith, *Civic Ideals: Conflicting Visions of Citizenship in U.S. History* (New Haven, CT: Yale University Press, 1997).

75. Linda Kerber raises this question in a study of the concept of statelessness: "Is it possible that the state *needs* its negation in order to know itself?" Kerber defines the stateless as a person who either does not claim allegiance to a country or lacks rights protected by a government. She suggests that the noncitizen status of black people, Indians, and women was historically a form of statelessness against which people understood American citizenship. See Kerber, "The Stateless as the Citizens' Other."

76. W. Caleb McDaniel, *The Problem of Democracy in the Age of Slavery: Garrisonian Abolitionists and Transatlantic Reform* (Baton Rouge: Louisiana State University Press, 2013).

77. "France," *North Star*, April 28, 1848.

78. Ibid.

79. On the centrality of a desire to belong for Douglass and other African Americans, see David Blight, *Frederick Douglass' Civil War: Keeping Faith in Jubilee* (Baton Rouge: Louisiana State University Press, 1989). This 1848 editorial bears interesting contrasts to Douglass's 1852 Fifth of July speech. Both share a goal of critiquing the nation's racial order, but in 1848,

Douglass spoke as a person who wanted to own the burden of American racism, while in 1852, he spoke as one who saw that that racism made it impossible for him to truly own either positive or negative aspects of his native country.

80. Richard Blackett notes that activists abroad shamed the United States while carefully avoiding absolute condemnation of the country. Steven Kantrowitz's work outlines the ways that a brotherhood was something more than freedom. My work here is to extend this critique of the nation's racial order, to argue that black activists wanted friendship or brotherhood or love but did not see it as sufficient protection. They understood the depths of prejudice and felt the only way to ensure that they would be secure members of American communities was to promote a raft of legal changes that would require states and individuals to accept them and provide them with a real relationship to governments in which they could express grievances and expect to be heard by those in positions of formal power. Blackett, *Building an Antislavery Wall*; Kantrowitz, *More Than Freedom*.

CHAPTER 4

1. For contemporary coverage of Dixon's case and the surrounding mob action, see "Kidnapping in New-York," *Liberator*, April 21, 1837; "The Slave Case," *Colored American*, April 29, 1837; "On Monday, John Davis . . . ," *Colored American*, May 27, 1837; "After a Long . . . ," *Colored American,* July 8, 1837, "Dixon Meeting," *Colored American*, July 15, 1837. The New-York Historical Society site "New-York Divided" has compiled a collection of evidence that forms a narrative of the controversy, accessed September 28, 2018, http://www.nydivided.org/popup/People/WilliamDixon.php. This chapter's title comes from a letter by the white abolitionist Henry Clarke Wright, dated Paterson, New Jersey, April 13, 1837, and published in the *Liberator*, April 21, 1837. Wright's claim is that in any potential hearing, an alleged fugitive faces the challenge of gathering evidence and then seeking a fair proceeding among lawmakers predisposed to protect the property rights of an alleged slaveowner. "Here is the great difficulty in all cases of runaways, or citizens claimed as such. The whole burden of proof is thrown on the colored man."

2. "The Account, Given Under the Head of *Court of Sessions* . . . ," *Plaindealer*, April 15, 1837, p. 314.

3. "Tremendous Riot in the Park," *Liberator*, April 21, 1837.

4. In part, laws to reclaim fugitive slaves were important to American people because protecting property was critical to the Lockean concept of freedom that had motivated many of the government's framers. The Constitution required that fugitives from "service or labour . . . shall be delivered up" to the person who claimed their labor, a protection of slaveowners' property rights but one that did not declare who was responsible for delivering a fugitive to a claimant. Southerners were anxious about that uncertainty and pushed for the 1793 law that gave slaveowners the sanction of federal law to go into free states to pursue and arrest their fugitive property. U.S. Constitution, Article IV, Section 2. On slave ownership and Lockean freedom, see Stephanie Smallwood, "Commodified Freedom: Interrogating the Limits of Anti-Slavery Ideology in the Early Republic," *Journal of the Early Republic* 24, no. 2 (Summer 2004): 289–298. On the 1793 law generally, see Thomas D. Morris, *Free Men All: The Personal Liberty Laws of the North, 1780–1861* (Baltimore: Johns Hopkins University Press, 1974), pp. 18–22.

5. On kidnapping in the North and black people's responses, see, for instance, Richard J. Bell, "Thence to Patty Cannon's: Gender, Family, and the Reverse Underground Railroad,"

Slavery and Abolition 37, no. 4 (April 2016): 661– 679; Hodges, *David Ruggles*; Eric Foner, *Gateway to Freedom: The Hidden History of the Underground Railroad* (New York: Norton, 2015); Carol Wilson, *Freedom at Risk: The Kidnapping of Free Blacks in America, 1780–1865* (Lexington: University Press of Kentucky, 1994).

6. Like white urbanites, black residents of antebellum cities took their politics to the street, and in these public events, we can understand the desires and interests of people who have not left extensive written records of their ideas. On popular political practices, see Gilje, *The Road to Mobocracy*; Waldstreicher, *In the Midst of Perpetual Fetes*; Newman, *Parades and the Politics of the Street*.

7. On black northerners' work to protect alleged fugitives, see Hodges, *David Ruggles*; Foner, *Gateway to Freedom*; Kantrowitz, *More Than Freedom*; Diemer, *The Politics of Black Citizenship*; Sarah L. H. Gronningsater, "'On Behalf of His Race and the Lemmon Slaves': Louis Napoleon, Northern Black Legal Culture, and the Politics of Sectional Crisis," *Journal of the Civil War Era* 7, no. 2 (June 2017): 206–241.

8. Kantrowitz and Diemer both explore the blended legal and extralegal actions that black people pursued in protecting fugitives, and they consider the development of personal liberty laws in Massachusetts and Pennsylvania, respectively. Vigilance work and fugitive rescues were two parts of a larger legal project, political activities that had the potential to and were at times explicitly directed toward reshaping the legal terms of black lives in the United States by making claims about the content of citizenship. Physical violence, rather than a "dimension [of] their assertion of citizenship," was a political statement with the potential to define the content of that uncertain legal status. See Kantrowitz, *More Than Freedom*, pp. 175–22, quotation from p. 179; Diemer, *The Politics of Black Citizenship*, pp. 94–138.

9. I have reflected here on the work of Dylan Penningroth and Anne Twitty to consider the connections between legal and extralegal tactics in black politics from slavery through emancipation. Both have explored the ways legal and extralegal actions together brought black people into contact with and shaped their interactions with formal legal authorities. In the slaveholding South and during the process of emancipation, extralegal realities such as people's reputations in their communities shaped the ways they interacted with formal legal processes. Black people used "loud talking" to establish that they had once been free or that they had possessed a particular piece of property, and judges often had to rely on those informal kinds of evidence in order to make informed decisions in legal proceedings. Extralegal actions thus constructed legal realities, rather than existing outside of or working against formal legal developments. Free black activists, like their enslaved southern brethren, used both legal and extralegal political forms, at times together, to work toward formal legal protections. Dylan Penningroth, *The Claims of Kinfolk: African American Property and Community in the Nineteenth-Century South* (Chapel Hill: University of North Carolina Press, 2003); Twitty, *Before Dred Scott*.

10. "From the N.Y. Tribune. National Free Soil Convention," *Frederick Douglass' Paper*, August 20, 1852.

11. James Kettner notes that by the 1820s, this clause suggesting that citizenship was connected to rights had become a hallmark of assumptions about the meaning of citizen status. Kettner, *The Development of American Citizenship, 1608–1870*, p. 287.

12. "More Slave Trouble," *Herald*, April 12, 1837. White abolitionist Henry Clarke Wright offers a useful description of Dixon's day in court and his brief statement in "Kidnapping in New-York," *Liberator*, April 21, 1837. On Riker's politics, see Hodges, *David Ruggles*, pp. 61–64.

13. Curry, *The Free Black in Urban America*, p. 250.

14. At their founding meeting, members called themselves "a committee to aid the people of color, legally to obtain their rights." But Graham Hodges notes that legal and extralegal work fit under the umbrella of "practical abolitionism." *The First Annual Report for the New York Committee of Vigilance for the Year 1837: Together with Important Facts Relative to their Proceedings* (New York: Piercy & Reed, 1837), p. 3; Hodges, *David Ruggles*, esp. pp. 88–92.

15. "New York Committee of Vigilance," *Colored American*, January 20, 1838. On the work Ruggles defined as "practical abolition," including aid to fugitive slaves, see Hodges, *David Ruggles*, pp. 84–94. Cornish also printed an argument from Joseph Pickering, a young white New York lawyer, who called access to jury trial "the birthright of every citizen" and acknowledged the significance of that presumption in American law. He proclaimed that any person, regardless of race, "is deemed, in judgment of law, to be free, until the contrary is established," a direct challenge to the country's racialized slave system. "Very Important Subject," *Colored American*, August 12, 1837.

16. *First Annual Report of the New York Committee of Vigilance, For the Year 1837, Together with Important Facts Relative to Their Proceedings* (New York: Piercy & Reed, Printers, 1837), esp. p. 13; Hodges, *David Ruggles*, pp. 84–94. On black New York, see Alexander, *African or American?*; Harris, *In the Shadow of Slavery*.

17. On the legal contexts of slavecatching and kidnapping in New York, see Hodges, *David Ruggles*, pp. 86–88; Foner, *Gateway to Freedom*, pp. 38–52; and especially Morris, *Free Men All*, pp. 53–58.

18. "Horrible Disgrace," *Colored American*, April 22, 1837. Slavecatchers boasted of the speed with which they could secure a captive in Judge Richard Riker's court. See Foner, *Gateway to Freedom*, p. 52.

19. "Dickson's Trial," *Colored American*, April 29, 1837.

20. Ibid. My use of "mob" reflects the work of Paul Gilje, who shows that mob action was a central aspect of popular politics in the early American republic. Gilje, *The Road to Mobocracy*.

21. "To the Thoughtless Part of Our Colored Citizens," *Colored American*, April 15, 1837. On gender and respectability in black politics, see Rael, *Black Identity and Black Protest in the Antebellum North*, esp. chap. 4. Black women did essential work in sustaining black communities and political bodies in the North, although nineteenth-century gender norms often left them marginalized in public spaces. See Dunbar, *A Fragile Freedom*; Psyche Williams-Forson, "What Did They Eat?"

22. "New York Committee of Vigilance," *Colored American*, January 20, 1838.

23. Morris, *Free Men All*, pp. 52–58.

24. "From the Emancipator. City Recorder—Kidnapping—and Free People of Color in New-York," *National Enquirer*, October 15, 1836.

25. "To the Thoughtless Part of our Colored Citizens," *Colored American*, April 15, 1837.

26. Ibid.

27. Ibid. In the aftermath of the riot, Cornish corrected a *New York Times* editorial that described a parade of the Clarkson Benevolent Society as a public protest against Dixon's apprehension. "Base Slander," *Colored American*, April 29, 1837. In national conventions during the early 1830s, black activists repeatedly advised against public processions because of their concern with respectability but also because of the increasing problem of racially motivated mob violence in struggles over public space. See "Minutes and Proceedings of the Second

Annual Convention," p. 27, and "Minutes and Proceedings of the First Annual Convention," in Bell, *Minutes of the Proceedings of the National Negro Conventions*. On the turn from mobbing to race riots, see Gilje, *The Road to Mobocracy*, pp. 121–170.

28. *Herald*, April 19, 1837; *Liberator*, April 21, 1837; Morris, *Free Men All*, p. 11. Dixon's council would have directed the writ *de homine replegiando* to a sheriff, paid a bond, and declared before a judge that the accused would return for a hearing when called.

29. "Trial by Jury" and "Kidnapping in New York," *National Enquirer*, April 29, 1837.

30. "Commonwealth of Massachusetts: Report," *Liberator*, April 21, 1837; Morris, *Free Men All*, pp. 64–65, 76–79.

31. "Law of New Jersey," *National Enquirer*, June 3, 1837; James J. Gigantino II, *The Ragged Road to Abolition: Slavery and Freedom in New Jersey, 1775–1865* (Philadelphia: University of Pennsylvania Press, 2015), esp. pp. 149–173. Generally, southern officials presumed that a black person was enslaved, and in setting out a required legal process for rendition of alleged fugitives, northern courts presumed that a black person was free. Still, many black northerners doubted that courts truly presumed freedom, arguing that lawmakers simply went through a required set of legal proceedings with the predetermined conclusion that a person was enslaved. On the legal structures relating to alleged fugitives generally, see Thomas Morris, *Southern Slavery and the Law* (Chapel Hill: University of North Carolina Press, 1996), pp. 2–28; Christopher L. M. Eisgruber, "Justice Story, Slavery, and the Natural Law Foundations of American Constitutionalism," *Chicago Law Review* 55, no. 1 (1988): 273–327.

32. "For the National Enquirer. Buckingham," *National Enquirer*, July 27, 1837.

33. On the breakdown of comity, especially in the Northeast, see Paul Finkelman, *An Imperfect Union: Slavery, Federalism, and Comity* (Chapel Hill: University of North Carolina Press, 1981), pp. 126–145; Morris, *Southern Slavery and the Law*, pp. 2–28.

34. Samuel Cornish and others at the newspaper helped knit together this news and the communities involved in the pages of the *Colored American*. See "Ohio Legislature," February 17, 1838; "Fugitive Slaves" and "Connecticut Coming Round," June 16, 1838; "From the Michigan Observer. A Bright Spot," August 18, 1838; "Public Meeting in Philadelphia," January 30, 1841; "Legislature," May 11, 1839; "A Voice from New Haven," August 1, 1840; and "Thomas C. Brown," July 15, 1837.

35. Joanna Brooks has suggested that race and class acted as barriers to restrict African Americans from accessing the public sphere and led them to construct a black counterpublic through their protest statements, institutions, meetings, and celebrations. But the central techniques of nineteenth-century African American politics—conventions, petitions, street processions, mob actions—were traditional early American political tools that inserted black protest forcefully into the antebellum public sphere. Black activists used traditional techniques to assert their essential Americanness, claiming a rightful place within their native country. On black politics and the public, see Joanna Brooks, "The Early American Public Sphere and the Emergence of a Black Print Counterpublic," *William and Mary Quarterly* 62, no. 1 (January 2005): 67–92; Geoff Eley, "Politics, Culture, and the Public Sphere," *Positions* 10, no. 1 (Spring 2002): 219–236..

36. "A Trial by Jury," *Colored American*, June 8, 1839; "From the Pennsylvania Freeman. Letter from Joshua Coffin," *Colored American*, June 8, 1839; "Jury Trial," *Colored American*, May 23, 1840; "Legislature," *Colored American*, May 11, 1839. Antislavery activists had earlier speculated that legislative shifts would create an opportunity to pass a jury trial law. See "From the Emancipator. Annual Meeting of the NY State Society," *Colored American*, September

22, 1838; Donald E. Fehrenbacher, *The Slaveholding Republic: An Account of the United States Government's Relations to Slavery* (New York: Oxford University Press, 2001).

37. Morris, *Free Men All*, pp. 71–93; Bruce Levine, *Half Slave and Half Free: The Roots of the Civil War* (New York: Hill and Wang, 1992); Leonard L. Richards, *The Slave Power: The Free North and Southern Domination* (Baton Rouge: Louisiana State University Press, 2000).

38. John W. Edmonds, ed., *Statutes at Large of the State of New York, Comprising the Revised Statutes, as they Existed on the 1st Day of July, 1862, and All the General Public Statutes Then in Force, with References to Judicial Decisions, and the Material Notes of the Revisers in Their Reports to the Legislature*, vol. IV (Albany, NY: Weare C. Little, 1863), pp. 518–522. The next week, lawmakers passed a measure to protect black New Yorkers after having been kidnapped, authorizing the governor to appoint agents to travel into other states or territories on rescue missions. Ibid., pp. 522–523.

39. "Jury Trial," *Colored American*, May 23, 1840.

40. On southerners' feeling that protecting black freedom threatened slavery, see Diemer, *The Politics of Black Citizenship*, esp. pp. 137–160.

41. For overviews of the arrest of Margaret Morgan and its place in the larger *Prigg* case, see H. Robert Baker, *Prigg v. Pennsylvania: Slavery, the Supreme Court, and the Ambivalent Constitution* (Lawrence: University of Kansas Press, 2012); Eisgruber, "Justice Story, Slavery, and the Natural Law Foundations of American Constitutionalism."

42. On Story's decision in *Prigg*, see Morris, *Free Men All*, pp. 94–106; Diemer, *The Politics of Black Citizenship*, pp. 119–120, 138–139.

43. "Freedom and Slavery," *Weekly Anglo-African*, March 10, 1842.

44. Morris, *Free Men All*, pp. 97–102.

45. "Decision of the Supreme Court," *Weekly Anglo-African*, March 17, 1842; "Freedom and Slavery," *Weekly Anglo-African*, March 10, 1842.

46. Horton and Horton, *In Hope of Liberty*, pp. 229–235.

47. For background on the committee, see Joseph A. Borome, "The Vigilant Committee of Philadelphia," *Pennsylvania Magazine of History and Biography* 92, no. 3 (July 1968): 320–351. Borome notes Purvis's well-recognized and extensive work as a station manager on the Underground Railroad. Vigilant Committee of Philadelphia Records, June 10, 1839. The committee's minutes of August 15, 1839, relate an incident in which committee members apprehended a man who intended selling a boy into slavery and brought the culprit before the alderman in order to prevent the youth's enslavement.

48. Vigilant Committee of Philadelphia Records, Case Records and Minutes, June 10, 1839. Historical Society of Pennsylvania.

49. Ibid.

50. On women's work in the domestic aspects of black northern politics, see Psyche Williams-Forson, "What Did They Eat?"

51. Vigilant Committee of Philadelphia Records, September 2, 1841.

52. For free black Americans, arguments for and appeals to a higher law were explicitly legal, not only moral appeals. They worked to secure tangible legal change to uphold their moral vision of the nation. James Oakes suggests these resonances of higher law, noting that both pro- and antislavery advocates invoked it in the antebellum period when they sought protections of their natural right to property and, in opposition, protections for a natural human right to freedom. James Oakes, *The Scorpion's Sting: Antislavery and the Coming of the Civil War* (New York: Norton, 2015), pp. 58–62. See also Jane Pease, "The Road to Higher Law," *New York History* 40, no. 2 (April 1959): 117–136.

53. "Inalienable Rights," *Liberator*, February 10, 1843. In their resistance to law, Ruggles and his black colleagues took part in an American tradition of conscientious objectors. For instance, in 1848, at a gathering of Ohio Quakers, one Friend asked pointedly, "Can we, as citizens of the United States, and above all, as professors of the benign doctrines of Christianity, give countenance to laws which we should deem unjust and oppressive if subjected to them ourselves[?]" *Address to the Citizens of the State of Ohio, Concerning What Are Called the Black Laws. Issued in Behalf of the Society of Friends of Indiana Yearly Meeting, by Their Meeting for Sufferings, Representing the Said Yearly Meeting in Its Recess [A Large Portion of the Members Reside in the State of Ohio]* (Cincinnati, OH: A. Pugh, 1848), p. 14. Also worth noting, the *Prigg* decision pushed William Lloyd Garrison to his vocal rejection of constitutional authority. Morris, *Free Men All*, p. 103. And it was that vision of resistance to slavery and the law that motivated John Dick's outrage at the legal proceedings surrounding the *Pearl* incident, a sentiment he revealed in the title of his editorial on the subject. See "Drayton and Sayres. Fined for What?" *North Star*, June 1, 1849.

54. On the ideological impulses behind the Fugitive Slave Act of 1850, see Morris, *Free Men All*, esp. pp. 130–132. Oakes notes that southerners claimed that man's right to property was the foundation of the natural law that preceded the U.S. Constitution. Oakes, *The Scorpion's Sting*, pp. 58–62.

55. "Can Congress Interfere with Slavery?" *North Star*, June 2, 1848.

56. Northerners and southerners ventured states' rights arguments in a utilitarian fashion rather than because of their convictions about the proper terms of federalism. The same southerners who demanded state sovereignty and seceded from the Union in 1861 to protect slavery had, in the late 1840s, led calls for a massive federal system to enforce their title to human property. And the northerners who endorsed personal liberty laws and bristled at slavecatchers invading their territory and violating their states' sovereignty would fight for the sanctity of Union and call upon a massive federal government to end slavery across the United States.

57. Morris, *Free Men All*, pp. 131–133. Congressmen, most notably John C. Calhoun, again raised the issue of southerners' rights to seize fugitives in early 1849. See "Mr. Calhoun's Manifesto. The Address of Southern Delegates in Congress to Their Constituents," *North Star*, February 9, 1849, and "Correspondence of the Tribune," *North Star*, January 19, 1849.

58. On the practice of "sojourning" and some of the ways black people used it to seek freedom, see Twitty, *Before Dred Scott*; Erica Armstrong Dunbar, *Never Caught: The Story of the Washington's Relentless Pursuit of their Runaway Slave, Ona Judge* (New York: Simon and Schuster, 2017).

59. "Decision in a Slave Case in Illinois," *North Star*, February 4, 1848; Paul Finkelman, *An Imperfect Union: Slavery, Federalism, and Comity* (Chapel Hill: University of North Carolina Press, 1981), p. 152. On Lincoln's work in the case, see Joseph A. Ranney, "In Praise of Whig Lawyering: A Commentary on Abraham Lincoln as Lawyer—and Politician," *Marquette Law Review* 93, no. 4 (Summer 2010): 1325–1331.

60. Freedom suits in particular were often decided based on state law. See, for instance, Judith Schaffer, *Slavery, the Civil Law, and the Supreme Court of Louisiana* (Baton Rouge: Louisiana State University Press, 1994), pp. 220–249; Twitty, *Before Dred Scott*, esp. pp. 155–179.

61. This narrative of the Crosswhite affair comes from *Giltner v. Gorham*, 4 McLean, 402; 6 *West. Law J.* 49 (Circuit Court, D. Michigan, 1848). See also Roy E. Finkenbine, "A Beacon of Liberty on the Great Lakes: Race Slavery and the Law in Antebellum Michigan," in *The History of Michigan Law*, ed. Paul Finkelman and Martin Hershock (Athens: Ohio University Press, 2006), pp. 83–107.

62. This law to protect black people was also a mechanism for control, requiring black people entering Michigan to provide a bond as security for good conduct and to document their freedom. See "An Act to Regulate Blacks and Mulattoes, and to Punish the Kidnapping of Such Persons," enacted April 13, 1827, in *Laws of the Territory of Michigan*, vol. II (Lansing, MI: W. S. George and Co., 1874), pp. 634–636; Finkenbine, "A Beacon of Liberty on the Great Lakes," pp. 83–84.

63. William Lloyd Garrison was the leading advocate of the idea that the U.S. Constitution was fundamentally, irreparably corrupt. See W. Caleb McDaniel, *The Problem of Democracy in the Age of Slavery: Garrisonian Abolitionists and Transatlantic Reform* (Baton Rouge: Louisiana State University Press, 2013); Sinha, *The Slave's Cause*, esp. pp. 462–470.

64. "The Crosswhite Case, Marshall, Michigan," *North Star*, April 6, 1849. For McLean's jury instructions, see *Giltner v. Gorham* (1848). On the outcome of *Giltner v. Gorham*, see Finkenbine, "A Beacon of Liberty," p. 90. Justice John McLean would most famously join Benjamin Curtis in a dissent to Roger Taney's decision in the *Dred Scott* case. On McLean's politics and jurisprudence, see Donald E. Fehrenbacher, *The Dred Scott Case: Its Significance in American Law and Politics* (Oxford: Oxford University Press, 1978), esp. pp. 233–234; Jeffrey M. Schmitt, "The Antislavery Judge Reconsidered," *Law and History Review* 29, no. 3 (August 2011): 797–834; Justin Buckley Dyer, "Lincolnian Natural Right, Dred Scott, and the Jurisprudence of John McLean," *Polity* 41, no. 1 (January 2009): 63–85.

65. "Detroit, December 6, 1848," *North Star*, December 15, 1848.

66. "Public Meeting of the Citizens of Detroit," *North Star*, December 29, 1848.

67. Ibid.

68. Ibid.

69. Ibid. See also "From the Model Worker. Crosswhite Case," *North Star*, April 7, 1849. On the 1793 law and southern concerns about its limitations, see Morris, *Free Men All*, pp. 16–22, 35–41.

70. Thomas Morris notes that federal legislators tried to contest the development of this proslavery law, including a proposal from Daniel Webster that would have allowed alleged fugitives to secure a jury trial simply by swearing an oath that they were not a fugitive. Congress did not take up that proposal, and while it might have been a measure designed to appease angry abolitionists, it suggests the larger debate that produced the 1850 Fugitive Slave Act. Morris, *Free Men All*, pp. 130–139.

71. *Senate Journal*, 31st Cong., 1st sess., March 4, 1850, pp. 451–455. On the process of compromise, see David M. Potter, *The Impending Crisis, 1848–1861* (New York: Harper and Rowe, 1976), pp. 90–120.

72. Seward's speech became notorious as a marker of the ways antislavery had penetrated the government at its highest levels. He joined a chorus of black activists who invoked and acted on a sense that divine principles of freedom trumped any obligation to follow man's laws that violated that principle. On this theory and practice of "higher law" abolitionism, see Morris, *Free Men All*, pp. 107–147, passim; Sinha, *The Slave's Cause*, pp. 490–499.

73. "Mason's Fugitive Slave Bill," *North Star*, February 22, 1850; "Weekly Review of the Congressional Proceedings," *North Star*, March 1 and 15, 1850; "We Cheerfully Yield . . . ," *North Star*, March 22, 1850; "XXXIst Congress—in Senate," *North Star*, April 12, 1850; Leonard Richards, *The Slave Power: The Free North and Southern Domination, 1780–1860* (Baton Rouge: Louisiana State University Press, 2000).

74. "An Act to Amend, and Supplementary to, the Act Entitled 'An Act Respecting Fugitives from Justice . . . ,'" 9 Stat. 462 (1850)}; Morris, *Free Men All*, pp. 145–147; Margot

Minardi, *Making Slavery History: Abolitionism and the Politics of Memory in Massachusetts* (New York: Oxford University Press, 2010), p. 135.

75. Steve Kantrowitz sketches a pattern of resistance to fugitive arrests in Boston that characterizes much of black northerners' response to arrests and legal proceedings before and after 1850. Often, a vigilance committee and members of a community learned of an arrest through word of mouth. Crowds gathered outside of courthouses in a show of dissatisfaction and force. At times, members of these crowds violently confronted authorities, particularly as officials attempted to transport a captive from a courtroom to a jail. At the same time, lawyers representing the accused sought writs of *habeas corpus* for respite from captivity. I have been struck by the ways these forms of politics worked together to demand legal change and, as in the case of William Dixon, the ways individuals like David Ruggles brought together legal and extralegal forms of protest. See Kantrowitz, *More Than Freedom*, esp. pp. 72–73.

76. "Meetings of the Colored Citizens of New York," *North Star*, October 24, 1850. Across the North, many lawmakers and other American people acquiesced to the Fugitive Slave Act in the early 1850s in the interest of preserving the Union or upholding property rights. Still, radical abolitionist actions continued in an effort to challenge the law, and states including Vermont, Ohio, and Massachusetts proposed and, in some cases, passed measures that would secure *habeas corpus* and other legal protections to alleged fugitives against the force of the federal law. The law did not determine all American lives, but it was a decisive force in ensuring the arrest of fugitives such as Anthony Burns, who was removed from Boston under a military escort in the summer of 1854. See Morris, *Free Men All*, pp. 148–167.

77. Ezekiel Porter Belden, *New-York, Past, Present, and Future; Comprising a History of the City of New-York, a Description of Its Present Condition, and an Estimate of Its Future Increase* (New York: Putnam, 1849), p. 83; on Cornish's founding, see Thomas Fisk Savage, *The Presbyterian Church of New York City* (New York: Presbytery of New York, 1949), p. 154; Foner, "Underground Railroad Sites in New York City and Brooklyn," *Gateway to Freedom*; Tom Calarco, *Places of the Underground Railroad: A Visual Guide* (Santa Barbara, CA: Greenwood, 2011), p. 217.

78. Quotations from "The Annual Congress of Fanatics," *New York Herald*, May 7, 1850. See also "The Moral, Philosophical, Religious, and Abolition Anniversaries for 1850," *New York Herald*, April 30, 1850; "The Great Annual Convention of the Blacks and Whites—Who Are the Real Disunionists?" *New York Herald*, May 6, 1850; "The Fanatical Convention—Public Opinion," *New York Herald*, May 8, 1850. The more extreme editors of the *New York Globe* wrote that "no public building—no not even the streets must be desecrated by such a proposed assemblage of traitors." "From the NY Globe. Mob Instructions," *North Star*, May 16, 1850. Douglass denounced the *Herald*, *Globe*, and *Journal of Commerce* for trying to incite a riot. "The Vigilance Committee Meeting," *North Star*, May 16, 1850.

79. "New York State Vigilance Committee," *New York Herald*, May 11, 1850. The prophecy is in Matthew 25:31–46. The *Herald* noted that Samuel Ringgold Ward read "the latter part of the 25th chapter."

80. "New York State Vigilance Committee," *New York Herald*, May 11, 1850, provides a detailed account of the meeting's disturbances, especially during Ward's message. See also "From the N.Y. Tribune. New York State Vigilance Committee" and "The Vigilance Committee Meeting," both in *North Star*, May 16, 1850. In that last article, Douglass noted that "the rioters and the police were several times brought into collision during the evening, but I believe no one experienced any bodily harm."

81. Elizabeth Pryor seeks to understand the power of black politics in part through the individuals who struggled to deny black travelers access to transit in Massachusetts, showing that formal segregation policies were a response to black political work. Pryor, *Colored Travelers*, pp. 76–90.

82. Sinha, *The Slave's Cause*, pp. 262–264.

83. "Meetings of the Colored Citizens of New York," *North Star*, October 24, 1850.

84. Ibid. Black activists' promotion of this brand of nullification followed in the footsteps of their earlier antebellum forbears, particularly the radicalism of the Garrisonians, although their reaching out to the state government for relief distinguished their work from that of their predecessors.

85. "Meetings of the Colored Citizens of New York."

86. Curry, *The Free Black in Urban America*, p. 245; *Herald*, April 19, 1837; *Liberator*, April 21, 1837; Morris, *Free Men All*, p. 11.

87. Douglass guessed that Dixon was concerned Douglass "might be a party to a second attempt to recapture him." Frederick Douglass, *My Bondage and My Freedom* (New York: Miller, Orton, and Mulligan, 1855), pp. 337–338.

88. All of these were critical chance developments in Douglass's own experience of slavery and his ultimate escape. See his autobiographies *Narrative of the Life of Frederick Douglass*, pp. 33–36; *My Bondage and My Freedom*, pp. 340–341; *The Life and Times of Frederick Douglass*, p. 249.

CHAPTER 5

1. On the *Dred Scott* case generally, see Donald E. Fehrenbacher, *The Dred Scott Case: Its Significance in American Law and Politics* (Oxford: Oxford University Press, 1978); Austin Allen, *Origins of the Dred Scott Case: Jacksonian Jurisprudence and the Supreme Court, 1837–1857* (Athens: University of Georgia Press, 2006). Fehrenbacher's analysis of Taney's ruling shows how central sectional interests—chiefly desires to expand slavery and preserve white supremacy—were to the chief justice. Among his key insights is that Taney was building an argument to support his political ends rather than reading law to understand the questions before the Court. Allen offers a more nuanced explanation of the Court's ruling, seeking to complicate the work of scholars like Fehrenbacher who place sectional politics at the heart of *Dred Scott*. He explores court decisions and personal writings from the justices to show that the decision also reflected desires to balance federal and state power, foster the developing national economy, and secure legal protections for corporations. While Taney's ruling certainly did more than simply promote sectional interests, Fehrenbacher observes that the justices were keenly aware of the stakes of their decisions amid an urgent sectional crisis. The urgency of that concern took precedence among a range of other projects of their jurisprudence, and some of the justices were especially interested in solving the problem of the future of slavery in the nation's law. See Fehrenbacher, *The Dred Scott Case*, pp. 305–307.

2. "Suffrage Convention of the Colored Citizens of New York, Troy, September 14, 1858," in *Proceedings of the Black State Conventions, 1840–1865*, vol. 1, ed. Philip S. Foner and George E. Walker (Philadelphia: Temple University Press, 1979), pp. 99–101. In 1857, the state legislature had agreed on an equal male suffrage amendment, but due to procedural errors and, according to one observer, the Republican Party's uncertain racial politics, lawmakers did not send the resolutions to the public for a vote. Phyllis F. Field, *The Politics of Race in New York:*

The Struggle for Black Suffrage in the Civil War Era (Ithaca, NY: Cornell University Press, 1982), pp. 104–108; David Blight, *Frederick Douglass' Civil War: Keeping Faith in Jubilee* (Baton Rouge: Louisiana State University Press, 1989), pp. 59–61. On race and the Republican Party, see Eric Foner, *Free Soil, Free Labor, Free Men: The Ideology of the Republican Party Before the Civil War* (New York: Oxford University Press, 1995).

3. C. Peter Ripley, ed., *The Black Abolitionist Papers*, vol. 4 (Chapel Hill: University of North Carolina Press, 1991).

4. "Suffrage Convention of the Colored Citizens of New York," p. 99.

5. *Dred Scott* loomed large for black activists in the late 1850s, and historians have illuminated much of the complexity of reactions to the ruling. Steven Kantrowitz emphasizes the ways black Bostonians used their fraught relationships with the Republican Party to challenge the decision and in particular emphasizes that activists were increasingly willing "to contemplate bloody, violent upheaval" as a political solution. Elizabeth Pryor notes similarly that the decision was an "inspiration for radicalism." Andrew Diemer shows that activists questioned whether they should persist in their loyalty to the nation, citing Robert Purvis's claim that "no allegiance is due from any man, or any class of men, to a Government founded and administered in iniquity." That language threatened that black people might decline loyalty to the government, but it also demanded change in the nation's legal structures, a public claim characteristic of black politics before *Dred Scott*. Activists understood that Taney's ruling had not "resolved . . . the question of black citizenship." After the decision, if they wondered "what reasons were there for hope," they could have reflected on their own political history and their knowledge of the pliable nature of law in the republic. These historians underscore that *Dred Scott* led black people to a profound questioning of their relationship with the United States, that it could inspire rage and despair and fatalism. I am interested here in exploring the reasons black people continued presenting themselves as Americans and the ways their responses to *Dred Scott* reflect not only emotional distress but also a strategic, persistent effort to define their legal position in the country. Taney tried to push black people out of American legal communities, and a key part of many activists' response was to ground themselves more firmly within those communities and continue to demand change in the law by pushing Taney to the margins. See Kantrowitz, *More Than Freedom*, pp. 224–262, quotations from pp. 224 and 262; Pryor, *Colored Travelers*, pp. 123–124; Diemer, *The Politics of Black Citizenship*, pp. 170–174.

6. "Suffrage Convention of the Colored Citizens of New York," p. 99.

7. For more details on Dred Scott's cases, see Paul Finkelman, "Scott v. Sandford: The Court's Most Dreadful Case and How It Changed History," *Chicago-Kent Law Review* 82, no. 3 (2007): 13–24.

8. Harriet Scott's marriage and her being gifted to Dr. Emerson were two legal facts at the center of her neglected role as Dred Scott's co-plaintiff. Lea S. Vandervelde and Sandhya Subramanian, "Mrs. Dred Scott," *Yale Law Journal* 106, no. 4 (1997): 1033–1123.

9. Quotation from Fehrenbacher, *The Dred Scott Case*, p. 264.

10. Dred and Harriet Scott sued for freedom in a federal court by claiming state citizenship. If successful, they might have set a precedent for fugitive slaves, real or alleged, to claim they were citizens of the state in which they were seized and seek a federal hearing against the person who claimed them, skirting the legal infrastructure that the 1850 Fugitive Slave Act had created. Allen, *Origins of the Dred Scott Case*, p. 161.

11. The policy of popular sovereignty had led to dozens of murders in 1854 as settlers struggled over the future of Kansas, part of the contentious political context of Dred Scott's suit. See Potter, *The Impending Crisis, 1848–1861*, pp. 199–224.

12. *Dred Scott, Plaintiff in Error, v. John F. A. Sandford*, 60 U.S. 393 (1857).

13. *Dred Scott v. Sandford*, 60 U.S. 393 (1857). On Taney's construction of a false consensus, see David Thomas Konig, "Constitutional Law and the Legitimation of History: The Enduring Force of Roger Taney's 'Opinion of the Court,'" in *The Dred Scott Case: Historical and Contemporary Perspectives on Race and Law*, ed. David Thomas Konig (Athens: Ohio University Press, 2010), p. 10.

14. *Dred Scott v. Sandford*, 60 U.S. 393 (1857).

15. On the uncertainties and inconsistencies in Taney's ruling on black people and citizenship, see Fehrenbacher, *The Dred Scott Case*, pp. 335–364.

16. *Dred Scott v. Sandford*, 60 U.S. 393 (1857).

17. On lawmakers' efforts to secure legal protections for black people, see, for instance, Thomas Morris, *Free Men All*, pp. 71–93; Robert P. Forbes, *The Missouri Compromise and Its Aftermath: Slavery and the Meaning of America* (Chapel Hill: University of North Carolina Press, 2007), pp. 108–118.

18. *Dred Scott v. Sandford*, 60 U.S. 393 (1857).

19. David Thomas Konig writes that Taney's historical interpretation "must be read as a carefully selective response to an ever louder assertion of black citizenship, which was presenting its own powerfully articulated historical counternarrative." Konig, "Constitutional Law and the Legitimation of History," pp. 12–13. Fehrenbacher suggests that the decision conveyed such inconsistencies because it was an argument on behalf of southern institutions rather than an interpretation of constitutional questions. Taney's ruling against black citizenship was a legal statement designed to leave states "in complete control of black men, whether free or slave." Fehrenbacher, *The Dred Scott Case*, esp. pp. 341–346.

20. Twitty, *Before Dred Scott*, esp. pp. 1–16; Kelly Kennington, *In the Shadow of Dred Scott: St. Louis Freedom Suits and the Legal Culture of Slavery in Antebellum America* (Athens: University of Georgia Press, 2017); David Thomas Konig, "The Long Road to Dred Scott: Personhood and the Rule of Law in the Trial Court Records of St. Louis Freedom Suits," *University of Missouri Kansas City Law Review* 75, no. 1 (Fall 2006): 54–79.

21. Pryor, *Colored Travelers*, pp. 121–125. As Pryor notes, "The Department of State's practice of passport rejections helped build the foundation of *Dred Scott*." By extension, black people's passport applications as claims to legal protections showed Taney that *Dred Scott* was an avenue to curtail black politics.

22. Some of Taney's supporters embraced his ruling for its potential to suppress black people beyond controlling the enslaved. William H. Welsh, a Democrat in Pennsylvania's state senate, agreed with Taney that the Constitution had created "a government of *white* men." Legalizing black citizenship, he warned, might displace white people from their jobs, their land, and their homes. Dr. John H. Van Evrie of New York saw Taney's ruling as a boon for his own scientific racism and felt it had aligned the nation's laws with those of nature. "The white man was superior—the negro was inferior—and in juxtaposition, society could only exist, and can only exist, by placing them in natural relation to each other, or by the social subordination, or so-called slavery of the negro." Pennsylvania General Assembly, Senate, *The Dred Scott Case. Report of Hon. William H. Welsh, in the Senate of Pennsylvania, May 11, 1857. From the Select Committee to Which Was Referred the Resolutions Relative to the Decision of the Supreme Court of the United States in the Dred Scott Case* (Harrisburg, 1857). For similar arguments and a digest of lawmakers' statements in favor of *Dred Scott*, see *The Rendition of Fugitive Slaves. The Acts of 1793 and 1850, and the Decisions of the Supreme Court Sustaining Them. The Dred Scott Case— What the Court Decided* (Washington, DC: National Democratic Campaign Committee, 1860);

Van Evrie, *The Dred Scott Decision: Opinion of Chief Justice Taney, with an Introduction* (New York: Van Evrie, Horton, and Co., 1859), p. iv.

23. "Suffrage Convention of the Colored Citizens of New York," pp. 99–100.

24. "Proceedings of a Convention of the Colored Men of Ohio. Held in the City of Cincinnati, on the 23rd, 24th, 25th, and 26th Days of November, 1858," in *Proceedings of the Black State Conventions, 1840–1865*, vol. 1, ed. Foner and Walker, p. 336.

25. "Greatly Pleased," *National Era*, May 7, 1857. The *Era* excerpted those comments from the *Boston Watchman and Reflector*.

26. Fehrenbacher, *The Dred Scott Case*, pp. 314–317.

27. "Rights of Free Negroes in Maine," *National Era*, August 27, 1857. Similarly, Whig state senators in Pennsylvania said that because of the proslavery decision, the Court had "forfeited that confidence and respect due to their exalted station." See Pennsylvania General Assembly, Senate, *Journal of the Senate of the Commonwealth of Pennsylvania of the Session Begun at Harrisburg, On the Sixth Day of January, A.D. 1857*, vol. 67 (Harrisburg: A. Boyd Hamilton, State Printer, 1857), p. 908.

28. Political party affiliation largely determined white lawmakers' responses to *Dred Scott*. Northern Democrats hoped *Dred Scott* could relieve sectional tensions with decisive answers to urgent questions about slavery. Southern Democrats were pleased with federal sanction for slavery's expansion. Democrats in the North and South called for obedience to the decision because they believed it would serve their interests. Republican newspapers and lawmakers denounced the opinion as a partisan stain on the Supreme Court's reputation. For instance, in 1858, Abraham Lincoln said the decision was the culmination of a Democratic Party conspiracy to spread slavery to all parts of the nation. "To meet and overthrow that dynasty," he announced, "is the work now before all those who would prevent that consummation." He presented *Dred Scott* as an existential threat to American freedom. Despite their impassioned opposition to the ruling, partisan concerns also discouraged Republicans from addressing the thorny issue of black people's legal status. Many accepted Taney's denial of black citizenship when they argued that because the Court ruled Scott's suit invalid, the subsequent statement that slavery was legal in all territories was unnecessary and lacked legal force. Fehrenbacher, *The Dred Scott Case*, pp. 417–443, 559; Michael P. Johnson, ed., *Abraham Lincoln, Slavery, and the Civil War*, 2nd ed. (Boston: Bedford St. Martin's, 2011), pp. 32–38, quotations from pp. 36 and 37. On anxieties and realities about conspiratorial southern power, see Leonard L. Richards, *Slave Power: The Free North and Southern Domination* (Baton Rouge: Louisiana State University Press, 2000). Taney's ruling gave legal sanction to the proslavery imperialism emanating from southern Democrats. See Johnson, *River of Dark Dreams*, pp. 303–422.

29. "Convention of the Colored Citizens of Massachusetts," *Proceedings of the Black State Conventions, 1840–1865*, vol. 2, ed. Foner and Walker, pp. 96–97.

30. William J. Watkins had petitioned unsuccessfully in 1853 for the state to permit black men to join extant militias. See Watkins, *Our Rights as Men: An Address Delivered in Boston, Before the Legislative Committee on the Militia* (Boston: Benjamin F. Roberts, 1853). On black militias, especially in Emancipation Day celebrations, see Jeffrey-Kerr Ritchie, *Rites of August First: Emancipation Day in the Black Atlantic World* (New York: Oxford University Press, 2007).

31. "Convention of the Colored Citizens of Massachusetts," p. 96. The account of the parade comes from *Liberator*, August 13, 1858. The Liberty Guard in 1857 had been the center of a race riot in Boston on the day of their first public parade. See "Miscellany, from the Boston Herald. First Public Parade of the Liberty Guard," *Liberator*, November 27, 1857. For more on

antebellum black militias, see Jeffery Kerr-Ritchie, *Rites of August First: Emancipation Day in the Black Atlantic World* (Baton Rouge: Louisiana State University Press, 2007), pp. 164–193.

32. On lying, regionalism, honor, and reputation in early American political culture, see Joanne Freeman, *Affairs of Honor: National Politics in the New Republic* (New Haven, CT: Yale University Press, 2002), esp. pp. 62–104.

33. Jean Barth Toll and Mildred S. Gilliam, eds., *Invisible Philadelphia: Community Through Voluntary Organizations* (Philadelphia: Atwater Kent Museum, 1995), pp. 660, 1010; "Philadelphia Negro Educator: Jacob C. White, Jr., 1837–1902," *Pennsylvania Magazine of History and Biography* 97, no. 1 (January 1973): 75–98; Tony Martin, "The Banneker Literary Institute of Philadelphia: African American Intellectual Activism Before the War of the Slave-holders' Rebellion," *Journal of African American History* 87, no. 3 (Summer 2002): 303–322.

34. *The Celebration of the Eighty-Third Anniversary of the Declaration of American Independence, by the Banneker Institute. Philadelphia, July 4th, 1859* (Philadelphia: W. S. Young, 1859), pp. 6–9.

35. Ibid., pp. 6–9.

36. Ibid., pp. 11–13, 21.

37. Ibid., p. 8.

38. "Convention of the Colored Citizens of Massachusetts," pp. 98–99.

39. The collection of items is described in "The Boston Massacre," *Liberator*, March 13, 1858, and has been analyzed in Elizabeth Rauh Bethel, *The Roots of African-American Identity: Memory and History in the Antebellum Free Communities* (New York: St. Martin's, 1997). Frequent reference was made to the fact that Attucks, along with one of his white comrades in the mob who lacked local family connections, was "buried from Faneuil Hall." Black leaders felt it very important that a black patriot had been celebrated with a funeral that began at one of the city's most important centers of protest, government, and business. See, for instance, *National Anti-Slavery Standard*, March 13, 1858, and Nell's speech in "The Boston Massacre," *Liberator*, March 12, 1858.

40. "The Boston Massacre," *Liberator*, March 12, 1858.

41. On the invocation of Attucks, see Mitch Kachun, "From Forgotten Founder to Indispensable Icon: Crispus Attucks, Black Citizenship, and Collective Memory, 1770–1865," *Journal of the Early Republic* 29, no. 2 (Summer 2009): 249–286; Steven Kantrowitz, "A Place for Colored Patriots: Crispus Attucks Among the Abolitionists, 1842–1863," *Massachusetts Historical Review* 11 (2009): 96–117.

42. "William J. Watkins at Albany," *Douglass' Monthly*, February 1859.

43. "Speech by Robert Purvis delivered at the City Assembly Rooms," *National Anti-Slavery Standard*, May 23, 1857. *Black Abolitionist* Papers Archive, accessed April 24, 2018, bap.chadwyck.com.

44. "From Our Philadelphia Correspondent," *Provincial Freeman*, March 28, 1857; "Mary Ann Shadd Cary to Frederick Douglass, 25 January 1849," *Black Abolitionist* Papers Archive, accessed May 11, 2018, http://bap.chadwyck.com.

45. "Republicanism of William H. Seward," *Provincial Freeman*, May 16, 1857. On Seward and his party's politics, see Foner, *Free Soil, Free Labor, Free Men.*

46. "Letter from William Still to James Miller McKim," in Ripley, *Black Abolitionist Papers.*

47. "Anglo African Nationality," *New-York Daily Tribune*, August 11, 1858; "African Civilization Society," *New-York Daily Tribune*, December 10, 1858. Frederick Douglass wrote disparagingly and perhaps without total accuracy of Garnet's society in "African Civilization Society,"

Douglass' Monthly, February 1859, accessed May 3, 2018, http://teachingamericanhistory.org/library/index.asp?document = 1031.

48. "Convention of the Colored Citizens of Massachusetts," p. 97.

49. On black Garrisonians and their politics, see McDaniel, *The Problem of Democracy in the Age of Slavery*, esp. pp. 66–86.

50. "Convention of the Colored Citizens of Massachusetts," pp. 97–99.

51. "The Dred Scott Decision," in *Two Speeches, by Frederick Douglass; One on West India Emancipation, Delivered at Canandiaigua, Aug. 4th, and the Other on the Dred Scott Decision, Delivered in New York, on the Occasion of the Anniversary of the American Abolition Society, May, 1857* (Rochester, NY: C. P. Dewey, n.d.).

52. Since the late eighteenth century, when Absalom Jones established St. Thomas's Episcopal, black churches had been centers for people to gather and worship as well as organize political ideas and activities. On local politics and Bethel AME, see Richard Newman, *Freedom's Prophet*, pp. 130–136. In addition to Newman, on the intersections between black religion and politics, see Sylvia Frey, *Water from the Rock: Black Resistance in a Revolutionary Age* (Princeton, NJ: Princeton University Press, 1991); Winston James, *The Struggles of John Brown Russwurm: Life and Writings of a Pan-Africanist Pioneer, 1799–1851* (New York: New York University Press, 2010).

53. Daniel R. Biddle and Murray Dubin, *Tasting Freedom: Octavius Catto and the Battle for Equality in Civil War America* (Philadelphia: Temple University Press, 2010), pp. 5–76; "W. T. Catto," *North Star*, October 20, 1848.

54. Albert J. Raboteau, *Slave Religion: The 'Invisible Institution' in the Antebellum South* (Oxford: Oxford University Press, 1978), pp. 311–312.

55. William Catto, *A Semi-Centenary Discourse . . .* (Philadelphia: Joseph M. Wilson, 1857), p. 7. A more cynical reading of this piece of Exodus might note that it was God who "hardened the heart of Pharaoh" and inspired him to chase down the Israelites whom he had briefly freed from bondage. Perhaps the same force had inspired the jurisprudence of Roger Taney, a man born into a society that taught him to believe in and defend white supremacy. If divine force could make the powerful villainous, perhaps it could not be relied upon to liberate the oppressed.

56. Catto, *A Semi-Centenary Discourse*, p. 3.

57. Ibid., p. 7.

58. "The Dred Scott Decision," pp. 27–31.

59. Douglass, "The Dred Scott Decision," pp. 35–36, 39–40, 45–46.

60. "Suffrage Convention of the Colored Citizens of New York," p. 99.

CHAPTER 6

1. William Still, *A Brief Narrative of the Struggle for the Rights of the Colored People of Philadelphia in the City Railway Cars; and a Defence of William Still, Relating to His Agency Touching the Passage of the Late Bill, &c. Read before a Large Public Meeting, Held in Liberty Hall, Lombard St. below Eighth, April 8th, 1867* (Philadelphia: Merrihew & Son, 1867), pp. 7–9. Still's narrative detailed a near decade of protest in pursuit of equal access to streetcars. But he also wrote with a personal motive, to explain "his agency" in that struggle in response to "enemies" who denounced him as elitist and pursued other "wicked efforts to blast my reputation." See pp. 1–2. In the 1870s, Still was working as a coal dealer out of an office on Washington Street in South Philadelphia, so he may have walked to that office after being forced out

of the train in 1863. See "William Still, Dealer in Lehigh & Schuylkill Coal, 1216, 1218 and 1220 Washington Avenue, Philadelphia" (Philadelphia, ca. 1875), Library Company of Philadelphia, accessed July 17, 2018, https://digital.librarycompany.org/islandora/object/digitool%3A105753.

2. Elizabeth Pryor examines the significance of transit restrictions in black northerners' lives, noting that Jim Crow as a term and a practice had its roots in discriminatory accommodations for black travelers in the antebellum North. For nineteenth-century black activists, fighting the Jim Crow car was a hallmark of their politics in pursuit of justice. See Pryor, *Colored Travelers*, pp. 76–102.

3. *Weekly Anglo-African*, November 11, 1865; *Philadelphia Inquirer*, November 15, 1865. See also *Ceremonies at the Reception of Welcome to the Colored Soldiers of Pennsylvania, in the City of Harrisburg, Nov. 14th, 1865, by the Garnet League: Together with the Report of the Committee of Arrangements, and the Resolutions of Vindication by the Garnet League, Defining Its Position with Reference to the Pennsylvania State Equal Rights League* (Harrisburg: Telegraph Steam Book and Job Office, 1866).

4. The processes of waging a war of unprecedented scale and the fact that enslaved black southerners looked to federal authorities as instruments of their emancipation produced critical new connections between African Americans and government authorities. These connections were liberating in critical ways but were also, for some, restrictive and physically harmful. See Eric Foner, *Reconstruction: America's Unfinished Revolution* (New York: Norton, 1988); Rosen, *Terror in the Heart of Freedom* Romeo, *Gender and the Jubilee*; Jim Downs, *Sick from Freedom: African American Illness and Suffering During the Civil War and Reconstruction* (New York: Oxford University Press, 2012); Tera Hunter, *Bound in Wedlock: Slave and Free Black Marriage in the Nineteenth Century* (Cambridge, MA: Harvard University Press, 2017).

5. Historians have explored the ways black politics developed across the Civil War era, focusing on changes and continuities through the period rather than framing it as a historical break. My project here is to expand the long history of the legal changes of Reconstruction by examining postwar legal developments in relation to the forms and goals of antebellum black politics that persisted through and beyond the war. See Kantrowitz, *More Than Freedom*; Masur, *An Example for All the Land*; Millington W. Bergeson-Lockwood, " 'In Accordance with the Spirit of the Times': African American Citizenship and the Civil Rights Act of 1866 in New England Law and Politics," in *The Greatest and the Grandest Act: The Civil Rights Act of 1866 from Reconstruction to Today*, ed. Christian G. Samito (Carbondale: Southern Illinois University Press, 2018), pp. 89–111.

6. "Convention of the Colored Inhabitants of the State of New York," in *Proceedings of the Black State Conventions 1840–1865*, vol. 1, ed. Philip S. Foner and George E. Walker (Philadelphia: Temple University Press, 1979), p. 21.

7. William Cooper Nell, *The Colored Patriots of the American Revolution* (Boston: Robert F. Walcutt, 1855), p. 10. Crispus Attucks was a central figure in Nell's work. Attucks, a black victim of the 1770 Boston Massacre, offered a compelling argument for activists claiming that they had been at the heart of the nation since its earliest origins. After publishing his book, Nell organized a series of Crispus Attucks Day celebrations, featuring remembrances of revolutionary patriotism and speeches by activists who deployed that history to push for legal change. See, for instance, "Ninetieth Anniversary of the Boston Massacre, March 5, 1770," *Liberator*, March 16, 1860. On the political meanings of Nell's work and the memory of Crispus Attucks, see Mitch Kachun, "From Forgotten Founder to Indispensable Icon: Crispus Attucks, Black Citizenship, and Collective Memory, 1770–1865," *Journal of the Early Republic* 29, no. 2 (Summer 2009): 249–286; Steven Kantrowitz, "A Place for Colored Patriots: Crispus Attucks Among the Abolitionists, 1842–1863," *Massachusetts Historical Review* 11 (2009): 97–117.

8. Jim Cullen, "'I's a Man Now': Gender and African American Men," and Darlene Clarke Hine and Ernestine Jenkins, "Black Men's History: Toward a Gendered Perspective," both in *A Question of Manhood: A Reader in U.S. Black Men's History and Masculinity*, ed. Darlene Clarke Hine and Ernestine Jenkins (Bloomington: University of Indiana Press, 1999), pp. 489–501; Amy Greenberg, *Manifest Manhood and the Antebellum American Empire* (New York: Cambridge University Press, 2005).

9. Kachun, "From Forgotten Founder to Indispensable Icon," p. 275.

10. Earlier, Massachusetts had also excluded black people from militia service, although lawmakers framed the exclusion as exemption from a burden. See *An Act, for Regulating and Governing the Militia of the Commonwealth of Massachusetts, and for Repealing All Laws Heretofore Made for That Purpose* (Boston: Adams and Nourse, 1786), p. 22.

11. U.S. War Office, Inspector General's Office, *Regulations for the Order and Discipline of the Troops of the United States, to Which Are Added the United States Militia Act Passed in Congress, May 1792, and the Militia Act of Massachusetts, Passed June 22, 1793. By Baron de Stuben, Late Major-General and Inspector-General of the Army of the United States* (Boston: Isaiah Thomas and E. T. Andrews for David West and John West, 1794), pp. 167–168.

12. Commonwealth of Massachusetts, House of Representatives, "Report on Sundry Petitions Respecting Distinctions of Color," February 25, 1839, Main Collection, New-York Historical Society. Many black people felt that the burden was politically valuable. In 1853, black Bostonian William Watkins spoke before Massachusetts lawmakers, representing a group of petitioners who sought state sanction for a proposed black militia. "All we demand of you," he asserted, "is that we be treated as men, that we be dealt with as all law-abiding citizens." To Watkins, a legal sanction of a black militia would help black men claim a legal position in the community and offer a foothold to a wider set of transformations toward racial equality. At its heart, the speech was about constructing a relationship between the government and black men as citizens. Watkins wanted "the Old Bay State [to] throw around us its protecting arm," to include African Americans as equal members of the legal community. His call for a sanctioned militia demanded a fundamental reorganization of the relationship between African Americans and the state. See Watkins, *Our Rights as Men*, pp. 2–4, 8–9, 19. On the militia campaign in the broader context of black Bostonians' politics, see Kantrowitz, *More Than Freedom*, pp. 198–204. On antebellum militias more broadly, see Jeffrey Kerr-Ritchie, *Rites of August First: Emancipation Day in the Black Atlantic World* (Baton Rouge: Louisiana State University Press, 2007), pp. 164–192; Mary Ellen Rowe, *Bulwark of the Republic: The American Militia in the Antebellum West* (Westport, CT: Praeger, 2003); Harry S. Laver, *Citizens More Than Soldiers: The Kentucky Militia and Society in the Early Republic* (Lincoln: University of Nebraska Press, 2007).

13. On the Liberty Guard's parade, see "Miscellany: First Public Parade of the Liberty Guard," *Liberator*, November 27, 1857. See also "Parade and Mobbing of a Colored Military Company," *Lowell Daily Citizen and News*, November 17, 1857. The parade was part of a robust tradition of black cultural and political events using public space in the North that stretched back at least as far as the Pinkster celebrations of the eighteenth century. See William Pierson, *Black Yankees: The Development of an Afro-American Subculture in Eighteenth-Century New England* (Amherst: University of Massachusetts Press, 1988); Douglas Egerton, *Death or Liberty: African Americans and Revolutionary America* (New York: Oxford University Press, 2009). An unsanctioned militia march would have been especially alarming to Americans in late 1857. In September of that year, the Nauvoo Legion, the territorial militia operating in Mormon Utah, killed more than 100 settlers passing through that territory en route to California. Federal

officials had previously deployed U.S. troops to suppress Mormon rebellion in the 1850s. See Ronald E. Walker, Richard E. Turley, and Glen M. Leonard, *Massacre at Meadow Mountains* (New York: Oxford University Press, 2008); Steven Hahn, *A Nation Without Borders: The United States and Its World in an Age of Civil Wars, 1830–1910* (New York: Penguin, 2017), p. 234; "Important News from Utah," *Evening Star*, November 19, 1857; "Utah Affairs—Captain Van Vliet at Washington," *San Francisco Bulletin*, December 1, 1857.

14. Diemer, *The Politics of Black Citizenship*, pp. 189–190. On the attempted rescue, see Benjamin Quarles, *Black Abolitionists* (New York: Oxford University Press, 1969), p. 214.

15. Green published that item in the *Philadelphia Press*, April 22, 1861. He collected this and other writings capturing the debate among black activists about the merits of black soldiering in *Letters and Discussions on the Formation of Colored Regiments, and the Duty of the Colored People in Regard to the Great Slaveholders' Rebellion, in the United States of America* (Philadelphia: Ringwalt & Brown, 1862). Quotations from pp. 3–4.

16. Chandra Manning, *What This Cruel War Was Over: Soldiers, Slavery, and the Civil War* (New York: Vintage, 2007), pp. 3–80.

17. "Black Regiments Proposed," *Douglass' Monthly*, May 1861.

18. "The Progress of the War," *Douglass' Monthly*, September 1861.

19. Lincoln subsequently fired Cameron, in part because of allegations of corruption, and appointed Edwin Stanton as secretary of war. See Laura Edwards, *A Legal History of the Civil War and Reconstruction: A Nation of Rights* (New York: Cambridge University Press, 2015), pp. 76–78.

20. James McPherson, *Battle Cry of Freedom: The Civil War Era* (New York: Oxford University Press), pp. 562–565. On the complex politics of black service, see also Carole Emberton, "Only Murder Makes Men: Reconsidering the Black Military Experience," *Journal of the Civil War Era* 2, no. 3 (September 2012): 369–393.

21. On the black men who took part in the meeting and the debates surrounding emigration among black Washingtonians, see Kate Masur, "The African American Delegation to President Lincoln: A Reappraisal," *Civil War History* 56, no. 2 (June 2010): 117–144.

22. Michael P. Johnson, ed., *Abraham Lincoln, Slavery, and the Civil War: Selected Writing and Speeches* (New York: Bedford/St. Martin's, 2010).

23. "Note from Philadelphia," *Pine and Palm*, May 25, 1862. The black activist William Henry Johnson wrote in his autobiography that he and a number of other young Philadelphians organized the Frank Johnson Guards in late 1859. Although he said that the "company had been organized more for display than for actual service," he also noted that the group was founded by "men connected with the Underground Railroad," which might suggest something of the martial actions its founders envisioned for the militia. *Autobiography of Dr. William Henry Johnson, Respectfully Dedicated to His Adopted Home, the Capital City of the Empire State* (Albany, NY: Argus Company, 1900), pp. 194–195. For more on the debates among black people about enlistment, see Kantrowitz, *More Than Freedom*, pp. 253–305; Christian G. Samito, *Becoming American Under Fire: Irish Americans, African Americans, and the Politics of Citizenship During the Civil War Era* (Ithaca, NY: Cornell University Press, 2009). Both authors explore black uncertainty about enlistment and the ways activists saw the potential of service. Here, I am interested in the specific lawmaking potential of statements that discouraged black enlistment on the grounds of African Americans' legal marginalization.

24. "Letter from Ohio," "How We Stand," and "A Word from the Country," all *Pine and Palm*, May 25, 1862; "Editorial Correspondence," *Pine and Palm*, June 22, 1861.

25. On this shared sense of the bond linking military service and rights, see Brian Taylor, "A Politics of Service: Black Northerners' Debates over Enlistment in the American Civil War," *Civil War History* 58, no. 4 (December 2012): 451–480.

26. Edwards, *A Legal History of the Civil War and Reconstruction*, pp. 64–82; Manning, *Troubled Refuge*.

27. On the fraught bonds that the war forged between freedpeople and the federal government, see especially Rosen, *Terror in the Heart of Freedom*, pp. 23–86, 222–242; Downs, *Sick from Freedom*; Romeo, *Gender and the Jubilee*.

28. In the antebellum period, major federal government decisions relating to African Americans, such as *Prigg v. Pennsylvania*, the 1850 Fugitive Slave Law, and the *Dred Scott* case, were spread across decades. During and after the Civil War, government policies defining black people's legal status changed rapidly, from slaves to contraband to freemen and ultimately to citizens.

29. Blight, *Frederick Douglass' Civil War*, pp. 150–153; James McPherson, *Marching Toward Freedom: Blacks in the Civil War* (New York: Knopf, 1968), pp. 16–19, 68–69, 91–96; McPherson, *Battle Cry of Freedom*, p. 564.

30. "Addresses of the Hon. W. D. Kelley, Miss Anna E. Dickinson, and Mr. Frederick Douglass, at a Mass Meeting, Held at National Hall, Philadelphia, July 6, 1863, for the Promotion of Colored Enlistments," 1863, Library Company of Philadelphia.

31. "For the Christian Recorder. Baltimore Correspondence," *Christian Recorder*, March 12, 1864.

32. "Massachusetts Black Corporal to the President," dated Morris Island, South Carolina, September 28, 1863, in *Freedom: A Documentary History of Emancipation, 1861–1867, ser. 2, The Black Military Experience*, ed. Ira Berlin, Joseph P. Reidy, and Leslie S. Rowland (New York: Cambridge University Press, 1992), pp. 385–386. While Gooding insisted that members of his regiment were not formerly enslaved and should not be paid under the doctrine of confiscation, he was careful not to devalue the work of contrabands on behalf of the Union cause. "But we do not wish to be understood, as rating our Service, of more Value to the Government, than the service of the exslave, their Service is undoubtedly worth much to the Nation, but Congress made express, provision touching their case."

33. "Soldiers of a Black Regiment to the President," dated Folly Island, South Carolina, July 16, 1864, in Berlin et al., *Freedom*, pp. 401–402.

34. "For the Christian Recorder. A Letter from a Soldier in New Orleans," *Christian Recorder*, July 16, 1864.

35. Congress agreed to pay back wages to the date of enlistment for soldiers who had been free when they began their service and to January 1, 1864, for all other soldiers. McPherson, *Battle Cry of Freedom*, p. 789.

36. On the forms of black southern politics that developed in the Civil War era, see, for instance, Hunter, *To 'Joy My Freedom*; Rosen, *Terror in the Heart of Freedom*; Thomas Holt, *Black over White: Negro Political Leadership in South Carolina During Reconstruction* (Champaign: University of Illinois Press, 1977); Steven Hahn, *A Nation Under Our Feet: Black Political Struggles in the Rural South from Slavery to the Great Migration* (Cambridge, MA: Harvard University Press, 2003).

37. Kate Masur highlights the significance of geography to black politics in the Civil War era, noting that black Washingtonians had distinctive opportunities to connect with the federal government and that congressional control of the District of Columbia made it a testing

ground for legal changes implemented during the period. See Masur, *An Example for All the Land*.

38. *Liberty, and Equality Before the Law. Proceedings of the Convention of the Colored People of Va., Held in the City of Alexandria, Aug. 2, 3, 4, 5, 1865* (Alexandria, VA: Cowing & Gillis, 1865). Library Company of Philadelphia.

39. Ibid.

40. Ibid., p. 10.

41. Andrew Diemer has highlighted the connections in northern and southern black politics in his study of Pennsylvania and Maryland. Those connections held new political potential in the aftermath of the Civil War. Diemer, *The Politics of Black Citizenship*.

42. "Anglo African Nationality," *New-York Daily Tribune*, August 11, 1858; "The African Civilization Society," *New-York Daily Tribune*, December 10, 1858; "African Civilization Society," *Douglass' Monthly*, February 1859.

43. *Liberty and Equality Before the Law*; On Fields Cook, see "Constitution of the Colored Men's Equal Rights League of Richmond," note 2, *Black Abolitionist* Papers Archive, accessed October 5, 2018, http://bap.chadwyck.com.proxy-um.researchport.umd.edu/search Bap/displayBapFulltext.do?QueryName = bap&ResultsID = 165ABBC9CEC&SortType = rele vance&fromPage = search&ItemNumber = 5&ItemID = 90076.

44. "To the Union Convention of Tennessee Assembled in the Capitol at Nashville," January 9, 1865, in Berlin et al., *Freedom*; McPherson, *Battle Cry of Freedom*, pp. 401–403.

45. "To the Union Convention of Tennessee Assembled in the Capitol at Nashville," pp. 811–816.

46. *Proceedings of the State Convention of Colored Men of the State of Tennessee, with the Addresses of the Convention to the White Loyal Citizens of Tennessee, and the Colored Citizens of Tennessee, Held at Nashville, Tenn., August 7th, 8th, 9th and 10th, 1865* (Nashville, TN: Daily Press and Times Job Office, 1865), Colored Conventions Project, accessed August 26, 2018, http://coloredconventions.org/items/show/522.

47. *First Annual Meeting of the National Equal Rights League, Held in Cleveland, Ohio, October 19th, 20th, and 21st, 1865* (Philadelphia: E. C. Markley & Son, 1865), pp. 4, 20.

48. Ibid.

49. Pennsylvania State Equal Rights League, "Memorial to the Honorable Senate and House of Representatives of the United States, in Congress Assembled" (Pennsylvania, 1866), pp. 2, 4–5.

50. Ibid., p. 2; Edwards, *A Legal History of the Civil War and Reconstruction*, p. 106.

51. Pennsylvania State Equal Rights League, "Memorial," pp. 2–3. As Laura Free has noted, these arguments sought to redefine the legal structures of the United States by claiming that racial equality and equal political participation were principles that lay at the heart of the nation's founding. See Laura Free, *Suffrage Reconstructed: Gender, Race, and Voting Rights in the Civil War Era* (Ithaca, NY: Cornell University Press, 2015), pp. 55–77.

52. "Pennsylvania State Equal Rights League," p. 1.

53. Ibid., p. 3.

54. Laura Edwards notes that the process of the war "allowed people to imagine the federal government as a more immediate presence in their lives." Edwards, *A Legal History of the Civil War and Reconstruction*, p. 6. For many Americans, black and white, this was a transformative way of thinking about government. But for a substantial set of black activists, it was a continuation of the imaginative work they had long conducted as they conjured a national government that would make real the egalitarian expressions of the U.S. Constitution and

protect them as American citizens. Free black people had long hoped for and worked toward a legal identity rooted in federal authority.

55. Pennsylvania State Equal Rights League, "Memorial," p. 3.

56. *Equal Suffrage: Address from the Colored Citizens of Norfolk, Va, to the People of the United States. Also an Account of the Agitation Among the Colored People of Virginia for Equal Rights. With an Appendix Concerning the Rights of Colored Witnesses Before the State Courts* (New Bedford, MA: E. Anthony and Sons, 1865), pp. 1, 4.

57. Edwards, *A Legal History of the Civil War and Reconstruction*, p. 99.

58. George Rutherglen, *Civil Rights in the Shadow of Slavery: The Constitution, Common Law, and the Civil Rights Act of 1866* (New York: Oxford University Press, 2013), pp. 40–69.

59. Civil Rights Act of 1866, 14 Stat. 27, secs. 1–2.

60. Laura Edwards notes that enslaved people's flight and the subsequent development of confiscation policy created a legal foundation for abolition because it shifted power over the institution of slavery to the federal government. Edwards, *A Legal History of the Civil War and Reconstruction*, pp. 66–82.

61. Rutherglen, *Civil Rights in the Shadow of Slavery*, pp. 50–52; Edwards, *A Legal History of the Civil War and Reconstruction*, pp. 4–5.

62. Edwards, *A Legal History of the Civil War and Reconstruction*, pp. 102–105.

63. For more on the connections between antebellum politics and postwar legal change, see Bergeson-Lockwood, "'In Accordance with the Spirit of the Times'"; Paul Finkelman, "Rehearsal for Reconstruction: Antebellum Origins of the Fourteenth Amendment," in *The Facts of Reconstruction*, ed. Eric Anderson and Alfred Moss Jr. (Baton Rouge: Louisiana State University Press, 1991), pp. 1–27.

64. "There Was a Festival Held . . . ," *Christian Recorder*, May 19, 1866.

65. "Life in the Churches," *Christian Recorder*, June 30, 1866.

66. *Civil Rights: Address of the Colored Citizens of Chicago to the Congress of the United States*, 39th Cong., 1st sess. (Washington, DC: House of Representatives, May 10, 1866), p. 1.

67. William Still wrote that black Philadelphians were subject to frequent "outrages" when they were permitted to ride inside of streetcars, which suggests the potential for violence in transit. Still, *A Brief Narrative*, pp. 3–4.

68. Vocal activists sought and secured the support of black Philadelphians. At one meeting in the streetcar fight, they secured a collection of $7.50. The following week, black men and women met at Philadelphia's Shiloh Baptist Church to offer their support to the streetcar protest, and an observer proudly reported that "the collection at this meeting was larger than at any previous meeting . . . ten dollars and eighty-three cents was collected." "Our Philadelphia Letter," *Weekly Anglo-African*, October 7, 1859; "Our Philadelphia Letter," *Weekly Anglo-African*, October 15, 1859. Similarly, William Kelley, in promoting equal access to the streetcars, wrote that their project, "though a local question, is immediately connected with the great policy of Equality before the Law, which is now offering itself to the national acceptance." William Kelley, *Why Colored People in Philadelphia Are Excluded from the Street Cars* (Philadelphia: Benjamin C. Bacon, 1866), p. 5.

69. "Letter from Philadelphia," *Weekly Anglo-African*, December 10, 1859.

70. William Kelley, *The Safeguards of Personal Liberty. An Address by Hon. Wm. D. Kelley, Delivered at Concert Hall, Thursday Evening, June 22, 1865* (Philadelphia: Social, Civil and Statistical Association of Colored People of Pennsylvania, 1865), p. 11.

71. Still, *A Brief Narrative*, p. 10.

72. *The Issues of the Hour: Negro Suffrage and Negro Equality, Address of State Central Committee* (Philadelphia: Office of the "Age," 1865).

73. This outlook was central to the violence visited on freed black people in the aftermath of the Civil War. Emancipation destabilized social hierarchies, and everyday actions therefore took on massive political stakes in the process of building a world without slavery. See especially Rosen, *Terror in the Heart of Freedom*; Hunter, *To 'Joy My Freedom*.

74. Still, *A Brief Narrative*, pp. 6, 8–9, 10.

75. Ibid.; Bergner, George, *The Legislative Record, Containing the Debates and Proceedings of the Pennsylvania Legislature, For the Session of 1867* (Harrisburg, PA: Printed at the Telegraph Steam Book and Job Office, 1867), p. 232; Ira V. Brown, "Pennsylvania and the Rights of the Negro, 1865–1887," *Pennsylvania History: A Journal of Mid-Atlantic Studies* 28, no. 1 (January 1961): 45–57.

76. "Caroline LeCount," in "A Great Thing for Our People: The Institute for Colored Youth in the Civil War Era," Villanova University Library, accessed June 21, 2018, https://exhibits.library.villanova.edu/institute-colored-youth/graduates/caroline-lecount-bio.

77. The Fourteenth Amendment was ratified only because the Reconstruction Acts provided for black suffrage in former Confederate states excluding Tennessee. Republicans had spoken in favor of black suffrage, and they would craft the Fifteenth Amendment as a step to secure it in 1869. But black activists in the 1860s could not foresee that constitutional development. They noted the limits of these earlier Reconstruction measures and demanded that black voting rights be embedded in the Constitution. In particular, they were unhappy that the language of the Civil Rights Act and the Fourteenth Amendment created a distance between suffrage and citizenship. See Edwards, *A Legal History of the Civil War and Reconstruction*, pp. 108–110; Rutherglen, *Civil Rights in the Shadow of Slavery*.

78. George Rutherglen's work is a history of civil rights struggles through the Civil Rights Act, a focus that outlines the legal possibilities and the highest ideas of its framers but at times discounts the ways black people thought and felt about the law, its value, and its limitations. Rutherglen, *Civil Rights in the Shadow of Slavery*, esp. pp. 40–69.

79. *Civil Rights: Address of the Colored Citizens of Chicago to the Congress of the United States.*

80. "Why Not Give Us Our Rights," *Christian Recorder*, July 14, 1866.

81. "It Is Not Safe," *Christian Recorder*, August 4, 1866.

82. "Trying Moment for the Colored People," *Christian Recorder*, March 10, 1866. The Civil Rights Act and the Fourteenth Amendment reflected contemporary ideas that rights fell into discrete categories, with civil rights distinct from political rights such as suffrage, jury service, and officeholding. Part of the reason black activists were disappointed with these legal changes is that they had offered alternative arguments about the relationships among different rights. Activists repeatedly argued that securing civil rights ought to be connected to formal political rights. Editors of the *Christian Recorder* described the project of the 1860s as "our contest for political equality, and the enjoyment of civil rights." If they were to remain distinct, black people expected that they would be secured together. Laura Edwards, *A Legal History of the Civil War and Reconstruction*, pp. 107–109.

EPILOGUE

1. *The Equality of All Men Before the Law Claimed and Defended; in Speeches by Hon. William D. Kelley, Wendell Phillips, and Frederick Douglass, and Letters from Elizur Wright and Wm. Heighton* (Boston: Press of Geo. C. Rand & Avery, 1865), pp. 36–39.

2. Edwards, *A Legal History of the Civil War and Reconstruction*, pp. 90–145; Michael Les Benedict, *Preserving the Constitution: Essays on Politics and the Constitution in the Reconstruction Era* (New York: Fordham University Press, 2006), esp. pp. 3–31; William E. Nelson, *The Fourteenth Amendment: From Political Principle to Judicial Doctrine* (Cambridge, MA: Harvard University Press, 1998).

3. *The Equality of All Men Before the Law Claimed and Defended*, pp. 36–39.

4. *National Anti-Slavery Standard*, July 7, 1866. Blight, *Frederick Douglass's Civil War*, p. 192.

5. *Proceedings of the National Convention of the Colored Men of America, Held in Washington, D.C., on January 13, 14, 15, and 16, 1869* (Washington, DC: Great Republic Book and Job Printing Establishment, 1869), p. 1.

6. Ibid., pp. 1–2.

7. The convention proceedings do not give an address for the Union League Hall, but it appears to have been located on Ninth Street NW just south of F Street NW and was a site for large meetings of labor and religious organizations in the late 1860s. See *Centennial History of the City of Washington, D.C.* (Dayton, OH: United Brethren Publishing House, 1892). "Colored National Labor Union" suggests that the location of the Union League Hall might have been at Ninth and F Streets NW, Washington, D.C., accessed August 29, 2018, http://www.communitywalk.com/location/colored_national_labor_union_1869/washington/dc/labor_organizations__historic/2942343. On the convention's second day, delegates moved to Israel Bethel AME Church, site of a black congregation that organized in the 1820s, which the minutes indicate was in the Capitol Hill neighborhood.

8. See, for instance, "A Very Numerous and Respectable Meeting . . . ," *Pennsylvania Freeman*, March 22, 1838; *Memorial of Thirty Thousand Disfranchised Citizens of Philadelphia, to the Honorable Senate and House of Representatives* (Philadelphia: Printed for the Memorialists, 1855).

9. *Proceedings of the National Convention of the Colored Men of America*, p. 16.

10. Edwards, *A Legal History of the Civil War and Reconstruction*, pp. 146–176.

11. On the political processes that separated black people from federal legal authority, see Pamela Brandwein, *Rethinking the Judicial Settlement of Reconstruction* (New York: Cambridge University Press, 2011). On the legal processes and violent limitations of Reconstruction generally, see Eric Foner, *Reconstruction: America's Unfinished Revolution* (New York: Harper, 1988); Romeo, *Gender and the Jubilee*; Rosen, *Terror in the Heart of Freedom*; Amy Dru Stanley, *From Bondage to Contract: Wage Labor, Marriage, and the Market in the Age of Slave Emancipation* (New York: Cambridge University Press, 1998).

12. "Colored Citizenship," *Christian Recorder*, September 14, 1861.

13. W. M. Brewer, "Henry Highland Garnet," *Journal of Negro History* 13, no. 1 (January 1928): 48–49.

14. John W. Cromwell, *The Negro in American History: Men and Women Eminent in the Evolution of the American of African Descent* (Washington, D.C.: American Negro Academy, 1914), p. 129.

15. Ibid., pp. 48–51; "Mister Garnet's Departure," *New York Times*, November 13, 1881; "Liberia," *Freedom's Journal*, February 14, 1829. On Garnet in Liberia, see William Seraile, "The Brief Diplomatic Career of Henry Highland Garnet," *Phylon* 46, no. 1 (1985): 71–81.

INDEX

abolition of slavery: as a political project, 76–78, 103, 131, 189 n.8; federal legislation (*see* Thirteenth Amendment); state legislation, 3, 18, 46

Adams, John Quincy, 50

African American newspapers, 2, 6, 13–14, 34–35, 51–53, 58, 189 n.9, 192 n.24, 194 n.12, 195 n.13, 205 n.53, 212 n.36; readership of, 13–14, 34, 53, 72, 99, 174. *See also specific newspapers*

African Civilization Society, 143, 164, 185

African Female Benevolent Society, 19

American Colonization Society: activities of, 34, 39, 55; as object of black protest, 2, 12–13, 15, 26, 39, 51–52; origins of, 2. *See also* colonization

American Moral Reform Society, 19–21

American Revolution: black military service in, 15, 119, 137–38, 151–53, 180, 230 n.7; in black politics, 25, 151–53, 180. *See also* Attucks, Crispus; black politics, use of military history

antislavery ideology, 63–66, 108, 112, 116–17, 141, 222 n.72. *See also* abolition of slavery, as a political project

Articles of Confederation: as a tool in black politics, 27, 68

Attucks, Crispus, 6, 137–40, 151–52, 228 n.39, 230 n.7. *See also* American Revolution, black military service in; black politics, use of military history

Banneker Institute, 137

Bates, Edward, U.S. attorney general, 4, 190 n.16

black conventions, 34, 39–41, 52–63, 73, 84–86, 127, 163–67, 182, 204 n.39, 207 n.74; Buffalo (1843), 57–68; New Bedford, Mass. (1858), 135–36, 138; New Haven (1840), 52–54; Philadelphia (1845), 38–40, 62–63; as sites for broad political participation, 6–7, 51–52, 57–58, 60, 162–67; Troy, NY (1858), 127, 130–31, 133–34

black politics: analysis of the U.S. Constitution in, 147, agrarianism in, 18–19, 30, 59–60, 197 n.30; and black separatism, 49; black women activists, 5, 7, 19, 94–102, 108, 122, 153; claims to role in building American communities, 16, 27, 31–34, 78, 149, 166, 169, 176, 182; and Christianity, 12–14, 87, 108, 143–47, 194 n.3; constitutional claims in, 27–28, 39, 61–62, 66–68, 74, 85, 115–16, 127–28, 130–33, 140–41, 143–44, 147, 160 (*see also* U.S. Constitution, Privileges and Immunities clause); education in, 13, 19–21, 60, 86, 88, 163, 178; and formal legal spaces, 15–16, 48, 101–2, 110, 114, 117, 121, 123–25, 131–32, 162, 171–73, 175; gender in, 7, 17–19, 33–34, 99–102, 122, 151, 153, 155; interstate connections in, 7, 11, 16, 23–25, 39, 51–63, 103–6 (*see also* black conventions); invocations of foreign events in, 14, 23, 70–78, 81–87, 89, 91–93 (*see also* Emancipation Day, British West Indies); labor in, 3, 16–17, 24, 196 n.25; lawbreaking as, 95–97, 100–102, 104, 107–8, 111–12, 115–18; 121–25, 152–54, 217 n.9; military service in, 25, 137–40, 151–53, 156, 158–63, 166–67, 176, 180; moral uplift in, 18–22, 32, 196 n.27; and personal security, 96, 98–102, 104–5, 107–9, 114–15, 121–25, 152, 223 n.75; promoting emigration in, 28, 34–37, 51, 140–43, 185–88, 195 n.16, 206 n.60; in public spaces, 94–100, 118–21, 136–37, 149–50, 152–54, 164, 168, 174–77, 192 n.22, 192 n.24, 231 n.13;; relationship to

ACKNOWLEDGMENTS

I feel incredibly fortunate to be able to thank all of the people who made this book possible. All that is good here is the product of years of intellectual and emotional collaboration. This project grew out of a graduate seminar with Joanne Freeman, who afterward remained a thoughtful reader and encouraging advisor. Jonathan Holloway offered invaluable time for conversations at critical moments. He raised penetrating questions that helped me navigate tangles of ideas, and he supported my broader development as a scholar and a person. David Blight was and remains a tremendously generous advisor. His immense intellectual curiosity urged me to continue asking and refining questions, and our discussions instilled confidence in my work.

My first training took place in the Department of History at Howard University. There, Edna Medford and Selwyn Carrington offered scholarly and personal mentorship and finely tuned criticism that led me to broaden my research and sharpen my writing. Dr. Medford in particular showed me the path to a life as a historian.

I am very happy to have connected with Bob Lockhart at the University of Pennsylvania Press. Bob has shepherded me through this process with patience when I wanted and speed when I needed. More important, he has been a sharp reader and inquisitor. I've very much enjoyed talking through this project with him, and it is immeasurably improved by his work.

Colleagues at the University of Maryland, College Park have welcomed me, pushed me, and provided me with space to develop this book. Phil Soergel helped me find and hold onto time for research and writing. I am glad to have been able to watch a bit of basketball and talk about black history with Ira Berlin. Elsa Barkley Brown is a model of intellectual rigor and of many varieties of generative academic labor. Mike Ross has been a terrific neighbor. He, along with Rick Bell, David Freund, and Leslie Rowland, offered vital criticism and encouragement as I revised this project.

I conducted research with the help of staff at Sterling Memorial Library; the New York Public Library, particularly the Schomburg Center for Research in Black Culture; the New-York Historical Society; the Library of Congress; the American Antiquarian Society; the Historical Society of Pennsylvania; and the Library Company of Philadelphia. I am grateful for research funding from the Gilder Lehrman Center at Yale University; the Albert M. Greenfield Foundation; the Graduate School at the University of Maryland, College Park; and the National Endowment for the Humanities. During several months of research at the Library Company of Philadelphia, I benefited from the knowledge and guidance of staff members Krystal Appiah, Connie King, Linda August, and Jim Green. I have developed this project through discussions with colleagues at Loyola University Chicago, the University of Memphis, the Gilder Lehrman Center, the McNeil Center for Early American Studies, SHEAR, the American Historical Association, the University of Miami, George Mason University, Durham University, the Society for U.S. Intellectual History, and the African American Intellectual History Society.

Most important, I have been overwhelmed by love and support from friends and family. Together, they have helped me understand how and why to be part of a community. Atkey moments, Ramona Bonner and David Wessel offered time and labor that helped me reshape this project. Thomas Bell, J. C. Cartwright, and Ryan Molina are my hilarious and loving brothers. I am thankful every day that they invited me to join the band. I had the privilege of building transformative relationships in graduate school. Caitlin Verboon first asked the question that became the core of this book, and it has been wonderful to have her as a friend and colleague in the years since. I spent countless hours working and, fortunately, not working with Richard Anderson, Ally Brantley, Ryan Hall, Dave Petruccelli, Max Scholz, and Nazanin Sullivan.

I feel especially blessed to have met Julia Wessel precisely when and where I did. Since then, her love and support have sustained me. I am delighted that Drew Bonner and Jennifer Spencer have further extended the family. They inspire me, and I treasure the time I share with my siblings and (usually) with Spencer and Cameron. In their own unique ways, my aunts Janet Pierre and Alice Bonner have been crucial to my growth. Finally, I dedicate this work to my parents. I strive to continue showing my appreciation for all of your labor, and I am so pleased to be able to share with you this small fruit.